STALKING
the
GREEN
FAIRY

JAMES VILLAS

STALKING

the

GREEN FAIRY

and
OTHER FANTASTIC
ADVENTURES IN
FOOD AND DRINK

Foreword by
JEREMIAH TOWER

WILEY

JOHN WILEY & SONS, INC.

To Jovan Trboyevic

Proud Serbian, peerless restaurateur, loyal mentor and friend

Published by John Wiley & Sons, Inc., Hoboken, New Jersey
Published simultaneously in Canada

For general information on our other products and services or for technical support, please contact our Customer Care Department within the United States at 800-762-2974, outside the United States at (317) 572-3993 or fax (317) 572-4002.

Wiley also publishes its books in a variety of electronic formats. Some content that appears in print may not be available in electronic books.

Library of Congress Cataloging-in-Publication Data:
     Villas, James.
       Stalking the green fairy and other fantastic adventures in food and drink / James Villas ; foreword by Jeremiah Tower.
          p.   cm.
       Includes bibliographical references and index.
       ISBN 0-471-27344-9 (cloth)
       1. Cookery (Vegetables). I. Title.
     TX801.V515 2004
     641.6'5--dc22
                                                  2003057099

Printed in the United States of America

10   9   8   7   6   5   4   3   2   1

CONTENTS

FOREWORD

JEREMIAH TOWER

"**A** COUNTRY IS NEVER AS POOR AS WHEN IT SEEMS FILLED WITH riches"—or so it appeared to me recently as I was crawling on my hands and knees halfway up the 120 feet to my apartment in New York's blacked-out darkness. Where this 2,084-year-old Chinese proverb popped out from I do not know, but blindness, if temporary, often produces extraordinary visions. As does the Green Fairy.

While reading this Villas manuscript, I poured another ounce of said absinthe into my glass in a race against time for ice and the light to read and wondered whether, perhaps, it was the mystery and fumes of the bitter green liqueur that was reaching back all those years. I had just completed my first investigative foray for James Villas by looking around London to see which brands of real absinthe were on sale, and here I was embarking on the second stage of my inquiries by tasting the one made by the Absinthe museum in France.

Guilt flowed more heavily than the lime-green liquid, because I knew my armchair investigation was a sham next to the positively Sherlockian discipline and brilliance of Villas on the scent of any culinary mystery he feels possessed to unravel. Villas has all the same fearless confidence as Holmes in the power of carefully laid out facts leading to conclusive opinion. And James Villas has never shied away from held and stated opinion. For him, it is the spice of the ragout or, as often in his case, the burgoo.

One of Villas's most successful opinions was stated loudly and clearly in 1976 as a result of one of the most fore-thinking culinary investigations ever: the revolutionary piece in Frank Zachary's *Town & Country* about the extraordinary revival of American regionalism in food in the United States (aka the new American food revolution). Jim Villas was its chief sleuth.

Now, in this new book, twenty-eight years later, Jim is at it again—into everything from "The Slime Factor" (when okra is delicious) and "Gustatory Goo" (all kinds of peanut butter) to "Sexy Soup" (*la vraie* onion soup). But he is never better than when "Foreign Foraging." There is a trip to Nice to find out again what was known but in its familiarity-bred contempt needed reaffirming, as in how a true *salade niçoise* is really made (certainly a peeve close to my heart), and a trip to Italy for the source of Parmesan cheese and to track down tiramisu in its "original, correct, unforgettable recipe."

But this is not a book with a geographical agenda. It is all about the love of food that is at its best when pristine, correct, delicious, and a lot of fun. Who else but Jim Villas could talk about most every American's favorite foods in a series of essays titled "Comfort Me with Meat Loaf"? Certainly anyone who can talk with passion about what makes a great Club sandwich—food that is near the top of my list of what makes me the most happy—gets my vote as culinary writer extraordinaire!

"There is nothing new in cooking. There are only newcomers to it. There are no new ways of transforming food from raw to cooked to be discovered. There are just more refined ways of doing these things perfected by more evolved humans with better sources to explore."

—MIRIAM UNGERER

DECLARATIONS OF A HUNGRY SLEUTH

I F IT'S TRUE THAT MOST OF US SPEND A THIRD OF OUR LIVES SLEEPING, I can only deduce that the remaining two-thirds of mine is devoted to eating, quaffing, cooking, foraging the globe, dining out, and either reading or writing about food and drink. Some people are addicted to cars, sports, exercise, and TV; others travel to sightsee, shop, visit museums, and attend theater. I exist primarily to nourish myself blissfully at all times, in all places, and on all types of victuals.

My unfeigned gourmandise is a very private fervor shared only with a happy few. I don't get along too well with more disciplined superficial foodies, who spend endless time talking about bogus gastronomic trends, offbeat ingredients, superstar restaurant chefs, and diets rather than, like myself, simply eating and drinking with wanton abandon. The single time I felt a tinge of shame over this obsession and mentioned it timidly to my doctor, his only feedback was in the form of requests for a good Texas chili recipe and my list of favorite Paris restaurants. I determined never to give it any more thought.

Over the past thirty years, I've gradually evolved a philosophy of gastronomy and a style of food writing that reflect the sacred, time-tested tenets of tradition while embracing any intelligent innovations that promise to contribute a worthwhile and lasting dimension to the ways we satisfy our hunger. My essays divulge no national or international boundaries, no blind prejudices or social status, and no unifying theme except the inordinate amount of detective work involved in the subjects that interest me.

I don't merely revere okra, exotic potato salads, brutally expensive French rosé Champagne, and tipping correctly in restaurants; I need to ferret out the interior motives, the histories and anecdotes, and the personal quirks behind my special preoccupations. Just as I once worked undercover as a table captain in a snazzy French restaurant to discover firsthand exactly what goes on behind the scenes, I've never been content simply extolling food and beverages in the abstract and reeling off dozens of overused recipes.

When, for example, the timeless subject of American prime steak seized my imagination (as it recently has that of millions of Atkins dieters), nothing would do but for me to stalk Midwestern feedlots, slaughterhouses, and local markets in search of the perfect steak, so I could explain why these days that sublime slab of meat is so incredibly scarce. Enamored with Scandinavian gravlax, I ventured deep into the fjords of Norway, not only to absorb the dish's mysterious lore but to learn from a native salmon farmer the absolutely definitive home-style way to prepare it. At one point, despite having tasted numerous restaurant versions of both tiramisu and Brunswick stew, these dishes seemed commonplace to me. Only after trekking through the northern provinces of Italy and the backwoods of Georgia and Virginia to get the lowdown on these recipes did I learn to appreciate them. I determined that most versions we encounter of each are utterly phony, and tapping the source brought them to life.

Likewise, other gustatory explorations intrigued me and inspired all sorts of stories. Nobody, for example, has ever before revealed that much of one of the world's greatest and most expensive cheeses, Parmigiano-Reggiano, is produced by none other than wealthy Italian aristocrats with bloodlines that reach back centuries. Even such humble topics as chicken salad and my beloved Club sandwich had me snooping around the United States and other countries in search of the most exciting, updated samples, encouraging folks to take a fresh approach.

It's not enough just to write about how wonderful onion soup is; I want to portray it more wistfully and romantically as the gustatory courtesan of the night I've known not just in the bistros of Paris but in the *tascas* of Lisbon, the beer halls of Denmark, and the pubs of London. Dig deep enough and you learn that Thomas Jefferson cultivated and loved iceberg lettuce, why all-American chowders can be traced back to seventeenth-century Nova Scotia and should play a much more prominent role in our current gastronomy, and how we've just begun to utilize our rich bounty of wild mushrooms and exotic seafood in ways we never imagined.

I liked uncovering the story of a Texas oil millionairess who adores pumpkin and the many unexpected ways it can be prepared so much that she wrote and privately published her own pumpkin cookbook. It was a thrill to address the otherwise hackneyed topic of *salade niçoise,* not only because I feel the dish has been inexcusably abused but because I've discovered luscious new examples on the French Riviera made with sardines instead of tuna, chickpeas instead of green beans, and diced turnips in place of potatoes. I can explain why there's damn good reason fastidious tipplers should now be drinking only imported vodkas and not the innocuous domestic swill; and, of course, there was my passionate pursuit of the elusive "green fairy."

The subjects into which I delve anxiously are disparate, often controversial, and range from the true secrets of San Francisco sourdough to absurdly neglected savory pies to my frank and unbridled zeal for lowly peanut butter and canned tuna. I break touchy ground by ranking our finest new regional micro beers on the same level as premium chardonnays and introducing unfamiliar sparkling wines that hold their own quite well against French Champagne at a fraction of the cost. With more than a little inbred enthusiasm from my Rebel background, I devote inordinate attention to the singular glory of Southern cookery and try to clear up a few appalling misconceptions. I expose candidly my own churlish grocery-shopping habits and provide substantial proof that, for better or worse, the vast majority of savvy Americans are becoming more loyal to gigantic price clubs sprouting nationwide than to all the upscale supermarkets, speciality food shops, and greengrocers combined. Since restaurants have always played a major role on my beat, I rant and rave about numerous aspects of the contemporary dining scene, tossing bouquets where they're deserved, excoriating the miscreants, and proffering insights and tips based on endless nights of shameless mastication, carousing, and hedonism.

Never has world gastronomy been more vibrant and challenging than during the late twentieth and early twenty-first centuries, a time when old values have been either discarded or reinterpreted, radical culinary innovations and techniques exploited to the fullest, a wealth of "new" global ingredients utilized to transform entire cuisines, and dining practices modified often beyond recognition. I've witnessed it all, involved myself intensely in most of the activity, and recorded any aspect that has aroused my curiosity. Many of the changes have been exciting and estimable, some are still confused, and others are downright ridiculous and perverted. Unlike certain other food writers, I have no fatuous inclination whatsoever to taste fresh cobra blood in Asia, sample 465 varieties of garlic grown on an Oklahoma farm, race to Spain's Costa Brava for a three-star chef's ducks' tongues with chopped oysters, or evaluate two dozen Eastern European mineral waters. My interest in fried turkey, pomegranate molasses, Starbucks coffee and green tea, Pacific Rim food, pasta machines, and tasting menus is minimal or nonexistent, and I remain stubbornly convinced that within a decade or less Americanized sushi, tuna roe, ostrich steaks, organic blue potatoes, apple martinis, vegetable juicers, and Oregon pinot gris will have followed in the dubious trail of alfalfa sprouts, sun-dried tomatoes, *cuisine minceur,* stratified sauces, oversize dinner plates, woks, and gamay rosés.

My basic stance on food and drink couldn't be more overt, and it's anchored by a personal code of principles I hold almost inalterable. First, I've never paid much attention to ludicrous trends, most of which come and go as quickly and blessedly as tidbits of shrimp with orange dust or beet carpaccio proffered in pretentious restaurants *du moment.* Nor have I allowed my tastes and convictions to be influenced significantly by the unruly ventures of professional celebrity chefs, or the pompous proclamations of fad-crazed food magazines, or the latest groovy cookbook. What does exert considerable impact on the subjects I write about is what I blithely call the gustatory heartbeat of America, meaning the traditions, flavors, serious innovations, and dining customs that most people comfortably associate with nourishing themselves well. James Beard once lectured me that Americans are fascinated with any foreign cuisine, unusual ingredient, and daring cooking technique, but what they'll always love instinctively more than anything else are engaging ideas about great meatloaf, juicy steaks, homespun pies, and other such treasured dishes that evoke our rich national and regional heritage. It was advice that I heeded and have never forgotten.

So does this imply that, in my crazy pursuits, I'm automatically hostile to any facet of the culinary revolution that does not adhere necessarily to a certain set of values perceived as the backbone of sensible eating and drinking? By no means! I extol sensuous new varieties of wild mushrooms, grains, and root vegetables; distinctive beans and leafy greens; modern cheeses and sausages; daikon, celeriac, and other beguiling vegetables and fruits; and salt cod, sardines, tilapia, and arctic char. And certainly not when I probe deeply into such virtually ignored topics as Southern pig, okra, and grits; gravlax and international seafood salads; microbrews, absinthe, and rosé Champagne; cooking with peanut butter and iceberg lettuce; Samster grocery shopping; and restaurant foods that simply don't travel.

While I never cease to scrutinize remote terrains and discover wondrous new flavors, no doubt part of my mission is not only to revisit, reassess, and redefine conventional subjects in order to give them fresh appeal but to convince professionals and amateurs alike that such seemingly prolix topics as chowder, steak, sourdough bread, Parmigiano-Reggiano cheese, fruitcake, vodka, and tipping in restaurants merit considerably more serious reflection if we're ever to evolve a truly balanced sophistication in the ways we eat, drink, cook, and dine out. There are without question patent advantages to utilizing some of the latest ingredients to hit the market, indulging judiciously in fusion cooking, sipping one peculiar wine or cocktail after another, and modifying our demeanor in restaurants to better suit the times, so long as we don't allow our global palates and eccentric dining habits to utterly destroy the very foundation on which intelligent gustatory and social pleasure must be based.

Over the centuries, gourmandise has had its champions in every civilized country of the world, but surely none has impressed me more or illustrated my philosophy with sterner gusto than the vigorous, portly, double-chinned figure of George Frideric Handel. While stories abound pertaining to the great composer's ravenous appetite and curiosity about food and drink during the many years he lived on Brook Street in London, perhaps the most salient relates how when dining alone one evening in a tavern and unable to decide between the roast partridge with juniper, beef braised in stout, and a new preparation of grouse, he simply ordered all three. After a long, restless delay, Handel finally signaled to the serving wench.

"Is there some reason you haven't served the food?" he huffed.

"But, Sire, we were waiting for your companions to arrive," the damsel explained.

"Well, I am the companions, so would you kindly bring my dinner?"

PART ONE

REBEL SCOUT

SOUTHERN PIG

PORK IS AND ALWAYS HAS BEEN MY FAVORITE MEAT, BUT, AFTER all, I was born and bred in North Carolina and have yet to meet a fellow Southerner who didn't respect, love, and, indeed, *understand* pig like no other American. So indelible are certain porcine memories of my youth in Charlotte, in fact, that you could say I was virtually weaned on the inimitable sight, aroma, and taste of hog in all its myriad and marvelous culinary manifestations.

Every other Saturday morning, for instance, the family ritually piled into the car and drove out to the shop on a huge working farm called Morrocroft so Mother could replenish our staples of fresh country bulk sausage, thick slabs of carefully cured back bacon, streak-o'-lean cooking meat, souse, and satiny liver mush. Come late summer each year, nothing was more exciting than making the trip up to W. G. Long's remote farm at Glendale Springs in the Blue Ridge Mountains to inspect, discuss, and eventually pick out two of the same hand-cured, slowly aged, moldy, luscious eighteen-pound country hams that today Mother and I still travel two and a half hours to procure.

And though it seems we were constantly attending one benefit pork barbecue or pig pickin' after another at churches, schools, country clubs, and private homes, what we awaited with utmost anticipation was the lavish spectacle thrown in October (yesterday and now) out at Mallard Creek Presbyterian Church, where the hog pits stretched thirty or more yards, and communal tables under a massive tent groaned with platters of chopped hickory-smoked pork barbecue, Brunswick stew, tangy coleslaw, and oozing pies and cakes, and politicians up for election from all over the state circulated, handing out fountain pens, calendars, and crazy little hats.

Today, pig is as much king on the Southern table as when I took my first bites of juicy pork roast with sweet potatoes, fried salty country ham with red-eye gravy, and pickled pig's feet, and no matter where I travel in Dixie, there's never a moment when I'm not sniffing out a new blend of country sausage, a different style of pork barbecue, or an increasingly rare but sapid hog's head stew. The state of Iowa might be number one in American swine production (North Carolina comes in second) and distribution; Chicago may still be called by some the "hog butcher for the world"; and no doubt Texans and Kansas Citians can talk with some authority about Chester Whites, Durocs, Spots, and other breeds of pig. But when it comes not only to the art of curing, smoking, seasoning, and cooking pig but also to outright consumption, nobody—repeat *nobody*—outperforms Southerners.

Even now, when the popularity of pork nationwide is reaching an all-time high (due primarily to much leaner hogs), rarely in markets outside the South do you find much more than standard chops and ribs, roasts, smoked ham and bacon, frozen sausage rolls, and maybe a little salt pork. The meat departments in Southern stores like Harris Teeter and Winn-Dixie, by contrast, boast vast sections devoted exclusively to pork products—a real pig spectacle that would baffle the unenlightened and gives credence to the adage that Southerners eat every part of a porker but the oink.

There, in addition to all the ordinary cuts, are gallon tubs of pork chitterlings (stomach lining) and lard; trays of fresh ears, jowls, snouts, liver, tongues, and knuckles; bags of stomachs and brains; packages of meaty pig's feet, country ham, fatback, ham hocks, and streak o' lean (lean salt pork); and containers of liver pudding, cracklin's (rendered, crisp skins), souse meat (or head cheese), and scrapple. Up North, I gave up a long time ago trying to find decent well-seasoned bulk sausage that contains the right proportions of lean meat and fat, but the last time I was home to stock up, I counted in one supermarket case no less than nine different brands of fresh whole-hog sausage just waiting to be pattied and fried for breakfast or used in stuffings, coatings, spoonbreads, sauces, and, yes, even pies and cakes.

Historically, the first domesticated pigs in the South were a herd of thirteen brought from Spain to southwest Florida in 1539 by Hernando de Soto. Since the animals proved to be so easily housed, fed, and cared for, they quickly became the region's main dietary staple. Not only was pork the most economical meat to produce, it was also one that could be successfully salted, smoked, air-dried, and preserved in other ways for long periods without losing its textural and palatal integrity.

Colonial Virginians ate such quantities of pig that one William Byrd reported jestfully that they were "prone to grunt rather than to speak." So infatuated was Thomas Jefferson with the potential of swine that he imported

Calcutta boars to cross-breed with his Virginia sows, and by the early nineteenth century, the exceptional hams produced in Smithfield from shoats that foraged in the surrounding peanut fields had already gained sun renown that even Queen Victoria had a standing order. Throughout the South, "pork-barrel legislation," "high-on-the-hog," having a "hoggish temper," doing something "whole-hog," and other such expressions became part of the vernacular, and there's more than a modicum of truth in the theory that the Confederacy lost the War Between the States partly because strategic pork supplies dwindled to the point where troops were literally half-starved when the vital commodity nearly disappeared.

From the bayous of Louisiana to the mountains of Tennessee and Alabama to the swampy low country of South Carolina and Georgia, the multiple ways that pig is utilized in the kitchen are staggering. All Southerners, of course, love a traditional, herby pork loin, shoulder, or fresh ham roasted with sweet potatoes or turnips, a plate of crispy spareribs, earthy pork stew with black-eyed peas or butter beans, and a regal country ham stuffed with any variety of greens or fruits. But move through the regions and you find pork-studded Kentucky burgoos, spicy ham and sausage pilaus in Charleston and Savannah, Cajun blood puddings, chitlin' hash and crunchy fried pig's ears throughout Mississippi, bacon and squash pudding, sausage spoon bread, pork pone pie, silky brains and scrambled eggs, crusty baked pig's feet, and deviled pork liver. What Rebel would dream of simmering "a mess of greens," peas, or beans without a ham hock or piece of side meat for flavor? Who can deny that even the most pristine cornbread is enhanced by a few cracklin's? And just the idea of frying chicken in vegetable shortening or lard that doesn't contain a little bacon grease is, well . . . Yankee!

It's been said that Southerners never agree on religion, politics, and barbecue, and all you have to do to see tempers flare on this last subject is to attend one of the outlandish barbecue champion cook-offs held annually in Lexington and Raleigh, North Carolina; Owenboro, Kentucky; Memphis, Tennessee; and Vienna, Georgia, not to mention the Southern Foodways Alliance Conference every fall in Oxford, Mississippi. It must first be understood that in the South, genuine pit-cooked barbecue means pig and only pig, since pig is the one meat that can absorb various flavorings and seasonings without losing its identity—which is why Texans (with all their beef and goat and chicken roasts) have never been considered true Southerners. Of course, every state—indeed, every region, county, and town—deems itself the world authority on barbecued pig. And in my home state of North

Carolina alone, passions run so deep over the fine distinctions between Eastern-style, Lexington-style, and Western-style barbecue (as well as the different styles of sauce, coleslaw, Brunswick stew, and hushpuppies served with the meat) that I learned never to air a preference on the complex and heated topic for fear of alienating family and losing friends. In my never-ending search for great barbecue (chopped with pieces of cracklin' mixed into the meat, if you please), I've eaten superior pig at Big Bob Gibson's in Decatur, Alabama; Piggy Park in Columbia, South Carolina; Goldies Trail in Vicksburg, Mississippi; Wilber's in Goldsboro, North Carolina, and dozens of other such down-home digs. But far be it from me to make any definitive proclamations now or in the future on what is without question the national dish of the South.

For nearly four centuries, the noble pig has sustained the South through development and prosperity, grief and glory, defeat and recovery. It has become a veritable symbol not only of survival, but of the gastronomic excellence that has come to define so many of the distinctive dishes that grace the Southern table. President Harry Truman from Missouri may not have been a legitimate Southerner, but no doubt he won over the hearts of Rebs from Maryland to Mississippi when he once declared, "No man should be allowed to be president who does not understand hogs."

Fresh Country Pork Sausage

MAKES 3 POUNDS SAUSAGE

2 pounds boneless pork shoulder, chilled
1 pound fresh pork fat, chilled
1 tablespoon salt
1 teaspoon freshly ground pepper
2 teaspoons ground dried sage
1 teaspoon crushed hot red pepper
3 tablespoons cold water

Cut the pork and pork fat into 2-inch chunks. Pass the chunks first through the coarse blade of a meat grinder, then through the fine blade into a mixing bowl.

Add all the remaining ingredients, moisten both hands with water, and knead the mixture with your hands till well blended and smooth. Form the sausage into a ball, wrap tightly in plastic wrap, and refrigerate until ready to use. (The sausage freezes well for up to 2 months.)

Sausage Spoon Bread

1 pound country pork sausage, commercial or fresh (see recipe on page 11)

2½ cups milk

1 cup cornmeal

8 tablespoons (1 stick) butter, softened

1 tablespoon sugar

1 teaspoon baking powder

1 teaspoon salt

4 large eggs, separated

½ cup grated sharp cheddar cheese

2 tablespoons minced onion

1 tablespoon prepared mustard

Break up the sausage well and fry in a large, heavy skillet over moderate heat, stirring until browned. When completely cooked, drain the sausage on paper towels and reserve.

Preheat the oven to 350°F.

In a large saucepan, scald the milk, heating till bubbles form around the edges of the pan. Gradually stir in the cornmeal, beat thoroughly with a spoon, and cook over low heat till thick. Remove from the heat and add the butter in pieces. Add the sugar, baking powder, and salt and beat well till the butter has melted. Set aside to cool.

In a small bowl, beat the egg yolks and stir them into the cooled cornmeal mixture. In a large bowl, beat the egg whites with an electric mixer till stiff peaks form; fold the whites into the cornmeal mixture. Add the cheese, onion, and mustard and mix lightly till well blended.

Pour the mixture into a medium-size buttered casserole or baking dish, sprinkle the reserved sausage evenly over the top, and bake till a straw inserted into the middle comes out clean, about 40 minutes.

Serve the spoon bread as a breakfast dish or on a brunch buffet.

Carolina Pork Barbecue with Spicy Vinegar Sauce

THE BARBECUE

One small bag hickory chips
(available at nurseries and
hardware stores)
One 10-pound bag charcoal
briquettes
One 6- to 7-pound boneless pork
shoulder (butt or picnic cut),
securely tied with butcher's string

THE SAUCE

1 quart cider vinegar
¼ cup Worcestershire sauce
1 cup ketchup
2 tablespoons prepared mustard
3 tablespoons light brown sugar
2 tablespoons salt
Freshly ground pepper to taste
1 tablespoon crushed hot red pepper

Soak 6 handfuls of hickory chips in water for 30 minutes.

Open one bottom and one top vent on a kettle grill. Place a small drip pan in the bottom of the grill, stack charcoal briquettes evenly around the pan, and ignite. When coals are gray on one side (after about 30 minutes), turn and sprinkle 2 handfuls of soaked chips evenly over the hot coals.

Situate the pork shoulder skin-side up in the center of the grill about 6 inches directly over the drip pan (not over the hot coals), lower the lid, and cook slowly for 2 hours. Replenish the coals and soaked chips as they burn up, but never allow coals to get too hot. Turn the pork, lower the lid, and cook 2 hours longer.

Meanwhile, prepare the sauce by combining all the ingredients in a large nonreactive saucepan. Stir well, bring to a simmer, and cook for 5 minutes. Remove from the heat and let stand for 2 hours.

Transfer the pork to a working surface, make deep gashes in the meat with a sharp knife, and baste liberally with the sauce. Replenish the coals and chips as needed (maintaining a low heat), replace the pork skin-side down on the grill, and cook for 2 hours longer, basting with the sauce from time to time.

Transfer the pork to a chopping board and remove the string. Remove and discard most (but not all) of the crisp skin and excess fat, and chop the meat coarsely with an impeccably clean hatchet, Chinese cleaver, or large, heavy chef's knife. Add just enough sauce to moisten the meat further and toss till well blended. Either serve the barbecue immediately with the remaining sauce on the side or refrigerate and reheat in the top of a double boiler over simmering water when ready to serve. (The barbecue can be frozen in individual containers for up to 3 months.)

Serve the barbecue plain or topped with coleslaw on a hamburger roll.

Pork Pie with Biscuit Crust

THE PIE FILLING

3 slices bacon
2 medium onions, chopped
1 celery rib, chopped
1 medium green bell pepper,
    cored, seeded, and chopped
1 garlic clove, minced
2 pounds lean, cooked pork, cut
    into small cubes
3 cups beef broth
2 tablespoons cornmeal
2 tablespoons tomato paste

2 tablespoons Worcestershire sauce
Tabasco to taste
1 teaspoon salt
Freshly ground pepper to taste

THE BISCUIT CRUST

2 cups all-purpose flour
2 teaspoons baking powder
1 teaspoon salt
3 tablespoons vegetable shortening
¾ cup milk
1 large egg, beaten

To make the pie filling, fry the bacon in a large, heavy skillet till almost crisp; drain on paper towels. Add the onions, celery, bell pepper, and garlic to the skillet and cook over moderate heat about 3 minutes, stirring. Crumble the cooked bacon over the vegetables, then add the pork, broth, cornmeal, tomato paste, Worcestershire, Tabasco, salt, and pepper, stirring till well blended. Simmer the mixture about 30 minutes, stirring, then transfer to a 2-quart baking dish or casserole.

Preheat the oven to 350°F.

To make the crust, combine the flour, baking powder, salt, and shortening in a mixing bowl and work mixture with the fingers till mealy. Add the milk and egg and stir till blended.

Spoon the batter over the top of the pork mixture and bake till the crust is golden brown, 40 to 45 minutes.

Baked Fresh Ham and
Sweet Potatoes with Orange Gravy

One 6- to 7-pound fresh ham
   (butt or shank)
6 to 8 finely crumbled dried sage
   leaves
Salt and freshly ground pepper to
   taste
4 cups water

6 medium-size sweet potatoes,
   peeled and quartered
3 tablespoons all-purpose flour
1 cup orange juice
3 tablespoons finely grated orange
   zest

Preheat the oven to 325°F.

Remove and discard any tough ham skin, score the fat at 2-inch intervals, and rub all sides of the ham with the sage and salt and pepper. Position the ham fat-side up on a wire rack in a roasting pan large enough to hold it and the potatoes. Add 2 cups of the water to the pan, cover, and bake about 2 hours, basting the ham from time to time with the pan juices.

Place the potatoes around the ham, cover, and continue baking about 30 minutes. Remove the cover and roast about 30 minutes longer or till a meat thermometer inserted into the ham registers 160°F and the potatoes are tender, basting once.

Transfer the ham and potatoes to a large, heated platter, remove rack from the pan, and pour off part of the fat. Over moderate heat, make the gravy by adding the remaining 2 cups of water to the pan and stirring and scraping the bottom and sides till juices are slightly reduced. Stirring constantly, sprinkle on the flour till well incorporated and the juices thicken. Add the orange juice and orange zest, return to a simmer, and continue stirring till the gravy thickens, 5 to 10 minutes. Taste for salt and pepper, pour the gravy into a gravy boat, and serve with the sliced ham and potatoes.

Pork Cracklin', Shrimp, and Pea Salad

2 cups diced streak-o'-lean cooking meat (lean salt pork) or slab bacon
2 pounds fresh medium-size shrimp
½ lemon
2½ cups cooked green peas
2 small dill pickles, diced
1 cup mayonnaise
3 tablespoons fresh lemon juice

3 tablespoons heavy cream
1 teaspoon prepared horseradish
Salt and freshly ground pepper to taste
Curly endive (chicory) leaves
2 medium-size ripe tomatoes, quartered, for garnish
3 hard-boiled eggs, peeled and quartered, for garnish

In a large, heavy skillet, render the diced cooking meat over moderate heat till crisp and golden brown, about 20 minutes, watching carefully and reducing the heat if the fat threatens to burn. Drain the cracklin's on paper towels and reserve.

Place the shrimp in a large saucepan with enough salted water to cover, squeeze the lemon into the water, then toss it in. Bring to a boil, remove from the heat, let stand 1 minute, then drain. When the shrimp are cool enough to handle, shell, devein, and place in a large mixing bowl. Add the peas and pickles, mix, and chill 1 hour, covered with plastic wrap.

In a small bowl, whisk together the mayonnaise, lemon juice, cream, horseradish, and salt and pepper till well blended. Add to the shrimp mixture and toss till ingredients are well coated.

Line a large salad bowl with the curly endive, mound the salad in the middle, sprinkle the top with the reserved cracklin's, and garnish with the tomatoes and eggs.

KING OF DIXIE STEWS

Whack!

Precise as a woodcutter's ax, Mr. Nunn's hatchet lopped off the mean old hen's neck in a single blow, sending the bird flapping around the dusty backyard as the proverbial chicken with its head cut off, causing the other pullets in the small henhouse to screech wildly, and scaring the dickens out of me.

"Here, son," our neighbor eventually directed after eviscerating the hen, scalding it momentarily in boiling water, plucking it clean of feathers, and wrapping it in newspaper. "Now, you take this right home to your granddaddy, and he'll fix you a big pot of Brunswick stew for supper."

Back at the house, Mother disjointed the plump chicken with her heavy butcher knife, handing the pieces to Paw Paw to brown evenly in bacon grease before adding to the iron pot some chopped onions, celery, and ripe tomatoes, a sizable ham hock, two or three red bird's-eye hot peppers, plenty of salt and pepper, and enough water to cover the ingredients. After everything had cooked slowly for a couple of hours, he then shredded the meats and returned them to the pot; added handfuls of fresh corn kernels, small butter beans, and sliced okra plus seasonings and a little more water; and continued the very slow simmering well into the afternoon, telling me to stir the pot regularly when he went outside to work in the garden. He measured nothing, paid little attention to the timing, never tasted his concoction once, and casually stirred in a few spoonfuls of mashed potatoes only when the stew had turned a pale orange and looked like it was ready to be thickened more.

Since those childhood days in North Carolina, I estimate that I must have ingested maybe five hundred gallons of Brunswick stew, half of which

I prepared myself, but never, not once, have I savored a version like the glorious ones that Paw Paw would throw together during summertime using those prodigiously pot-bellied fresh hens of Mr. Nunn's. Served with nothing but Mother's homemade cornbread, or in smaller bowls alongside plates of pit-cooked, chopped pork barbecue, vinegary coleslaw, and hush puppies, the stew was thick, earthy, perfectly balanced, and utterly sumptuous.

I've eaten Brunswick stew made with squirrel, turkey, possum, lamb, fresh pork, beef, rabbit, and even goat. I've had it with and without okra, shredded cabbage, rice, chili powder, curry, apple cider, and sherry. Some renditions have been sensational, others credible, and still others plain down ridiculous. Obviously, I'm very serious about the stuff. I'm forever scouting new locales throughout the South, I throw at least three big Brunswick stew parties at my house every year, I consider myself the consummate aficionado, and I'd claim to be a world authority if only—if only that persistent, nagging memory of Paw Paw's mysterious, ineffable stew were not always present to remind me how cruel the quest for perfection remains.

That Brunswick stew is a quintessential Southern creation traditionally cooked in huge, black, iron cauldrons is no more open to debate than the fact that its natural venues are lavish church barbecues, fish fries, political rallies, civic fund-raisers, tobacco curings, family reunions, and other such communal gatherings which necessitate feeding vast numbers of people. Broach the topics of its origins and what constitutes an authentic stew, however, and boy, does the fur begin to fly in the key states of Georgia, Virginia, and North Carolina.

Residents of the Georgia coastal Low Country swear that the first vat was fired up by natives in the vicinity of Brunswick, Georgia in 1898 at a July Fourth celebration, and, to make the claim official, the town has mounted the original pot on a concrete podium at the Welcome Center on Highway 17.

"That's nothing but nonsense," counters the head of the Stewmasters Association at Lawrenceville in Brunswick County, Virginia, the area proclaimed by the Virginia Legislature to be the irrefutable home of Brunswick stew—and a region where there seems to be a different charity cook-off every weekend of the year. "We have documents to prove that Brunswick stew was first made in our county back in 1828 by 'Uncle Jimmy' Matthews, a black cook who prepared it with squirrel, onions, butter, and stale bread while a Dr. Creed Haskins and his buddies were on a hunting expedition—and that's seventy years before those Georgia Crackers' date."

Brunswick County, North Carolina, is also part of the feud, but although there can be no question that some of the best Brunswick stew on earth is found at dozens of legendary barbecue joints in the eastern part of the state, Georgians and Virginians hardly consider Tarheels real contenders: they don't have much impressive Brunswick stew history and they don't even *respect* it enough to serve it primarily as a main course. As for the rest of the South, a consensus of opinion in Georgia, Virginia, and North Carolina is that those folks should simply stick with their burgoos and bogs and perloos and gumbos and other poor cousins of the more noble Brunswick stew.

If you think the never-ending war pertaining to the origins of Brunswick stew is intense, that's staid bickering compared with the blazing controversy over the correct ingredients, the right cooking time and texture, the color, and whether it's best eaten with cornbread or hush puppies or biscuits. Due to strict federal legislation forbidding the sale of uninspected game animals shot in the wild, plus the fact that most urban squirrels now feed more on garbage than nuts, the days are long gone when Brunswick stew was made with the furred creatures favored by our culinary ancestors. As a result, the primary ingredient today in most Brunswick stews is chicken—ideally a stout, flavor-packed hen simmered till the meat is falling apart and can be casily shredded—plus another meat like ham hock or fatback or beef.

Of course, certain Rebels have their own radical ideas about the stew, but when somebody like Wilbur King of King's barbecue in Kinston, North Carolina, wanted not long ago to include Brunswick stew made only with pork in his mail-order business, Oink Express, it came as a shock to learn that, according to another federal regulation, nothing can be called genuine Brunswick stew unless it contains at least two meats.

"They said it can be possum or cat if you want," King complains, "but it has to have two."

Personally, I'm now strictly a chicken and smoked ham hock stewhead, having determined years back that the beef chuck I was adding to my Brunswick stew made it taste more like a beef stew or thick vegetable pottage than the distinctive victual it's supposed to be.

As to secondary ingredients, the possibilities are so disparate that I have no intention of inciting more wrath among enthusiasts by indulging vicariously in futile suggestions and disputes. Instead, I'll simply relate the official items adopted by the Stewmasters Association of Brunswick County, Virginia, sponsors of the hotly competitive annual championship cook-off between Virginians and Georgians at Brunswick's Mineral Springs Bed and Breakfast to determine once and for all for the umpteenth time who produces the greatest Brunswick stew: potatoes, onions, tomatoes, lima beans, corn, butter, salt, black pepper, hot red pepper, sugar, plus one additional thickening ingredient. "Adding any additional ingredient(s) will disqualify the stew from being an original Brunswick stew," a strong footnote to the bylaw reads.

Well, on second thought, I just can't let that pass, for the simple reason that no Brunswick stew worthy of the iron pot it's cooked in is right without okra. Maybe that's what those Virginians mean by "one additional thickening ingredient," but, if so, it should be spelled out in no uncertain terms. North Carolinians, Georgians, and even Alabamans all know that Brunswick stew is simply not Brunswick stew without the special flavoring and thickening agent of okra—and Virginians should know that, too. Brunswick stew without okra is like black-eyed peas without sidemeat.

Nor can I refrain from commenting very briefly on what other ingredients I deem appropriate and inappropriate for a sublime Brunswick stew. Unless you want your stew to taste like some fancy French ragout, never use stock or broth in place of plain old water for the liquid base. In addition to the chicken and some form of flavorful pork (smoked ham hock, fatback, bacon, streak-o'-lean, or shoulder), I find nothing wrong with a little chopped celery, bell pepper, carrot, and garlic; a few dashes of Worcestershire and Tabasco sauces; and maybe a discreet sprinkling of paprika or herbs. Green beans or peas, shredded cabbage, and rice, on the other hand, have no place in Brunswick stew. And, as far as I'm concerned, those who add such utterly alien ingredients as lamb, chopped apples, ketchup, curry or chili powder, and liquid smoke must have learned to cook up North or out in California.

And while I'm at it, there are a few final things that tend to irk me about the way some people (including many putative experts) fix Brunswick stew. First, shortcutting the process by using skinless, boned chicken is nothing less than sacrilege for the simple reason that skin and bones add so much rich flavor to the stew during the initial simmer (and, after all, the bones and some skin are discarded when the meat is shredded). Second, pouring sugar (white or brown) into Brunswick stew is almost as muddle-minded as putting it in cornbread and biscuits. If you must have a sweet edge to your stew, just add a few chopped carrots. And third, since the main purpose of cubed potatoes is to thicken the stew, they should either be allowed to cook long enough to practically disintegrate or be mashed and stirred in at the end—not left floating around as in a chowder.

The only thing worse than a thin, liquidy Brunswick stew is one that is stodgy. In South Carolina, Georgia, and much of the Deep South, the stew often has a tendency to be soupy, while up in Virginia, competition stewmasters insist vehemently that the texture is right only when a wooden stirring paddle stands upright in the stew. In my experience, North Carolinians generally seem to attain the ideal consistency, meaning that while the finished stew contains some liquid, it can be eaten as easily with a fork as with a spoon.

Fortunately, there are a few cardinal rules in making Brunswick stew about which all Southerners are in near total agreement, the most important being the pot in which it's simmered. Of course, no home cook is expected to invest in a traditional, cumbrous, three-legged, cast-iron cauldron like the ones seen at competition cook-offs. But since nothing scorches worse than Brunswick stew prepared in a cheap, light-gauge metal vessel, it's absolutely essential to use the heaviest iron or stainless-steel pot possible. (Experts say they can somehow tell a difference when the stew is cooked in a well-seasoned, black, cast-iron pot, and I agree.)

Brunswick stew can never be rushed. While throughout the South cooking times vary almost as much as the ingredients, the uncontested canon is that any Brunswick stew must be simmered very slowly long enough to allow the ingredients to fuse, the flavors to meld, and the characteristic pale to reddish orange color to develop; the heat should be such that the stew barely bubbles. The larger the quantity, of course, the longer the stew needs to be cooked. The minimum time for even four or five quarts is no less than about three and one-half hours (and, please, no twaddle about the vegetables not being al dente). As one Virginia stewmaster pronounces, "In a perfect Brunswick stew, 'bout the only ingredients you oughta be able to make out at the end are the limas and corn."

Perhaps what takes the most patience is the almost constant stirring required to prevent the stew from scorching once the shredded meats are added. Professionals at big cook-offs and benefits literally take turns stirring their stews nonstop with the paddles hour after hour, and although I'm not quite that precautious at home, I, like many another Southerner, have learned from more than one nearly cremated disaster never to leave the pot longer than ten or fifteen minutes.

No doubt I'll esteem Brunswick stew as one of the South's most glorious contributions to world gastronomy till my dying day, but the truth is that, after a gentle reprimand I received not long ago from a wise waitress at Wilber's Barbecue in Goldsboro, North Carolina, I've just about resolved from this point on to distance myself from all the heated fuss about the stew. There I was with friends perched over a Chick-n-Que platter, raving blissfully over the thick, aromatic, luscious Brunswick stew and asking the busy waitress endless questions about types of chicken and potatoes, and cooking times, and why the stew was so reddish. Finally, in utter exasperation, she popped her order pad impatiently in the palm of her hand, looked down at me with a motherly smile, and uttered, "Honey, why don't you just hush up and eat your stew?"

North Carolina–Style Brunswick Stew

Although I'm forever modifying the recipe, this is basically the standard Brunswick stew I've been making for decades and the style found in most North Carolina barbecue joints. I prefer to use all fresh vegetables, but when they're unavailable or don't look too good, I have no qualms about using canned tomatoes and frozen corn, okra, and limas. Like my granddaddy, and unlike most Tarheels who let potatoes cook with the other ingredients, I like to thicken my stew at the end with mashed potatoes in order to control the texture. A classic North Carolina stew such as this one can be eaten with either a fork or a spoon.

4 slices bacon
¼ cup vegetable oil
One 6-pound stewing chicken (hen), cut up, rinsed, and patted dry
2 medium onions, chopped
2 celery ribs (leaves included), chopped
1 carrot, scraped and dried
1 medium smoked ham hock, trimmed
3 large ripe tomatoes, chopped and juices retained

1 small dried hot red pepper, seeded and minced
1 tablespoon Worcestershire sauce
1 teaspoon paprika
Salt and freshly ground pepper to taste
1½ cups fresh or frozen corn kernels
1½ cups fresh or frozen sliced okra
1½ cups fresh or frozen small lima beans
1½ cups mashed boiled potatoes

In a large cast-iron or heavy stainless-steel pot, fry the bacon till crisp over moderately high heat. Drain on paper towels, crumble, and reserve.

Add the oil to the bacon grease, add the chicken pieces, and brown on all sides; transfer to a platter. Reduce the heat to moderate, add the onions, celery, and carrot and cook 3 minutes, stirring. Return the chicken to the pot and add the ham hock, tomatoes with their juices, hot pepper, Worcestershire, paprika, and salt and pepper. Add enough water to cover the ingredients by 1 inch, stir, bring to a steady simmer, skimming any scum off the surface, cover, and cook 2½ to 3 hours, or till the chicken is very tender.

With a slotted spoon, remove the chicken and ham hock. When cool enough to handle, remove and discard the bones and any skin; shred the meats and return them to the pot. Add the corn, okra, limas, and reserved bacon, return the stew to a simmer, and cook, uncovered, 1 hour, stirring every 10 minutes for the first half-hour, then constantly.

Add the mashed potatoes and continue stirring about 15 minutes, or till the stew is nicely thickened. Taste and, if necessary, adjust the seasoning.

Ladle the stew into large soup bowls.

Virginia-Style Brunswick Stew

The recipe for this typically thick, reddish-orange stew designed to feed a small crowd comes from a member of the Brunswick County, Virginia, Stewmasters Association. Since he uses skinned and boned chicken, no shredding is necessary; the chicken simply falls apart during the cooking process. He gradually adds the margarine and seasonings, tasting the stew periodically till he gets just the right savor. Ideally, this stew should be so thick that a fork positioned in the center stands upright.

5½ pounds skinned and boned roasted chicken parts (thighs are best)

6 ounces fatback or salt pork, chopped

4 pounds all-purpose potatoes, peeled and cubed

2½ pounds onions, peeled and chopped

8 tablespoons (1 stick) margarine or unsalted butter

3 tablespoons salt

3 tablespoons sugar

1½ teaspoons freshly ground pepper

1½ teaspoons cayenne

1½ quarts (6 cups) canned crushed tomatoes (juices included)

2½ quarts (10 cups) small fresh or frozen lima beans

1½ quarts (6 cups) fresh or frozen corn kernels

Place the chicken parts and fatback in a 12-quart cast-iron or heavy stainless-steel pot and add enough water to cover by 1 inch. Bring to a boil, reduce the heat to a steady simmer, and cook uncovered 1½ hours, or till the chicken is very tender.

Add the potatoes, onions, 2 tablespoons of the margarine, 1 tablespoon each salt and sugar, and pinches of black pepper and cayenne. Return to a simmer and cook about 1 hour longer, or till the potatoes are tender, stirring about every 15 minutes.

Add the tomatoes plus their juices, another 2 tablespoons of the margarine, 1 tablespoon each salt and sugar, and pinches of the black pepper and cayenne. Return to a simmer and cook, stirring, 10 minutes.

Add the limas, another 2 tablespoons of the margarine, and the remaining salt, sugar, black pepper, and cayenne. Return to a simmer and cook about 1 hour, or till the limas are soft, stirring steadily or at least every 10 minutes.

Add the corn and remaining margarine, return to a simmer, and cook, stirring constantly, 15 to 20 minutes longer, or till the stew is very thick. Taste and, if necessary, adjust the seasoning.

Ladle the stew into large soup bowls.

Georgia-Style Brunswick Stew

SERVES 10 TO 12

Unlike Virginia and North Carolina Brunswick stews, most Georgia versions contain not only chicken and pork but also beef. Although the stew is thickened with both potatoes and okra, enough liquid is usually retained to produce an almost soupy texture. And unlike the other two reddish-orange styles, the color of this one is quite pale.

8 slices bacon

Two 3-pound chickens, cut up and patted dry

1½ pounds boneless beef round or chuck, trimmed of excess fat, cut into 1-inch pieces, and patted dry

3 large onions, chopped

2 celery ribs (leaves included), chopped

1 medium green bell pepper, seeded and chopped

Vegetable oil, if needed

1 medium smoked ham hock, trimmed

One 28-ounce can tomatoes, chopped, juices reserved

3 medium baking potatoes, peeled and cubed

2 small hot red peppers, seeded and minced

1 teaspoon dried thyme

1 teaspoon dried basil

Salt and freshly ground pepper to taste

2½ cups fresh or frozen corn kernels

2½ cups fresh or frozen small lima beans

2 cups fresh or frozen sliced okra

In a large cast-iron or heavy stainless-steel pot, fry the bacon till crisp over moderate heat. Drain on paper towels, crumble, and reserve.

In batches, add the chicken pieces to the pot, brown on all sides, and transfer to a platter. Add the beef to the pot, brown on all sides, and transfer to the platter. Add the onions, celery, and bell pepper. Cook, stirring often, till softened, adding a little oil if necessary.

Return the chicken and beef to the pot and add the ham hock, tomatoes plus their juices, potatoes, hot peppers, thyme, basil, and salt and pepper. Add enough water to cover by 1½ inches and stir well. Bring to a moderate boil, reduce the heat to low, and simmer, covered, about 1½ hours, or till the chicken is very tender, skimming the surface from time to time.

With a slotted spoon, remove the chicken and continue to simmer the stew 1½ hours longer, stirring from time to time. When the chicken is cool enough to handle, remove and discard the skin and bones, shred the meat, and set aside.

Add the corn, limas, and okra to the pot, stir, return the heat to low, and let simmer, uncovered, about 30 minutes, stirring often. Remove the ham hock; pick the meat from the bone, shred, and return to the pot along with the shredded chicken and reserved bacon. Return to the simmer and continue cooking, uncovered, 30 minutes longer, stirring almost constantly. Taste and, if necessary, adjust the seasoning.

Ladle the stew into large soup bowls.

THE SLIME FACTOR

ALTHOUGH AMERICAN FOOD LOVERS CAN BE A SAVVY, ENGAGing, and wildly curious breed, I must say that sometimes they frustrate me to the point of distraction. Without blinking an eye, they'll tuck into a dozen or so lubricious fresh oysters or snails, or mound a sludge of extremely ripe, runny brie or St.-Marcellin cheese on a piece of bread, or swoon ecstatically over squishy morsels of sushi. No one objects in the least to an underfried sunny-side up egg with viscid albumen flowing all over the plate, while the really groovy and obsessed totally disregard the nauseating, disgusting odor of a Malaysian durian fruit just to taste its rich, oozing flesh. Few of these gastromaniacs, in fact, are intimidated by the slick, unctuous, or mucilaginous texture of any number of foods. But confront them with one of the great staples of Southern cookery, namely okra, and there echoes the familiar, age-old, tiresome howl of "Eek, it's so sliiimy."

Well, the truth is that most non-Southerners can quite easily and quickly develop an infatuation for grits, spoon bread, and pimento cheese; and they might eventually take to salty country ham, pot likker, chowchow, and even brains and eggs. But not till they overcome the slime factor of okra and learn how glorious these pods can be will they ever fully grasp an essence of Southern cooking. Simply boiled, steamed, fried, sautéed, stewed, or pickled; incorporated into luscious soups, stews, mulls, ragouts, pilaus, and bogs; used to thicken classic gumbos and make fritters, omelettes, and salads—the versatility of okra is so amazing that it's nothing less than shocking that the vegetable has yet to capture the imagination of amateur and professional cooks outside the South.

The reason for okra's neglect certainly cannot be attributed to its unavailability, since, after all, it can be found frozen year-round all over the country (well, almost all over) and fresh during summer and early fall in most markets. Nor can blame be laid on any difficult cooking techniques necessary to transform the vegetable into numerous toothsome dishes. As for the flavor, suffice it that I've never once served nuggets of fried okra (the safest preparation to initiate the unenlightened) at a cocktail party or as a side dish that the bowl wasn't left empty and the moans of delight audible.

So the one and only explanation is the slime factor, meaning the substance (which is actually no more than a form of carbohydrate) that seeps from the pods when they're cooked beyond a certain stage (and, to be truthful, okra overcooked to a gummy, mushy mess is appalling). That I find this excuse to be narrow-minded and downright childish should be obvious, especially in view of the putative sophistication of America's contemporary eating habits.

Southerners, of course, have no problem with a blissfully smooth okra and crabmeat soup; sautéed shrimp, okra, and tomatoes; and okra and ham pilau (better know in the Carolina Low Country as "limpin' susan"). And what, for heaven's sake, would Creole gumbo, Brunswick stew, and burgoo be without the flavor and thickening power of okra?

All I can say about others' squeamish perception of okra is that it's high time they get over their prejudice, learn to cook it correctly, and embrace the pod as the wonder it is. I mean, after all, if I can learn to find occasional virtue in that rock heavy, gross, indigestible Yankee obsession called a bagel, not to mention a silly confection known as an egg cream, others can be just as bighearted about okra.

Egyptians most likely cultivated okra, a flowering hibiscus plant, as early as the twelfth century, though there's some evidence that it was popular in Asia long before that. In any case, the tropical or subtropical vegetable eventually became a staple throughout most of the Middle East, Greece, Spain, Madagascar, and, above all, Africa, and was introduced into the Western Hemisphere by Ethiopian and Angolan slaves in the seventeenth century. Called *ochinggombo* or *kingombo* by the Africans, okra came to be known in the American South simply as *gumbo* ("the vegetable"), which, in turn, evolved into the famous Creole stew of Louisiana and various other gumbos of the Carolina Low Country. (Technically, when okra appeared on the scene, it often displaced filé powder made from dried sassafras leaves as the preferred thickener, and subsequently gave its name to the stew.) Meanwhile, in the Caribbean, there developed such classic okra dishes as callaloo, coo-

coo, and foo-foo, but nowhere in the New World did the pods establish a firmer culinary foundation than in the temperate southern colonies.

Today, as in the past, okra is always harvested unripe since, if allowed to ripen, it becomes fibrous and indigestible. At its freshest, the taste is clean, slightly tart, and distinctive. Used whole or cut in cross-sections and cooked properly, the whole pods or sliced discs are crisp under the teeth and exude a minimum of the viscous (but sapid) substance that offends so many sissies. (Frying okra, by the way, eliminates all traces of slime.) Southerners know never to buy fresh okra that is not fully green and firm. Pods should be no longer than three inches, and any that is grayish, spotty, bruised, woody, or that bends in the least should be rejected. (Young, tender pods can be easily pierced with a fingernail.) Impeccable pods have a prickly fuzz along the ridges that should be wiped off under running water, and since fresh okra is highly perishable, it should be refrigerated immediately and cooked within a day or so.

To keep whole pods from "weeping," remove the stems but never cut into the caps to expose the mucilaginous seeds. Although freezing whole or cut okra does alter the texture and can affect the flavor, I find nothing really objectionable about frozen okra for soups, stews, and certain braised dishes. I'm convinced, on the other hand, that okra intended to be battered and fried, pickled, or used in salads and omelettes must be fresh. The only cardinal rule is that, except when okra is needed mainly as a thickener for soups, gumbos, and the like, it should never be overcooked. Simply boiled or steamed whole okra pods require no more than about five to seven minutes of simmering, or just till tender.

Now, much as Southerners relish okra and tomatoes, okra succotash, "limpin' susan," seafood and okra gumbo, Brunswick stew, pickled okra, and above all, crisply fried okra, never, by any stretch of the culinary imagination, would the pod be perceived as an "elegant" vegetable or used to create refined dishes. Gifted professional chefs have managed in recent years to elevate and give new definition to such other humble ingredients as grits, ham hocks, black-eyed peas, sweet potatoes, and catfish, but the one item that seems to defy experimentation and innovation is okra—at least so far. Maybe it's because the vegetable is so texturally temperamental, or because its distinctive flavor can challenge that of many other ingredients, or because most cooks truly believe that there's simply no way to improve upon the classic okra dishes codified centuries ago. I think I've discussed okra with every major Southern chef—not to mention a few hundred home cooks, food writers, and cooking teachers—and they all have such respect for this vegetable that no one has so much as suggested any new ways to cook it. It's like witnessing even the most outlandish French chef back down when the subject of potato gratin is broached, or hearing an Italian expert stammer when asked the different ways to prepare gnocchi. Some foods are sui generis in terms of culinary flexibility, and okra is one of them.

This is certainly not to say that okra dishes are not to be found in some of the South's most prestigious restaurants—not when I've had a delectable okra, green bean, and Jerusalem artichoke vinaigrette at Fearrington House, in Chapel Hill, North Carolina, or when Anson in Charleston, South Carolina, serves okra succotash or fried okra with numerous ambitious fish preparations, or when the venerable Commander's Palace, in New Orleans, has both an inimitable Creole seafood and okra gumbo and classic maque choux (sautéed okra, corn, onion, bell pepper, and bacon) on its upscale menu. But as I've discovered over and over in my quest for great okra dishes, the pod's rightful place (other than in private homes) is in no-nonsense family restaurants, country-style cafés, and a few old-fashioned hotel dining rooms.

The okra gumbo at the legendary Mrs. Wilkes' Boarding House, in Savannah, Georgia, for instance, is still as revered as their chipped roast beef hash, green rice, and blackberry cobbler. And anybody who's ever turned a lazy Susan at the Dinner Bell, in McComb, Mississippi, remembers the crunchy fried okra as much as the rabbit stew, barbecued ribs, and moist pound cake. Pilgrimages are made to homey Crook's Corner in Chapel Hill, North Carolina, just to order the sumptuous jambalaya with okra. Even when I insisted not long ago that locals in Nashville, Tennessee, take me to the shabby Loveless Motel and Restaurant outside town to try the much-touted country ham, fried chicken, and biscuits with sorghum syrup, what impressed me most was a small bowl of bacony okra and tomatoes.

I've raved over the steamed okra with black-eyed peas and fried okra battered in buttermilk and cracker crumbs at Mary Mac's Tea Room in Atlanta; Louis Osteen's shrimp stewed with okra and tomatoes at the Fish Camp Bar on Pawleys Island, South Carolina; and plain, succulent, buttered okra at John's restaurant in Birmingham, Alabama. But where I've almost met my match with okra is at a lively haunt in Charleston, South Carolina, called Slightly North of Broad, better known to locals as SNOBS. There they serve a luscious okra, shrimp, and oyster stew and a spicy okra jambalaya; they serve okra gumbo, fried okra, and sautéed oysters and okra; and they serve lethal martinis and bloody Marys garnished with pickled okra. SNOBS is a serious okra haven, and I knew that hope springs eternal when one waiter told me that they have almost as many "foreign" customs as Rebs ordering the okra dishes.

Literary sons and daughters of the South have sung the praises of okra for centuries, but perhaps none has captured the pod's glory more passionately than the contemporary novelist James Dickey did in *Jericho:* "It is time to eat. Here is supper. Black-eyed peas with ham hock . . . fried okra . . . country cornbread . . . sweet potato pie. . . . You've just done it, for who but a god could come up with the divine fact of okra?"

Stewed Okra and Tomatoes

SERVES 4 TO 6

4 slices bacon
2 small onions, chopped
1 large garlic clove, minced
1½ pounds small firm, fresh okra, stems removed, washed well, and cut into ¾-inch rounds
4 ripe but firm large tomatoes, peeled and chopped

1 small dried hot red pepper, seeded and finely chopped
2 teaspoons salt
Freshly ground pepper to taste
Pinch of dried thyme
Pinch of dried basil
Boiled white rice

In a large, heavy, nonreactive skillet (not cast-iron or aluminum), fry the bacon over moderate heat till crisp. Drain on paper towels, crumble, and set aside.

Pour off all but about 2 tablespoons of fat from the skillet. Add the onions and garlic and cook, stirring, about 5 minutes. Add the okra, tomatoes, hot pepper, salt, pepper, thyme, and basil. Reduce the heat to low, cover, and simmer till the okra and tomatoes are just soft, about 20 minutes, stirring once or twice.

Serve over rice and sprinkle the top of each serving with crumbled bacon.

Maryland Okra, Barley, and Crabmeat Soup

3 to 4 slices bacon, diced

1 medium onion, finely chopped

2 veal knuckles, trimmed of excess fat

1 pound small firm, fresh okra, stems removed, washed well, and cut in half

5 ripe medium tomatoes, peeled and quartered

3 parsley sprigs, stems removed and leaves chopped

3 quarts water

1 cup pearl barley, washed

½ teaspoon salt

⅛ teaspoon pepper

3 dashes Tabasco

Kernels cut from 3 ears fresh corn

½ pound fresh crabmeat

In a skillet, fry the bacon over moderate heat till almost crisp; drain on paper towels. Pour off all but about 1 tablespoon fat from the skillet. Add the onion to the fat and sauté till soft, about 5 minutes. Reserve with the bacon.

In a large, heavy, nonreactive pot (not cast-iron or aluminum), combine the veal knuckles, okra, tomatoes, parsley, and water. Stir in the barley and season with the salt, pepper, and Tabasco. Bring to a boil, skim the surface, reduce the heat to low, cover, and simmer slowly about 3 hours, skimming if necessary.

Add the corn and crabmeat, and simmer about 1 hour longer. Stir in the reserved bacon and onion. Season with additional salt, pepper, and Tabasco to taste.

Creole Seafood and Okra Gumbo

MAKES ABOUT 4 QUARTS

¾ cup vegetable oil
¾ cup all-purpose flour
3 medium onions, finely chopped
3 celery ribs, finely chopped
3 small green bell peppers, seeded and finely chopped
4 garlic cloves, minced
1 teaspoon cayenne
⅛ teaspoon dried oregano, crumbled
⅛ teaspoon dried basil, crumbled
3 bay leaves
Salt and pepper to taste

2 teaspoons Worcestershire sauce
2½ quarts water
½ pound smoked sausage, cut into ¼-inch rounds
½ pound small firm, fresh okra, stems removed, washed well, and cut into rounds
1 quart fresh shucked oysters (liquor included)
1 pound fresh medium shrimp, peeled and deveined
¾ pound crabmeat
Boiled white rice

In a large, heavy pot, heat the oil over moderately high heat till very hot. Slowly add the flour and cook, stirring constantly with a wooden spoon, till the roux is mahogany in color, 3 to 5 minutes; never allow it to burn in the least. (If the roux shows any black spots, you have to start again from scratch.)

Reduce the heat to moderate and add the onions, celery, bell peppers, and garlic. Cook, stirring often, about 3 minutes, scraping the bottom of the pot. Add the cayenne, oregano, basil, bay leaves, salt and pepper, and Worcestershire; stir well. Add the water, stirring constantly, then add the sausage and okra. Bring to a boil, reduce heat to low, and simmer, uncovered, 1 hour, skimming the surface and stirring from time to time to prevent sticking.

Add the oysters plus their liquor, the shrimp, and the crabmeat. Bring to a boil, reduce the heat to low, and simmer 10 to 15 minutes, or till the gumbo is thick and smooth.

Serve the gumbo over rice in soup bowls.

Batter-Fried Okra

1½ pounds small firm, fresh okra
1 cup cornmeal or fine cracker
 crumbs
1 teaspoon salt
Freshly ground pepper to taste

1 cup buttermilk
1 large egg, beaten
Tabasco to taste
Lard or vegetable shortening, for
 deep fat frying.

Heat the oven to 200°F.

Rinse the okra well, remove the stems, and either leave the pods whole or cut into ½-inch rounds. Bring a large pot of water to a boil, add the okra, and parboil 2 minutes. Drain in a colander, refresh under cold running water, and pat dry with paper towels.

In a shallow bowl, combine the cornmeal, salt, pepper, buttermilk, egg, and Tabasco. Beat till the batter is smooth.

In a large, heavy iron skillet, heat enough lard or shortening to reach about ½ inch up the sides till very hot, about 375°F on a deep-frying thermometer. Dip the okra in batches into the batter till well coated, allowing excess batter to drain off, then drop into the fat and fry till golden brown and crisp, 3 to 4 minutes. With a slotted spoon, transfer the okra to a large cookie sheet covered with paper towels and keep warm in the oven till all is fried. If you like, sprinkle with a little extra salt. Serve hot with cocktails or as a side dish.

Pickled Okra

3½ pounds small firm, fresh okra
4 teaspoons dill seeds
4 small fresh hot red peppers
4 small fresh hot green peppers
8 garlic cloves, peeled

4 cups distilled white vinegar (5%)
1 cup water
6 tablespoons salt

Trim the stems off the okra. Rinse the pods well and pat dry.

Sterilize four 1-pint canning jars and place ½ teaspoon dill seeds in the bottom of each. Pack the okra into the jars, taking care not bruise them. Add another ½ teaspoon dill seeds and 1 of each color hot pepper and 2 garlic cloves to each jar.

In a large nonreactive saucepan (not cast-iron or aluminum), combine the vinegar, water, and salt. Bring to a boil and pour equal amounts of the liquid over the okra to ¼ inch from the tops of the jars. Seal and store in a cool area at least 1 month before serving or giving away as gifts. Serve the okra chilled and refrigerate after opening.

TRUE GRITS

I'M HAVING A VERY FRUSTRATING EXPERIENCE AT A LARGE SUPER-
market on Long Island.

"Grits," I repeat for the third time to a clerk. "Could you please tell me
where the grits are located? I've been searching everywhere."

"Grapes?" she mutters.

"No, not grapes. Grits. G..r..i..t..s. Just ordinary corn grits that you eat
for breakfast. Kind of like porridge. I know Quaker makes some."

Utterly baffled, she thinks they might be shelved with the oatmeal, but
I tell her I've already checked there, and what we're looking for is ground
corn—like coarse cornmeal. Ah, maybe the flour section, then the cereals,
and next the rices. No luck, so we finally traipse to a higher authority at the
information counter.

"Groats?" the savvy-looking young man asks rather proudly.

"No, not groats, grits," I articulate with growing impatience. "Southern
grits—like very rough corn grains or meal—that come in boxes or packages
or bags and that you boil till they're smooth and creamy."

"Oh, like pabulum."

"No, sir, it's not like pabulum," I almost rage. "I can't believe you people have never heard of grits—plain, old-fashioned hominy grits."

"Ah, hominy," he sort of boasts. "Why didn't you say so? Sure, we have
cans of hominy—in the gourmet section, aisle 13."

Of course, I'm accustomed even in the South to all the linguistic confusion over hominy and grits, but, sure enough, there in the "gourmet" section
are exactly three round boxes of Quaker Quick Grits not far from the canned
hominy. That's not really what I want, but I buy a box since I'm desperate
and have no alternative. Normally in East Hampton, I'm never without at

least a half dozen packages of superior Jim Dandy grits (made by the Martha Washington folks in Tennessee) and a few big sacks of whole-grain, stone-ground grits (from a mill in Brevard, North Carolina). But since I haven't been home to Charlotte to stock up for a much longer period of time than usual, I'm reduced to searching for any brand and style I can find. And I tell you, it's like being in the South and asking for a bialy.

Not that all Yankees and other non-Southerners are exactly ignorant of grits as one of the cardinal staples of the Southern kitchen. Most have certainly heard of them, some have tasted them when traveling in the South, and since they do seem to be available nationwide in limited quantities, I have to assume that a few cooks actually buy and prepare them. But to even suggest that grits are truly known, respected, and loved anywhere in this country but the South would be absurd. I remember once having breakfast with a New York colleague at a pretty fancy hotel in Memphis when hot grits were served automatically with our eggs and bacon.

"What's that?" he asked curiously, staring at the small bowls. "Looks almost like rice."

"Grits," I virtually howled, salting and putting pats of butter on both portions. "Just stir 'em a little and taste them."

"Hummm," he mumbled after the second forkful. "Interesting. What are they made from?"

Suffice it that by the time I'd finished my short lecture on exactly how grits are produced and how they're even better baked with cheese, turned into a soufflé or casserole, or battered and fried, the near convert had wiped his bowl clean and even dipped his fork into mine. The man was learning the glory of grits. People usually do. If he ever moved to the South, no doubt he'd eventually become a grits addict like every other Reb.

Needless to say, I've been eating grits day and night in every form imaginable ever since I was above my mother's knee helping her stir a mess to creamy perfection. For breakfast, it's plain grits saturated with butter, grits and eggs, grits and red-eye gravy (made from fried country ham), grits and sausage, and cheese grits. At brunches, I've served with some success all types of puddings, casseroles, and spoon breads made with grits. In the evening, I love nothing more than buttered or baked grits with a runny herb omelette, or to batter and fry up cold leftover grits in squares to eat with cocktails, or to bake for unsuspecting friends a crusted grits soufflé flavored with any number of compatible ingredients. When traveling around the

South, I look for restaurants with shrimp and grits, grillades and grits, or grunts (small fried fish) and grits on the menu. And to me, a real find is a diner, hotel, or private home that prides itself on hominy ham biscuits, hominy waffles, and a toasted grits bread called Southern crumpets. I simply can't imagine life without grits.

Exactly why Southerners have always been so devoted to grits, while others have to acquire the taste, is not easy for me to understand. One possible explanation is historical, based on the supposition that what the initial settlers in the London Company at Jamestown, Virginia, were offered by friendly Indians in 1607 were bowls of a hot substance consisting of boiled maize seasoned with salt and probably bear fat, called *rockahominie.* If true, this would make grits (or, in the parlance of the Carolina Low Country, "hominy grits") the first genuine American food.

In any case, evidently the settlers liked the dish so much that they not only anglicized the name to "hominy" but contrived a milling process by which dried corn kernels (so plentiful throughout the South) could be ground into smaller particles. Gradually, grits became as important to the Southern diet as buttermilk biscuits and cornbread, relished as much in earlier days by Thomas Jefferson, Andrew Jackson, the French Marquis de Lafayette, and, yes, even Ulysses Grant as by President Jimmy Carter, author Truman Capote, and fashion designer Geoffrey Beene in our own time. As to the origin of the term *grits* itself, the account is simple: *grytt* was an Old English word for bran.

Today, much too much unnecessary fuss—even in the South—is made about the difference between hominy and grits, which are basically one and the same. Technically, when whole white, hard kernels of corn are soaked in a solution of water and lye (or wood ash) to remove the outer hulls, the result is the softened germs (or "eyes") of the kernels, called *hominy.* When hominy is then dried and coarsely ground, you have grits. (And when dried hominy is then finely ground, the end product is cornmeal.) Soft (or "pearl") hominy is sold as a canned vegetable and either simply heated with a piece of cooking meat (lean salt pork) or incorporated into various dishes. The finest, and rarest, grits are made from mature corn kernels that have been neither degerminated nor treated with lye but simply stone- or water-ground and bolted (sifted) to remove the husks. They contain no preservatives.

Southern purists wouldn't dream of cooking commercial "quick" or "instant" grits and make extraordinary efforts to find mills that still do things the old-fashioned way. (One Charleston, South Carolina, chef and food writer, John Martin Taylor—better known as "Hoppin' John"—goes so far as to have grits ground to his exact specifications at a small mill in the mountains of Georgia.) Rest assured that there is a noticeable difference between the bleached, blander grains found in supermarkets and full-flavored, stone-ground grits that must be kept refrigerated or frozen and cooked slowly for at least one hour. But if my own fastidious mother, who eats grits almost round the clock, doesn't object too vehemently to "quick" grits when the bespoke aristocrats are difficult to come by, I see no reason why others can't adapt to this acceptable and more readily available substitute. Where she and I both do draw a definite line is with overly processed "instant" grits, which are simply mixed with boiling water and served immediately. This tasteless mush is fit only for the hogs.

There are really no special tricks to cooking good grits so long as you use the right pot and exercise more than a little patience. The ideal pot is enameled cast-iron or stainless-steel with a heavy bottom, both of which allow for a slow, steady simmer with the least risk of sticking. (Savannah cookbook author and grits expert Damon Lee Fowler suggests a Crock-Pot as an acceptable alternative.) Most grits are simply boiled in water, but for a creamier texture, milk, chicken broth, or even half-and-half are often substituted. To attain the perfect degree of creamy thickness, natural, stone-ground grits must be simmered very slowly—with frequent stirring—for at least one hour. As for the "quick" variety, Southerners disregard the careless directions to boil only five minutes, aware that even these grits need up to thirty minutes in the pot for fine, smooth texture. Some folks say that adding salt while the grits are cooking keeps them from sticking; others insist that this prevents them from absorbing enough liquid while releasing the necessary starch for a creamy texture. In either case, grits without salt are as insipid as unsalted mashed potatoes.

What really perplexes me today is why most of our supposedly bold, innovative chefs around the country eager to exploit regional American cookery are not paying the least amount of attention to grits. I mean, these guileless rascals get all excited about couscous, kasha, bulgar, and polenta, but mention grits to them and their eyes go blank. The best professional Southern chefs, on the other hand, are developing elaborate dishes with grits that would have been unimaginable just fifteen years ago. At the nationally esteemed Highland Bar & Grill in Birmingham, Alabama, for example, master chef Frank Stitt prepares not only memorable cheese grits timbales with country ham and wild mushrooms but also a very stylish rabbit with grits. Louis Osteen's preserved duck over fried grits and his catfish and grits with black-eyed sauce at Louis's at Pawleys (Island) restaurant are worth a special trip to the coastal South Carolina Low Country. And I'd return again and again to Crook's Corner in Chapel Hill, North Carolina (home of my alma mater), just to overindulge in the creamy shrimp and grits enhanced by a lusty mushroom and bacon sauce. Close by in Durham at the celebrated Magnolia Grill, chef Ben Barker has created a stunning crawfish and grits cake that had me swooning; while down in New Orleans, Tory McThail at the legendary Commander's Palace prides himself as much on succulent pork grillades and grits as on grits and goat cheese topped with veal medallions and mushroom ragout. Slowly but surely there is evolving a veritable grits cuisine all over the South, a sophisticated phenomenon that excites any Southerner accustomed only to buttered breakfast grits—and one that could well add a whole new dimension to American cookery in general if chefs outside the region paid a little closer attention.

Now, in case you still suffer under the misapprehension that grits are little more than some remote item relegated strictly to tables of the American South, perhaps I should relate that, ironically and incredibly, the exact same dish has for ages figured prominently in one of the world's most exotic cuisines, namely that of the Republic of Georgia, just south of Russia. This momentous revelation was made by none other than my close, adventurous friend and fellow food writer Paula Wolfert, who, after tasting a sublime, soothing dish in Georgia called *elargi*, composed mainly of coarsely ground dried corn and either fresh mozzarella-style or smoked cheese, brought back packages of the rough particles, sent a large envelope to my mother in North Carolina, and asked her to critique the grains. "Paula, honey," mother responded in almost no time, "I don't know anything about this Georgia you visited over there near the Black Sea, but I can tell you that in the Georgia where I was born, what you sent me would be classified as just plain old grits." What Mother did not tell Paula was that, once slowly boiled, the grains are little more than old-fashioned Southern corn mush—or, to use the fancier Italian term, polenta.

Finally, anybody who thinks I take grits too seriously really should attend the annual World Grits Festival held every April in St. George, South Carolina, and witness the thousands who view grits as nothing less than a religious experience. There, they crown a Grits Queen, cheer at the Grits Parade, visit a working gristmill, and, to be sure, award prizes for the best and most original grits recipes. Some of the winning dishes have been a Rio Grande Grits Casserole, Grits Yorkshire Pudding, Grits with Artichokes and Bacon, Butterscotch Grits, and Peachy Grits Cheesecake. It's all quite a spectacle. And although the recipe competition can be nerve-racking, I'm giving lots of thought to submitting my Grits and Wild Mushroom Soufflé for consideration next spring.

Mail Order for Stone-Ground Grits

Anson Mills
2013 Greene Street
Columbia, South Carolina 29205
843-709-7399
www.ansonmills.com

Morgan Mill
201 Morgan Mill Road
Brevard, North Carolina 28712
828-862-4084

Hoppin' John's On-Line (Charleston, South Carolina)
800-828-4412
www.hoppinjohns.com

Falls Mill
134 Falls Mill Road
Belvidere, Tennessee 37306
931-469-7161
www.fallsmill.com

Nora Mill Granary
7107 South Main Street
Helen, Georgia 30545
800-927-2375
www.noramill.com

Baked Cheese Grits

3 cups water

2 teaspoons salt

1 cup quick grits

3 cups milk

4 large eggs, beaten

1 cup grated extra-sharp cheddar
   cheese

1 teaspoon Worcestershire sauce

8 ounces (2 sticks) butter, softened
   and cut into pieces

Freshly ground pepper

In a large, heavy saucepan, combine the water and salt, bring to a brisk boil, and slowly sift the grits through the fingers of one hand into the water while stirring with the other. Reduce the heat to a gentle simmer and continue cooking about 20 minutes, or till the grits start to thicken, stirring frequently. Add 2 cups of the milk, return mixture to a boil, reduce the heat to a simmer, and continue cooking about 15 minutes, or till the grits have thickened. Remove the pan from the heat.

Preheat the oven to 350°F. Grease a 2-quart baking dish and set aside.

Return pan to the heat, add the remaining 1 cup milk, the beaten eggs, cheese, Worcestershire, butter, and pepper. Stir till the butter has melted and the mixture is smooth. Scrape into the prepared baking dish and bake about 1 hour, or till a knife inserted in the center comes out clean. Serve piping hot as a breakfast dish or with a baked ham dinner.

Shrimp and Grits

THE GRITS

5 cups water

1 teaspoon salt

1 cup grits (stone-ground or quick)

2 tablespoons butter

THE SHRIMP

2 pounds small fresh shrimp

2 tablespoons butter

2 tablespoons bacon grease

2 small onions, finely chopped

½ small green bell pepper, seeded
     and finely chopped

¼ cup all-purpose flour

Salt and pepper to taste

To cook the grits, combine the water and salt in a large, heavy saucepan, bring to a brisk boil, and slowly sift the grits through the fingers of one hand into the water while stirring with the other. Reduce the heat to a gentle simmer and continue cooking till the grits are thick and creamy, 30 minutes to 1 hour, stirring frequently to prevent sticking. Add the butter, stir till well blended, cover, and keep warm till ready to serve.

To prepare the shrimp, place them in a large saucepan with enough water to just cover. Bring to a boil, remove pan from the heat, let stand 1 minute, then drain, reserving the cooking liquid in a bowl. Peel and devein shrimp.

In a large, heavy skillet, heat the butter and bacon grease over moderate heat. Add the onions and green pepper and cook, stirring often, about 8 minutes. Sprinkle the flour over the top and continue to stir till the mixture begins to brown, about 2 minutes. Gradually add about 2 cups of the reserved shrimp cooking liquid and whisk briskly till the gravy is smooth. Add the shrimp, season with salt and pepper, and cook, stirring, for 2 minutes, adding a little more cooking liquid if the gravy seems too thick.

Serve the shrimp and gravy over large spoonfuls of grits.

Grits and Wild Mushroom Soufflé

1 ounce dried cèpe mushrooms

3 cups water

1½ teaspoons salt

1 cup grits (stone-ground or quick)

6 ounces (1½ sticks) butter, softened and cut into pieces, plus 4 tablespoons melted

1 tablespoon bacon grease

2 teaspoons Worcestershire sauce

Freshly ground pepper to taste

6 large eggs, beaten

½ cup dry bread crumbs

In a small bowl, soak the dried mushrooms in 1 cup of warm water for 30 minutes. Pick them over to remove any grit, rinse well, pat dry, and chop finely; set aside. Strain the mushroom liquor through cheesecloth into a bowl and reserve separately.

Grease a 2- to 2½-quart casserole or baking dish and set aside.

In a large, heavy saucepan, combine the water, reserved mushroom liquor, and salt. Bring to a brisk boil and slowly sift the grits through the fingers of one hand into the water while stirring with the other. Reduce the heat to low, cover, and simmer for 15 minutes, stirring occasionally.

Preheat the oven to 350°F.

Remove the saucepan of grits from the heat. Add the softened butter, bacon grease, Worcestershire, and pepper, stirring till well blended and the butter has melted. Add the eggs and mushrooms, stir till well blended and smooth. Scrape the mixture into the prepared casserole.

Sprinkle the bread crumbs over the top and drizzle the melted butter evenly over the crumbs. Bake till the soufflé is puffy and the top is golden brown, about 45 minutes. Serve piping hot with country ham biscuits and a tart green or fruit salad.

Damon Fowler's Green Grits

4 cups water
1 cup stone-ground grits
Salt to taste
2 tablespoons butter
4 scallions (white and 2 inches of green), thinly sliced
1 package (10 ounces) frozen whole leaf spinach, thawed, squeezed dry, and coarsely chopped
½ cup heavy cream
1½ cups freshly grated Parmigiano-Reggiano cheese
Freshly ground pepper
2 large eggs, beaten

In a large, heavy pot, bring the water to a brisk boil and slowly add the grits in a steady stream, stirring constantly. Reduce the heat to a gentle simmer, loosely cover the pot, and cook the grits about 1 hour, or till thick and creamy, stirring frequently at first, then occasionally as the grits begin to thicken. Add salt, let simmer a few more minutes to absorb the seasoning, and set aside, covered to keep warm.

Preheat the oven to 350°F. Grease a 10-inch round casserole and set aside.

In a large, heavy skillet or Dutch oven, melt the butter over moderate heat. Add the scallions and cook, stirring, till wilted, 3 to 4 minutes. Add the spinach, let heat through, about 2 minutes, and remove from the heat.

Stir the cream into the warm grits till smooth. Add the spinach, 1 cup of the cheese, and salt and pepper; stir till well blended. Add the eggs and beat with a spoon till the mixture is well blended and smooth. Scrape the mixture into the prepared casserole and sprinkle the remaining cheese on top. Bake in center of the oven till the eggs are set and the top is browned, 35 to 40 minutes. Serve piping hot.

PC AND PROUD OF IT

"Son," Mother would scold playfully at the kitchen table while feeding chunks of sharp cheddar and strips of sweet pimento into the meat grinder as I turned the handle and picked at the mixture collecting in a bowl, "if you keep eating that, I'm not going to have one iota left to make your or anybody else's sandwiches. Now, stop it this minute and just grind."

She would then carefully examine the mixture and maybe drop a little more cheese or pimento into the grinder if the blend didn't look exactly right to her expert eye. Taking the bowl to a counter, she next would casually add a few globs of homemade mayonnaise, a quick squeeze of fresh lemon juice, dash of Worcestershire, and sprinkling of cayenne and mash everything with a fork till the concoction was smooth as silk and ready for her to sample.

"Here, honey, taste this," she'd direct proudly, handing me the other half of a cracker topped with the tangy spread. "If I say so myself, that's pretty good pimento cheese."

Although time has a cruel way of dissipating childhood memories, one that has remained crystal clear for me is that of helping Mother make pimento cheese for the delectable sandwiches she routinely packed into my metal school lunch box when I was a lad growing up in North Carolina. Also included in the bright red and white container might have been a fried chicken drumstick or zesty country ham biscuit, carrot sticks, a fat juicy pear, and a few homemade cookies. But what I really loved and never, ever tired of were her soft, pungent pimento cheese sandwiches on whole wheat bread with just enough of the luscious spread oozing from the edges onto the waxed paper wrapping to make for a good initial lick.

Pimento cheese? When I mention the name to most non-Southerners, I can almost be guaranteed little more than a puzzled stare. But utter those two words in front of anybody from Dixie, and the same ecstatic smile will twinkle as when the subject of buttermilk biscuits or chopped pork barbecue or peach cobbler is broached. Long before the term "politically correct" was conceived, "PC" connoted generally only one thing in the South: the simple, piquant, utterly addictive combination of grated cheddar cheese, diced pimentos, cayenne pepper, and mayonnaise, which is spread on crackers and sandwiches, stuffed into celery stalks and cherry tomatoes, incorporated in salads, turned into dips and festive balls, and used as a topping on grilled burgers and various breads. For the record, it's been quaintly called Southern pâté; nobody in his or her right mind would ever spell *pimento* with a second "i"; and the correct pronunciation of the spread is "pa-MEN-uh" cheese.

You can search food dictionaries till you're blue in the face and never find a reference to pimento cheese, and the only cookbooks that include recipes for the stuff are those written by Southerners. When, where, and how pimento cheese originated remains a total mystery, but then, nobody in the South really cares. All that matters is that a day never pass without a jar or crock of fresh PC in the refrigerator to dip into when the urge strikes, when folks show up unexpectedly at the house, or when there's a quick lunch to prepare.

If Southerners manifest an inordinate passion for this unique spread, it's equally true that arguments become heated when the question of what constitutes great pimento cheese is raised. There does seem to be common agreement amongst the wise that the cheese must be the finest sharp or extra-sharp cheddar available and the mayonnaise top grade (which means only fresh, Duke's, or Hellmann's), but there all civility stops. To attain the best texture, for example, should the cheese be finely grated or coarsely shredded or run through a meat grinder the way my mother still does? Must the spread be mixed and mashed with a fork the old-fashioned way, or can an electric mixer or food processor yield comparable results? What are the ideal proportions of cheese to pimentos to mayo? And does pale pimento cheese made with white cheddar instead of traditional orange-dyed really pass for classic pimento cheese?

These are cardinal considerations, to be sure, but the fur really begins to fly when optional ingredients are debated: chopped celery, onions, hard-boiled eggs, garlic, jalapeños, parsley, herbs, and bacon; lemon juice, sugar, horseradish, Worcestershire sauce, and Tabasco; and additional cheeses such as Parmesan, cottage, and cream. There's one lady down in Nashville who includes Durkee's sauce and Dijon mustard in her pimento cheese; another at Lake Wylie, North Carolina, who's convinced that evaporated milk gives her mixture exceptional smoothness; and Ruth Fales, co-owner of the Pinckney Café in Charleston, South Carolina, who couldn't imagine making PC without a few chopped green olives. For these and hundreds of other serious enthusiasts, homemade pimento cheese is a very emotional topic, though never quite as controversial as the horrifying alternative of using any one of the many prepared versions available in small tubs at all Southern supermarkets. The least said about commercial pimento cheese the better. None other than the renowned North Carolina author Reynolds Price once summed it up best when he likened these products to "congealed insecticides."

Over the years, I've made pimento cheese every way conceivable, and while I'd never be so reckless as to dictate a strict formula for a spread that lends itself to endless interpretation and experiment, I do have my own strong convictions and prejudices. First of all, since the marriage of cheddar and pimentos is blessed from on high and must therefore be treated with respect, never should any other ingredient be allowed to alter or nullify these primary flavors—which is why I personally disapprove of adding garlic, sugar, vinegar, bulb onions, and horseradish or inordinate amounts of chili peppers, crumbled bacon, assertive mustard, Worcestershire, and Tabasco. Nor do I ever salt a basic spread due to the salty nature of the cheese and mayonnaise—not to mention such acceptable additives as olives, bacon, and mustard. Today I use only Hellmann's mayonnaise, careful as with any other ingredient not to overwhelm the cheese and pimentos.

I'm obsessed with the cheddar intended for PC and am forever in search of premium styles. When I was a child, Mother's butcher shop always had enormous wheels of sharp, gloriously mellow country cheddar we called "rat cheese" (and it was my duty at home to set mousetraps in the basement with tiny morsels), but those days are long gone. Well-aged (at least twelve months), extra-sharp cheddar found in some supermarkets is respectable enough (A&P's Master Choice New York State brand is my favorite). But what I really seek out are such exceptional artisanal products as Vermont's Cabot, Crowley, Shelburne, and white Grafton; Oregon's Colby, white Tillamook, and Jack; any all-natural Canadian cheddar; and, noblest of all, a real, cream-colored, English farmhouse cheddar or feisty Cheshire. Anybody who would try to make pimento cheese with that appalling processed American cheese or Velveeta needs serious psychiatric help.

I'm equally grouchy about using genuine pimentos versus ordinary roasted red bell peppers, not only because of the former's superior flavor but also because the canning liquid is ideal for thinning overly dense pimento cheese. Unbeknownst to most, and contrary to certain confusing etymological implications, the large, red, heart-shaped pimento pepper (indigenous to the Americas and taken back to Spain by Columbus) is *not* the same as its humbler red bell cousin and can make all the difference between extraordinary and mediocre pimento cheese. Although most pimento production and packing is done in the South, whole, sliced, and diced canned pimentos are available at supermarkets nationwide in 4- and 7-ounce jars. I'm almost as adamant about using plenty of pimentos in my PC as about mixing the spread to a slightly coarse consistency with a fork, and I even toss pimentos into certain doughs and batters to produce such savory marvels as pimento-cheese straws, cocktail biscuits, and muffins.

Although I consider myself as much a PC aficionado as the next Reb, the sad irony is that I've still never quite succeeded in creating what I perceive to be the ideal spread. I'm not alone, for if you challenge any honest Southerner to augur once and for all a definition of the world's perfect pimento cheese, the elusive and frustrating response remains the same: Mom's.

My Everyday Pimento Cheese

MAKES ABOUT 3 CUPS

½ pound extra-sharp white
  Vermont cheddar cheese
½ pound extra-sharp New York
  State cheddar cheese
One 7-ounce jar pimentos, drained

½ teaspoon freshly ground pepper
Salt to taste
Cayenne to taste
⅔ cup Hellmann's mayonnaise

Finely grate the two cheeses into a mixing bowl. On a plate, mash the pimentos well with a fork till they're very pulpy. Add them to the cheeses along with the pepper, salt, and cayenne and mix till well blended. Using the fork, fold in the mayonnaise and mash till the spread is smooth, adding a little more mayonnaise if it appears too dry.

Scrape the spread into a jar or crock, cover well, and refrigerate at least 2 hours before serving with crackers or using to make pimento-cheese sandwiches. Keeps up to 4 days tightly covered in the refrigerator.

Deluxe Southern Pimento Cheese

MAKES ABOUT 3½ CUPS

1 pound extra-sharp aged cheddar cheese

3 tablespoons grated genuine Parmesan cheese

One 7-ounce jar pimentos, drained, diced, and liquid reserved

½ cup finely chopped green olives

1 teaspoon fresh lemon juice

1 teaspoon Worcestershire sauce

Cayenne to taste

⅔ cup mayonnaise, or to taste

Grate the cheddar coarsely into a mixing bowl, add the Parmesan, pimentos, and olives, and mix well with a fork. Add the lemon juice, Worcestershire, cayenne, and mayonnaise and stir and mash the mixture with the fork till well blended and almost a chunky paste. (If too thick, add a little of the reserved pimento liquid.)

Scrape the mixture into a jar or crock, cover well, and refrigerate at least 2 hours before using as a spread or stuffing for vegetables. Keeps up to 4 days tightly covered in the refrigerator.

Spicy Pimento Cheese Dip

MAKES 2 CUPS

6 ounces white Vermont cheddar cheese

1 jar (4 ounces) pimentos, drained and finely chopped

1 can (2 ounces) finely chopped chile peppers

1 tablespoon finely chopped chives

3 ounces cream cheese, softened

½ cup sour cream

½ cup V-8 juice

Grate the cheese finely into a mixing bowl, add the pimentos, chile peppers, and chives, and stir well. Add the cream cheese, sour cream, and V-8 juice and beat the mixture with an electric beater till light and smooth.

Scrape the mixture into a crock, cover with plastic wrap, and chill at least 2 hours before serving with crackers or raw vegetables.

Pimento Cheese Cocktail Biscuits

½ pound extra-sharp aged cheddar
  cheese, room temperature
8 ounces (2 sticks) butter, softened
  and cut into pieces
One 4-ounce jar pimentos, well
  drained on paper towels and
  finely diced

¼ teaspoon salt
Big dash cayenne
2 cups all-purpose flour
Pecan halves

Preheat the oven to 350°F.

Grate the cheese very finely into a mixing bowl. Add the butter, pimentos, salt, and cayenne and mix with the hands till well blended. Add the flour gradually and mix with the hands till the dough is firm and smooth, adding a little more flour if necessary.

Roll the pieces of dough between the palms of your hands into balls the size of large marbles and place about 1 inch apart on 2 ungreased baking sheets.

Press a pecan half into the center of each ball and bake till slightly browned but still fairly soft, about 20 minutes. Let the biscuits cool completely, then store in tightly sealed tins.

DEBUNKING FRUITCAKE

STORED INCONSPICUOUSLY ON THE BOTTOM SHELF OF MY refrigerator are two rare fruitcakes in tightly sealed tins, one dated 1979, the other 1985. The larger and more venerable of the two was made and given to me by my Georgia-born mother one Christmas with the explicit instruction that the cake must be allowed to age and mellow for at least one year before serving. The second fruitcake I myself baked, following the same family "receipt," for an elaborate Christmas Eve feast I once planned. Though I've pinched bits off the edges to sample them over the years, they are both so special, so evocative, so aromatic, so utterly seductive that I've simply never had the nerve to actually cut them.

Shortly before the holidays every year, I open the tins, remove the foil and bourbon-drenched cloths (to be truthful, used cotton T-shirts) in which the cakes are tightly wrapped, sprinkle them with more whiskey, and swaddle them with fresh moist cloths. My sincere intention always is finally to serve the older of these prized beauties instead of the more recent rendition, to share the ripened treasure with family and friends, to show others what truly great vintage fruitcake is all about. Then, guilt-ridden, I decide we'll try the less pedigreed '85 (and give the noble '79 just one more year "on the bourbon"). Then, nervously, I taste a smidgen and begin to wonder whether perhaps the '85 might not ultimately surpass the '79 in both flavor and texture with just a little more coddling. I approach vintage fruitcake with the same trepidation I approach the rare burgundies in my wine cellar.

Having finally resolved that this embarrassing nonsense should never begin again, last fall, as usual, I baked a few big fruitcakes, gave two away in fine Southern tradition, wrapped up another to be served over Christmas, and casually stashed the last one in the cool basement for any dessert emergencies that might arise at future dinner parties. The Christmas cake was fine, up to standard and infinitely superior, as always, to those commercial things that have given fruitcake such a bad name. And I was proud when guests finished off every morsel. The problem began, however, when spring came and necessity forced me to resort to the almost forgotten cake aging quietly downstairs.

No sooner had I pried open the tin than my senses were stunned by that familiar intoxicating aroma of homemade fruitcake undergoing the mysterious and unpredictable natural process that can sometimes—but not always—transform a mere mound of baked batter into a gustatory miracle. The colors of both the cake and crystallized-fruit decoration had already begun to deepen; the texture was now much softer, almost supple as I pressed the top with one finger. And when I pinched off a tiny bite, the beautifully balanced, blended flavors of fruits and nuts and spices and good whiskey exploded in my mouth. That evening, my sympathetic guests went without dessert. I reannointed the splendid specimen with a little more bourbon to reinforce flavor and keep the cake sound and returned it to the basement, determined then and there to serve it before, during, and after the upcoming Christmas . . . maybe.

Although fruitcake can be traced back at least to an ancient Roman-baked mixture of dried fruits, seeds, nuts, and the honey wine called *satura*—and while it has modern derivatives throughout the world (German stollen, Portuguese *morgado,* Italian *panforte,* Caribbean black cake, English Christmas pudding and simnel cake)—nowhere over the centuries has the cake evolved as an intrinsic part of the culture as it has in the American South. Needless to say, everyone in this country is as familiar with fruitcake as with meatloaf. If in recent times this confection has become the object of every bad gastronomic joke imaginable, it is only because most Americans, exposed increasingly to little more than those wretched store-bought or mail-order products, do not know, or have forgotten, what great fruitcake tastes like. This sad predicament applies as much to our professional chefs as to most home cooks, which I suppose is why, disgracefully, the last item you can expect to find on restaurant dessert menus is some form of fruitcake.

Southerners like my mother, on the other hand, not only still prepare the same luscious cakes made by their mothers and grandmothers and great-grandmothers but also spend days in the fall planning their baking schedules, searching for just the right ingredients, and indulging in a culinary and social tradition that is as sacred as the preparation of authentic pork barbecue. Southerners are fiercely proud of their fruitcakes. They eat them all year round, and arguments can become heated when it comes to which ingredients are correct, exactly how a cake should be mixed, and the length of time it must be aged. Because of their high alcohol and sugar content, fruitcakes that are moistened from time to time with additional spirits and kept in sealed containers can be preserved for years, even decades; and there are still Southern cooks who love nothing more than to prepare a very special "heirloom cake" intended to be passed down from one generation of the family to the next—and that is no wild exaggeration.

Nobody ever evoked the spirit of fruitcake-making in the South like Truman Capote in "A Christmas Memory": "The black stove, stoked with coal and firewood, glows like a lighted pumpkin. Eggbeaters whirl, spoons spin round in bowls of butter and sugar, vanilla sweetens the air, ginger spices it; melting, nose-tingling odors saturate the kitchen, suffuse the house, drift out to the world on puffs of chimney smoke. In four days our work is done. Thirty-one cakes, dampened with whiskey, bask on window sills and shelves."

Even if certain details of Capote's setting and ceremony differ from those used in the same ritual I've observed at home ever since I was old enough to wield a blade, help Mother mix the batter, and abscond with a few crystallized cherries, the essence of the age-old experience is there. "No, honey," confesses Mother (who cannot recall so much as tasting a "bought cake"), "I don't guess much has changed even since I was a girl. Of course, in those days, Mama and her friends had to wait till October when Cousin Berta sent the pecans up from Monticello before planning their 'spend-the-day' fruitcake parties. And of course, back then we had to *shell* all those pecans— pecans for a dozen, maybe fifteen cakes. Lord, that was a job. And Mama also used blackberry wine instead of bourbon since my grandmother disapproved of whiskey but not of wine. Can you just imagine? Other than that, I reckon I've always made fruitcake exactly the way they did."

And—slight prejudice aside—what a fruitcake it is. I can assure you that I've sampled fruitcake in one form or another in every corner of the South and around the globe, and never, not once, has any version of this cake aroused my passion like the dark, well-aged work of art that has been a hallmark of my family's kitchen for at least five generations. This is the cake I knew as a toddler, the one I watched my Georgia grandmother and great-grandmother compose, the marvel my mother continues to turn out every year in every size conceivable, and, indeed, the cake every serious cook in America should strive to emulate or even transform into a personal success.

Ideally, this quintessential fruitcake should be made at least a year in advance of serving, wrapped well and put in an airtight container, stored in the refrigerator to mellow, and pampered with occasional dousings of bourbon, cognac, rum, or sweet wine. If your patience tends to strain easily, however, don't worry. Even in infancy, the cake has the ability to produce instant gratification. Perhaps even more important, it also serves to illustrate how, in these days of excessive novelty, still another honest, genuine, American culinary masterpiece cries out for renewed recognition and serious creative attention.

The Perfect Southern Fruitcake

MAKES ONE 5½-POUND AND TWO 2½-POUND FRUITCAKES

1 pound golden raisins
1 pound dark raisins
½ pound crystallized citron, coarsely chopped
¼ pound crystallized orange peel, coarsely chopped
¼ pound crystallized lemon peel, coarsely chopped
1 pound crystallized pineapple, coarsely chopped
1 pound crystallized cherries, cut in half
1 pound dates, pitted and coarsely chopped
2 pounds shelled pecans, coarsely broken up
4 cups sifted all-purpose flour

1 pound (4 sticks) butter, softened
2 cups sugar
1 dozen large eggs
1 teaspoon ground cinnamon
½ teaspoon ground cloves
½ teaspoon grated nutmeg
¼ teaspoon ground ginger
1 teaspoon salt
2 teaspoons pure vanilla extract
2 teaspoons pure almond extract
1¼ cups bourbon, plus more for sprinkling and soaking
Light corn syrup
Crystallized cherries, pineapple, and pecan halves, for decoration

In a large mixing bowl, combine the golden and dark raisins, crystallized citron, orange peel, lemon peel, pineapple, and cherries, dates, and pecans. Add half the flour and mix till the ingredients are well coated.

In another very large bowl, cream the butter with an electric mixer, add the sugar, and beat till light and fluffy. Add the eggs one at a time, beating well after each addition. Add the remaining flour, the cinnamon, cloves, nutmeg, ginger, salt, vanilla, and almond extract and mix with a wooden spoon till well blended. Add the fruit-and-nut mixture to the batter along with ¾ cup of bourbon. Using your hands, mix the batter well.

Preheat the oven to 250°F.

Grease and lightly flour the bottom and sides of one 10" x 4" tube pan and two 8" x 4½" x 2½" loaf pans. Line each with heavy brown paper, extending it 1 inch above the pans. Grease the brown paper, scrape the batter into the pans, and, using your hands, pack the batter firmly to ½ inch below the tops of the pans. Cover the tops with sheets of wax paper.

Place a shallow pan of water on the lower rack of the oven and place the cake pans on the middle rack. Bake the smaller loaf cakes about 3½ hours and the large tube cake about 4 hours, or till a straw inserted in the middle comes out clean, removing the wax paper during the final 15 minutes of baking. (Do not overcook the cakes; watch the timing of each and check doneness periodically with the straw.)

Remove the cakes from the oven. Immediately sprinkle each with 2 tablespoons more bourbon, and let cool in the pans. Soak 3 double-layer pieces of cheesecloth large enough to envelope each cake in bourbon, squeezing the excess from the cloth. Remove the cakes from the pans by lifting up the brown paper, and discard the paper. Brush the tops of the cakes with corn syrup, decorate with crystallized cherries, pineapple, and pecans, and let dry. Wrap the cakes securely in cheesecloth and store in airtight containers at least 1 month before cutting. (To age the cakes longer, wrap tightly in foil and store in the refrigerator, sprinkling the cheesecloth with bourbon or another spirit every 6 months.)

A FEW CRUCIAL WORDS
ABOUT SOUTHERN ICE' TEA

WHILE I SUPPOSE MOST AMERICANS HAVE A GLASS OF ICED TEA from time to time during summer, Southerners couldn't survive without the brew on a daily basis twelve months of the year. We drink it whenever and wherever food is served—morning, noon, and night—and we drink it anytime just to be drinking it. We drink it at casual brunches, picnics, church suppers, cookouts, and formal dinners. We drink it at bridge luncheons, bereavement buffets, beach parties, political rallies, pig pickin's, football games, and holiday feasts. And we drink as much of it in fancy restaurants as at barbecue joints and diners. My mother has even been known to drink it at breakfast when the weather's really scorching, and since she's never, ever without a pitcher of tea at the back of the kitchen counter or in the refrigerator, it's nothing unusual for her to ask a visitor, "Honey, how 'bout a glass of tea?" (meaning, of course, "ice' tea").

Despite our inordinate devotion to bourbon whiskey, the truly sacred beverage of the South is ice' tea, and has been ever since ice became readily available in the mid-nineteenth century. (Little wonder, also, that the only tea leaves grown in the United States are on Wadmalaw Island, off the coast of South Carolina.) The varieties are endless, though it's important to point out that most Southerners have no use whatsoever for weirdly flavored teas. Plain old ice' tea is nothing but carefully brewed orange pekoe, but there's also sugar tea (highly sweetened), mint tea (with bruised fresh mint leaves), lemon tea, and sun tea (a gallon container of cold water and tea placed in the hot sun for three or four hours to develop ultimate flavor). The pitchers you see at most restaurants, diners, cafés, and my own house are usually full of sugar tea. I also like a squeeze of lemon in my ice' tea, but Mother wouldn't dream of destroying the natural flavor of her everyday brew with sugar or lemon or anything else. "I know to sweeten my pitcher of tea when I'm entertaining since most people love sugar tea," she states with a frown, "but frankly I have no use for it in private." And that's that.

So engrained has ice' tea become in Southern culture over the decades that even such legendary alcoholic libations as St. Cecilia's Punch or Goalpost Punch or Cotillion Punch are based on the brewing of tea leaves. Same is true with the ice' Russian tea, spiced cider tea, and orange tea that hostesses often serve at bridge luncheons, charity league get-togethers, social get-togethers, and elaborate funeral receptions. Given our equal passion for fine sour mash, I'm surprised somebody hasn't come up with an ice' whiskey tea to make guests particularly happy.

Today, health fanatics outside the South make a big to-do about using only bottled water to make tea and coffee, but Southerners don't pay any attention to all that nonsense. The main thing to remember about making good ice' tea is to double the number of tea bags or amount of loose tea you'd normally use for hot tea since the ice will dilute the tea—and nothing on earth is more insipid than weak ice' tea. Also, be sure to brew it in a nonreactive pot to prevent a bitter metallic taste. (Big tip: ice' tea is almost as good brewed in a drip coffeemaker as in a pot.) Tea cooled to room temperature should remain crystal clear; but if for some mysterious reason the tea clouds when stored in the refrigerator, simply add a little hot water to clear it before serving.

To make a pitcher of perfect Southern ice' tea, place one bag or one teaspoon of loose tea leaves per glass in a nonreactive pot. Bring another large pot of fresh *cold* water to boil (don't ask me why the water must be cold to start), pour over the tea, cover, and let steep 10 minutes or till desired strength. Let cool to room temperature, then either squeeze and discard the tea bags or strain the loose tea leaves while pouring the brewed tea into a large pitcher. Sweeten the tea to taste if desired, pour over lots of ice cubes (not crushed ice) in tall glasses, serve lemon wedges on the side, and whistle "Dixie."

PART TWO

STAR-SPANGLED ADVENTURES

CHEAPSKATE SHOPPING

I N ALL-AMERICAN STYLE, EVERYTHING IN SIGHT IS BIG. THE PARK-
ing lot, packed with behemoth, expensive SUVs, would dwarf a football
field. The oversized shopping carts might well be used to transport mini
whales instead of groceries. Inside, the concrete floor space could be measured in acres rather than square yards, and it would not be inconceivable to
drive a Volkswagen Bug between the immense aisles. There are indeed wash-
ing machines and tires and computers and huge pup tents for sale, but by far
the largest and most populated area is where profusions of foods, drinks,
condiments, cooking supplies, and numerous other kitchen items are stacked
up almost to the soaring ceiling. You don't come here to pick up a single box
or package or bunch or bottle of this and that as in a normal supermarket.
You come here to buy by gallon tubs, and one-by-two-feet cartons, and giant
flats, and colossal vats—much as professional chefs would do. Most of the
customers themselves are, well . . . stout, the average body weight being
maybe two hundred pounds—male and female, upper, middle, and lower
class, rich and poor. These people look big, think big, act big, and certainly
shop big, and what they particularly share besides a strapping appetite is an
addiction to enormous quantities of everyday (and a few not so ordinary)
provisions at bargain prices. Welcome to Sam's Club, of which I count myself
a long-standing, relatively loyal, and often stunned member.

To understand the phenomenon of Sam's Club (or Costco, or B.J.'s, or any
of the other no-frills warehouse clubs spread about the country), you must first
disabuse yourself of almost everything you see today in glossy food magazines,
voguish newspaper food columns, trendy cookbooks, and on television's Food
Network. These self-styled arbiters of what's happening on the food scene
would have you believe that the vast majority of Americans are now shopping

at upscale Dean & Delucas and quaint farmers' markets; paying top dollar for pots and pans at Williams Sonoma; emulating the cutting-edge recipes and cooking techniques of Nancy Silverton and Michel Richard; and purring over dainty portions of sushi; daikon ravioli seasoned with fleur de sel, sage flowers, or Aleppo oil; and diver scallops with Meyer lemon peel and angled loofah. Nothing, of course, could be further from the truth, as the wizards behind all the contemporary propaganda would discover if they'd ever set foot in a Sam's and observed the swarming masses loading up on cut-rate 4-pound shrink-wrapped cartons of canned tuna, gallon jars of dilled pickles, 3-pound foil trays of frozen chicken taquitos and shrimp scampi, 5-pound packages of hot dogs, and crates of beer and Gatorade. No doubt there is an ever-growing segment of the population that is both eager to taste (and possibly prepare) pearl couscous, nori, and elk sausage, and willing to pay outrageous prices for truffle oil, pomegranate molasses, and Nantucket clam bellies. But to even insinuate that these blossoming foodies are posing a serious challenge to the shopping and eating habits of this nation's Samsters is nothing less than a triumph of naiveté.

Let me next disabuse you of any idea that Wal-Mart, Big K-Mart, Target, and the other supposedly discount superstores that stock groceries and beverages can begin to compete with a price club like Sam's in terms of sheer magnitude, selection, and cost. Dedicated Samsters have no more time for these secondary emporiums than serious shoppers at Home Depot or Lowe's have for neighborhood hardware stores charging $40 for a standard peppermill. Yes, it is possible at these places to find on sale small bottles of Dijon mustard, extra-virgin olive oil, and Yukon Gold potatoes. But since most Samsters aren't interested in such fanciful, undersized, and still overpriced articles, they're infinitely more comfortable with gallon buckets of French's ballpark mustard at a mere $2.88, stupendous bottles of regular olive or vegetable oil at no more than about $5, and plain old Idahoes at a sensible 39¢ a pound. Likewise, why bother, for heaven's sake, with expensive, puny supermarket sizes when, by buying in bulk at a relative fraction of the cost, you can leave Sam's with 7½-pound cans of Bush's baked beans, 3½-pound jars of Planter's Cocktail Peanuts, 45 packages of Quaker Instant Oatmeal, 20-inch frozen pizzas with all the toppings, and herculean fresh boned pork loins. Only a fool shops for staples at K-Mart or Target—not to mention ordinary supermarkets, extortionate 7-Elevens, fashionable greengrocers, and custom meat markets. If food mavens like Alice Waters ever crossed the threshold of Sam's, they'd no doubt go into immediate coronary arrest.

Although the U.S. discount-store industry can actually be traced back to 1954, when Sol Price founded FedMart, it was not till he and his son, Robert, launched the first Price Club in 1976 that the modern concept of membership shopping based on low-margin merchandizing, brand-name quality, and "cheap, steep, and deep" came into full focus. Sam's Club followed in 1983 when Sam Walton, creative genius also of Wal-Mart, opened the first warehouse club in Midwest City, Oklahoma, followed by two additional clubs in Kansas City, Missouri, and Dallas, Texas. Initially, the stores were operated as members-only outlets catering exclusively to eligible business owners and their families, but eventually the scope was extended to include any deal seekers in the public at large willing to pay an annual membership fee. Today, with more than 500 clubs nationwide, 46 million members, and annual revenues of around $30 billion, Sam's is a commodities wonder—and growing in leaps and bounds every day.

My introduction to Sam's occurred some years ago when a very polished lady friend of mine, who consumes M&Ms day and night the way others nibble compulsively on tiny pretzels, said she'd heard the club sold the pricey candy in whopping 3-pound bags at some unheard-of discount. At around this same time, I was jolted breathlessly one afternoon to notice on a neighbor's kitchen counter a massive container of Hellmann's mayonnaise approximately the size of a gasoline can, only to learn that the source was none other than the friendly Sam's Club located about thirty miles from my home. He then went on to expose in his spacious pantry or deep freeze a 10-pound box of baking soda, monstrous cans of Hunt's tomato sauce, 2½-pound jars of Jif peanut butter, a whole 16-pound beef rib eye, and jumbo packages of cut-up chicken, bacon, hamburger, New Zealand lamb chops, and who knows what other poultry and meats. My eyes popped in disbelief when I studied some of the prices, but it was the Hellmann's, Jif, and a 10-pound boneless pork loin priced at $1.68 per pound that inspired me to drive over to the club, pay the annual $35 membership fee, and indulge in my first orgy of shopping. (One reason I remain loyal to Sam's, by the way, is because the regular membership fee at places like Costco and Price Club is an inflated $45. Also, I learned on the sly that when my membership at Sam's expires, I can get a one-day free pass and load up on a couple of months worth of supplies by paying only a negligible 10 percent of the total cost when I check out.)

Now, I'm not the least embarrassed to confess that, generally, I'm a notorious cheapskate grocery and beverage shopper, a trait that appalls and irritates my friends but one that not only keeps me abreast of what virtually all foods, wines, beers, sundry delicacies, and the like should cost but saves me thousands of hard-earned dollars a year. Each and every week, with ball-point in hand, I pore over in advance each and every supermarket and wine circular tossed in my driveway, analyzing my present and future needs, scrutinizing and comparing the sale prices, and, when absolutely necessary, clipping damnable coupons. Consequently, it's no exaggeration to say that I normally shop in at least one supermarket every day of my life when not traveling, and that it's not unusual for me to browse through wine and liquor shops maybe twice a week even when I am traveling. Some people simply view this habit of mine as an abnormal compulsion; my own loving mother classifies it as a certifiable sickness.

By no means do I want anybody to get the idea that I'm a shopping yahoo who settles for mediocre foods and drinks just to save a dime the way so many other Samsters do. No indeed. I will not, for example, eat canned fruits or vegetables, frozen microwave dinners (in fact, I don't own a microwave), commercial cookies, or instant anything. And the two times I tried packaged stove-top stuffing and a boxed pound-cake mix, I flushed the results of each down the disposal. I've never been able to bring myself (even for the sake of professional research) to sample frozen chicken teriyaki strips, French-toast sticks, instant beef pot roast, Dum Dum Pops, or Mountain Dew—although I am a little curious about Bumbleberry Blossoms and a snack combination of nuts, raisins, and M&Ms called Mountain Trail Mix that seasoned Samsters seem to relish. Though it is painful to shell out big bucks for smoked Scotch salmon, fresh caviar and morels, branzino, hazelnut oil, and St.-Marcellin cheese at specialty food markets and fancy delis, I do drum up the courage to splurge if the urge or need is overwhelming, but even when shopping for these luxury products, rest assured that I've memorized and am guided by the price differences at various locales—no matter how minute.

Of course what staggers me, what really drives me up the wall, is watching some Americans all over the country shop with no regard whatsoever for bargains, which in my opinion is the height of stupidity. I've stood flabbergasted at a Jewel supermarket outside Chicago as a woman with a screaming child quickly grabbed an outrageously priced box of ordinary bran flakes cereal when another was on sale for almost half the cost. Observing an obvious housewife at a King Kullen on Long Island choose a $4.99 package of

Hormel bacon over a much less expensive store brand (unaware that there's virtually no difference in the quality of American bacon—it's all pretty lousy) made my flesh crawl. And when recently, at a Winn-Dixie in Charlotte, North Carolina, a young, intelligent-looking man snatched a $4.17 carton of Florida's Natural premium orange juice from the shelf, oblivious to the same size of Tropicana on sale for $2.00, all I wanted to do was shake him hard and bellow, Why, Why, Why?

I remember my pulse throbbing at the sight of a rather orchidaceous lady at the customized meat counter of a Ralph's market in Beverly Hills imperiously ordering a butcher to cut four lamb chops (size unspecified) to the tune of $10.99 a pound, disdainful (or ignorant) of the obviously identical packaged chops clearly on sale in the nearby display case for $6.99 the pound. Routinely in Manhattan and on Long Island, I'm mortified by nitwits who sail through Citarella, Grace's Market, Barefoot Contessa, and other such posh food boutiques grabbing criminally priced iceberg lettuce, containers of coleslaw and potato salad, bottles of ordinary jams and ketchups, loaves of Pepperidge Farm bread and gummy bagels, and even paper towels and napkins. And as for the unenlightened foodies in every state of the nation who somehow find more virtue in a tasteless, highly overrated, so-called organic chicken tagged at $8 than in a very similar bird on sale for a more realistic 69¢ a pound, all I can say is that those folks either have money to burn or should be forced to attend a blind taste-testing of American chickens.

Not, mind you, that Samsters are always the most careful and discerning players in the grocery arena. It's true that most can spot a good deal a mile away, but there are also some who are so enraptured by volume shopping that they fail to determine whether an item might be cheaper on sale at a supermarket than at Sam's. (Naturally, this necessitates constantly scrutinizing supermarket circulars, as I do, plus always carrying a pocket calculator, as I also do.) To wit: Not long ago, I was tickled pink to find quart bottles of my beloved Hellmann's mayo (the normal price of which can soar to a preposterous $4.19 or more) at one supermarket for $1.69 with a two-bottle limit. Sam's price for a gallon container is $8.37, or $2.09 a quart. Of course, a truly steadfast Samster might argue that the supermarket sale is a very rare and restricted opportunity, whereas the gallon will last much longer and is always available at the same low price. To which I could respond that, when quarts of Hellmann's are discounted so incredibly, I don't think twice about buying my first two legitimate bottles, returning from the parking lot two, maybe three or four times, checking out at different counters, and lugging home the equivalent of two gallons for a savings of $3.20 over Sam's. Okay, not a phenomenal amount for all the inconvenience, but every buck does count these days, and besides, nothing is more comforting and gratifying than beating any system.

Much as I admire Samsters' wise frugality, I must say it does amaze me the way some load up on provisions as if planning for a nuclear holocaust. During one of my excursions, for instance, I was contemplating whether to buy a 4½-pound box of minute rice for a remarkable $3.86 when I observed a fairly young, buxom, but beautifully tailored woman with an alligator purse pulling one overloaded cart while pushing another that was already half filled. Glancing furtively at the first, I was able to make out burly cans of Green Giant mushrooms, Hormel chili with beans, and Del Monte fruit cocktail; an 18-pack carton of Vienna sausages; hulking bottles of garlic and onion powder; a couple of oversized boxes of Ritz crackers and three 20-ounce bags of Wise potato chips; a duo of weighty Pam cooking spray aerosols; two strapping containers of Hershey's chocolate syrup; a flat of Bud; and enormous aluminum trays of frozen mac & cheese, lasagne, meatballs, pork egg rolls, and heaven knows what else.

As we both headed for the spacious produce department and mile-long fresh meat and poultry cases, she stopped momentarily, as I did, to sample a small slab of steak a clerk was frying at a tasting station. (Sam's has lots of tasting stations, and the aromas can be intoxicating or nauseating.) She casually popped the meat into her mouth, chewed with conviction, then turned to me and pronounced "Umm, delicious!" before proceeding to haul a sack of oranges over the side of the second cart and pluck an 8-pound package of ground beef chuck and 4-pound tray of Italian-style sausages from the meat counter. Now utterly intrigued by this confident, compelling creature negotiating two mountains of food and drink, I purposely followed her to the checkout area, only to see that she was soon joined by a healthy-looking man with two well-fed school-age children with their own over-flowing cart in tow. While the clerk swiped or aimed a price gun at each item in the carts (maybe a ten-minute process), the four happy shoppers nibbled from a megabag of fun-size candy bars, and by the time the carts had been refilled (there's no such thing as useless plastic shopping bags at Sam's), the gent had pulled out a platinum MasterCard and signed a chit totaling some $340 plus change. I caught last sight of the family from a short distance in the parking lot as they loaded their goods into the back of a big, sleek, dark blue Mercedes SUV.

Although I rarely shop at Sam's with such reckless abandon, I can't deny that I'm virtually helpless when confronted with any number of supersized staples at such rock-bottom prices. Nor does it make a particle of difference that I could probably purchase an entire side of Angus beef or wheel of Parmigiano-Reggiano for what my periodic jaunts to Sam's cost me annually in gas. But, for better or worse, there's never a time when my home itself does not resemble a food-and-drink warehouse stocked with enough essentials not only to nourish me comfortably on a monthly basis but to accommodate most plans for entertaining. That much of my discounted stash ends up being outdated, stale, rancid, freezer-burned, or bug-infested by the time I use it is a ridiculous reality I simply try to ignore—just like the wasted gasoline.

Partially surveying my present inventory of provisions bought primarily at Sam's, I see that in the kitchen cabinets alone are twenty-seven 6-ounce cans of Star-Kist solid white albacore tuna, three 48-ounce bottles of Heinz ketchup, two 5-pound boxes of baking soda, and six 2½-pound jars of Skippy peanut butter. Under a work table rests two cardboard boxes with six 5-pound bags of flour each and five 10-pound bags of sugar (all double-wrapped in plastic to ward against tiny varmints). Stacked high in a hall closet are seven large boxes of assorted crackers, two 3-pound boxes of raisin bran crunch cereal (which I really don't eat much), two 3½-pound containers of Planters Cocktail Peanuts (salted), three 20-ounce bags of crinkly potato chips, and two 4½-pound boxes of minute rice. And right alongside shelves of wines and homemade pickles and preserves in the basement are four 39-ounce cans of Folger's decaffeinated coffee, two 1-gallon jars of extra-large kosher dill pickles, mammoth cans of garbanzo beans and Italian tomatoes, maybe fifteen various 10¾-ounce cans of Campbell's soup, and, of course, no less than four 1-gallon containers of Hellmann's mayo—not to mention a couple of flats of both Samuel Adams beer and Coke, twenty-three rolls of paper towels, and a 3,000-square-foot roll of Reynolds plastic wrap stored on the concrete floor. Since some of the oranges, grapefruits, cantaloupes, lettuces, and breads in the refrigerator are now on the verge of rotting or turning moldy, I won't bother discussing those. But I do know that in the freezer are about a dozen nicely marbled strip steaks, a turkey breast, two 5-pound beef rump roasts, a dozen or so chuck hamburgers, and some type of battered ground chicken nuggets that looked interesting to serve with cocktails but that I haven't tasted yet. (I yearn to buy a deep freeze, but I don't dare.) Perhaps I should add that I live here alone.

While some people might be aghast at the prospect of dealing with such large quantities of supplies, I have most of it down pretty much to an art—give or take a few over-the-hill fruits and vegetables. It does present something of a problem wondering what to do with the remainder of a giant drum of canned tomato sauce after I've used just enough to make *ragù* for pasta and the freezer is overflowing. And when a murky, viscous film forms on top of an opened 46-ounce jar of stuffed olives, I do have to debate whether to patiently skim the disgusting muck off and rinse what olives I want to use through my fingers, or just dump everything down the disposal and swallow the cost. Transferring mayonnaise from gallon buckets to quart jars that will fit conveniently in the fridge is, admittedly, a messy task resulting in mayo all over my hands, on the counter, down the sides of the jars, and sometimes across the front of my shirt, but I'm gradually perfecting the knack. I've also learned a few tricks about gouging two or three strips of bacon from a frozen 4-pound package I've forgotten to partially thaw, as well as how to sterilize and skillfully fill empty balsamic vinegar bottles with soy sauce from a metal 1-gallon can to keep it from going rancid. I used to think I was just plain dumb to store an extra industrial-sized cylinder of plastic wrap (unavailable, by the way, in supermarkets) that wouldn't be used for at least three years, but then it dawned on me that not only would the film never deteriorate but that the price was sure to go up by the time I needed a new roll.

It goes without saying that food snobs obsessed with the causes of white sapote, wild sockeye gravlax, prune-pit oil, Tarocco blood oranges, Prosecco, and Masamoto knives would have nothing but disdain for the banality and parsimony implicit in Samster shopping, to which all I can say is, tough cheese. Like it or not, Samsters are setting an important precedent in America, and if others are unsettled by the way millions so far choose to nourish themselves according to a certain set of tightwad principles that don't necessarily embrace a high degree of culinary sophistication, so be it. As for myself, I'll no doubt always succumb to the sporadic temptation to spend shocking amounts at carriage-trade shops on such supernal treats as fresh white truffles, goose foie gras, and Château d'Yquem. But rest assured that when I'm not in the grips of rash hedonism, most of my time away from supermarkets will be spent roaming the aisles of Sam's, stocking up while saving the big bucks necessary to keep me in steady supply of rare Spanish Jabugo ham and afloat in French rosé Champagne.

Not, mind you, that price clubs in America are not presently undergoing such rapid and radical changes that even I find it hard to keep up with what's going on. Recently, for example, I learned that Costco was elevating at least some of warehouse shopping to a sophisticated new plateau by installing tanks of live lobsters, stocking walls of premium wines (including Dom Pérignon), and hiring white-coated butchers to custom-cut racks of lamb, huge pork tenderloins, and extra-thick strip steaks—all at deeply discounted prices and all based on the strategy of mixing class with mass. Wondering if Sam's was challenging Costco's ambitious effort to attract more fastidious, moneyed customers, I consequently returned to my outlet and found new voluminous cases of sushi and smoked salmon, 2½-pound containers of genuine Greek feta cheese, 3-liter bottles of extra-virgin olive oil and 1-liter ones of balsamic vinegar, boneless legs of lamb, and whole 13-pound beef rib eyes. No doubt venerable Sam's is as capable of upgrading part of its operation as any of the enterprising upstarts, and rest assured that I'll be the first to load up on cut-rate live lobsters, fresh Long Island ducks, wild mushrooms, and Château Talbot when they make their first appearance. While the competition on more exotic goods heats up, however, I'm quite content maintaining loyalty to Sam's, benefiting from any lofty changes, and of course, saving that important ten bucks on the membership fee over the other clubs.

Actually, not long ago I was beginning to feel a bit guilty about my obsessive volume shopping, skinflint ways, and gustatory compromises. Then, just in the nick of time, I happened to read an illustrated interview with Daniel Boulud, probably the greatest and most famous chef in America. Predictably, there was lots of talk about his love of caviar, and Champagne, and farm-raised chickens, and Fiji water, but he also fessed up to a penchant for hot dogs, peanuts, and potato chips. That impressed me, but what really caught my eye was a small photo taken in his home kitchen that revealed on a counter the most gigantic bag of Pepperidge Farm Goldfish and boxes of Newman's Own popcorn I'd ever seen. Of course, I have no way of knowing for sure without calling the chef personally, but I really do bet an imperial tin of fresh beluga that Boulud is a closet Samster.

PRIMAL STEAK

THE MOST RECENT OFFICIAL VERDICT BY THE UNOFFICIAL American health jury is in: fats are good, protein is good, red meat is good, and consequently, one answer to the national problem of obesity is a steak diet. Plain and simple. It seems that Dr. Atkins was right all along, and the high-carbohydrate, high-fiber, high Omega-3, high Mediterranean this-and-that killjoys are now wringing their hands, as are a few million pasta fiends, white-rice addicts, and bagel freaks. Steak lovers, on the other hand, relieved of their periodic hunger, deprivation, and guilt, couldn't be more jubilant as they indulge their passion shamelessly and watch the pounds miraculously melt away. If cholesterol and all those other evils pose a stubborn problem, some dedicated carnivores are now even exploiting a solution I learned about years ago: pop a Lopid or Tricor once a day, forget all about lipids, and eat away like a Flintstone.

That's the good news. The bad news pertains to the steaks themselves, or rather to the difficulties involved in satisfying our eternal quest for bovine perfection. Contrary to what everybody is led to believe, the ideal American steak cannot be found at even the most respected butchers in our largest cities. It cannot be found in any of the upscale, hideously expensive steak houses that seem to multiply more rapidly each year. And it damn sure doesn't exist in the meat cases of supermarkets. The sad truth is that most people have never tasted a perfect steak. I have. Not that often and not that easily, but certainly enough times over the past few decades to know what absolute steak perfection is all about and where to find it.

So who am I to make such a claim, especially in a country where steak reigns supreme at the dinner table, where at any one moment twelve million beef animals are being fed or finished for national consumption, and where the average citizen devours something like 113 pounds of beef annually—even those not on a steak diet? There's no doubt that my insinuations will spark the wrath of thousands of meat distributors, buyers, butchers, and restaurateurs, not to mention that countless number of backyard enthusiasts who are convinced that the thick red slabs cooked on their charcoal or overpriced gas grills are, give or take a few gristles and sinews, of the finest quality. But the fact is that you'll probably go the rest of your life and never savor an ultimate steak like the ones I discovered at a small, family-run Midwestern market and still purchase when I'm in the vicinity or when a caring friend is good enough to lug a nice supply back East to me on a plane. So why don't I just have the luscious steaks shipped to me? Simple: the good folks who own the market don't ship—they don't have to.

My search for the perfect steak was not undertaken without some premise. When I lived in Missouri some years ago, a friend whose father owned a small meat-packing plant in St. Joseph once prepared for me a two-inch-thick Kansas City sirloin strip that sent shock waves through every cell in my mouth. Informed that this was one of many such Prime Angus steaks never shipped from the area but put aside for local consumption, I studied the prize as carefully as possible, fixing in my food-oriented brain its remarkable characteristics. I'd never before seen, much less eaten, such a steak, but there could be no doubt: it had to be an aristocrat. The meat had been properly dry-aged for thirty days, the color could be most closely described as purplish-red, the marbling of the lean was prominent, and the partial encasement of white fat had to be at least an inch thick. After the strip was grilled to medium-rare, it took but a single luscious bite to convince me I was eating an exceptionally flavored, fine-textured, fork-tender, flawless piece of meat.

After that, I must have ingested over six hundred pounds of beef, either in some of the country's most legendary restaurants or at home, and, without exception, I never failed to meet with some degree of disappointment. I rummaged through stacks of supposedly choice cuts on meat counters; I believed butchers when they told me I was buying the finest Prime; and I paid astronomical prices in steak houses for what were touted as the country's finest dry-aged hunks of meat—all in the hope that somewhere, somehow, I might relish an impeccable steak at least once more before my liver gave out. From time to time I would find respectable, even delicious beef, but there was always something that made it less than ideal. A sirloin that was juicy and flavorful had the texture of tawed leather. A filet that was tender as marshmallow but, lacking natural fat, was tasteless. A porterhouse that appeared to have character in its raw form, once cooked, was full of connective tissue (gristle) and had probably been artificially tenderized in one way or another.

Eventually, it became evident to me and to those who shared in my gustatory exploits that, contrary to what everyone thinks—and certainly despite all the hype about how the best Midwestern beef is automatically shipped to such obviously lucrative markets as New York City, Los Angeles, Chicago, and other metropolises that can charge top dollar—the finest Prime steak in the nation simply is not generally found in these blue-chip locales.

I wanted to know why. If the perfect steak I once tasted indeed still existed, according to the history of the meat-processing business, it had to reside in the Midwest, more than likely in a small, privately owned processing plant that supplied superior beef only to a local area.

Suffice it that I eventually found the steak I was seeking, but only after stalking God knows how many huge stockyards, breeding stations, feedlots, and aging lockers, and after talking with well-informed experts in various divisions of the industry. The name of the market was Snow's Meat Locker, located on some offbeat side street in Kansas City, Kansas, not a fifteen-minute car ride across the state line from the fashionable Country Club Plaza in Kansas City, Missouri. As I hopefully anticipated, it was one of the few remaining family enterprises in the entire Midwest that still slaughtered, aged, processed, and sold its beef right on the premises.

Even more important was that during his many years in business, the owner, I. O. Snow, had never sold a pound of his meat outside Kansas City.

"In all, I've been dealing with meat fifty-four years," he began, "and I've never had to ship out. There're enough folks around here who know good beef, and they know I handle the best you can buy. Just look at that line of customers standing out there at the counter."

I glanced from the small office out at the crowd, then watched as he pushed his large frame back in an old swivel-style chair and wrapped a rubber band around a fat roll of greenbacks.

"No sir, you won't find this type of beef back where you're from, and one day you might not find it here. The way those big companies are fooling around with tenderizers and preservatives and all those flash-frozen methods, it's a wonder most people ever taste a natural steak."

Pulling himself up, he then headed out back toward the spacious meat lockers lined with hanging carcasses that weighed five hundred to seven hundred pounds each and were in the process of being aged for thirty days at a temperature of thirty-five degrees with minimum humidity.

"Now here's a side of perfect Prime Angus," he continued, grabbing a mammoth flank that displayed the standard purple inspection stamp. "The day's slowly approaching when this grade of beef will be something of the past. See all this thick fat under the ribs? 'Gobby' we call it. Well, that's what gives this steer a Prime grade, but people just aren't willing to pay for that much extra fat to get a good-flavored, tender steak. When cattlemen finally get the [lean] product they're aiming at by crossbreeding and feed modification, this carcass won't exist."

Although beef carcasses are still graded by federal inspectors as Prime, Choice, and Select (depending on form, the amount and distribution of fat, the color and marbling of the flesh, and the quality of the bone), there's no doubt that the rapid progress being made in the scientifically controlled diet and selective breeding of cattle is gradually producing more standardized animals as well as a somewhat modified grading system. Today, practically all domestic livestock is fattened in U.S. feedlots not only on corn but also high-protein grains, soybeans, and hybrid sorghums. Furthermore, according to the U.S. Department of Agriculture, the diet of about 75 percent of the thirty million cattle slaughtered each year is supplemented by synthetic hormones, which make the animals fatten faster on less grain.

To meet the public's growing demand for good beef, even greater efforts are being made by registered cattle breeders to develop more refined animals through crossbreeding. I've talked to lots of cattlemen, and whether they come from Missouri, Kansas, Nebraska, or Texas, most seem in common agreement that the most important developments in the industry pertain to specialized crossbreeding, and some authorities predict a three-way terminal cross in breeding will be the ultimate step in producing what will fill the meat counters of the future. As Don Shead, head butcher at Snow's, told me recently, "The slaughter steer or heifer will be the product of an Angus-Charolais mother cow, for example, bred back to a Hereford or Shorthorn, or bred artificially to one of the large European breeds that have made their mark on the American cattle industry."

From all this, it doesn't take a wizard to pinpoint the industry's ideal: an animal that grows rapidly, reaches an early maturity, utilizes its feed efficiently, reproduces regularly and with minimum calving problems, and yields not a Prime but an excellent Choice carcass. In other words, the goal is to produce streamlined cattle that carry not more than 5 percent fat (a Prime steer averages around 15 percent) and provide uniformly lean and tender cuts of beef.

The fact that at least 90 percent of our slaughter animals are now of Choice grade or better testifies already to the success of many experimental programs. Still, I find it interesting, if not terrifying, to envisage how the average consumer (not to mention the professional epicure) will react if and when the steaks displayed in retail markets and restaurants are nearly identical in color, texture, size, and even taste. If this stage of development is actually realized by the beef industry, it will undoubtedly please many of those mindful of substantial savings, as well as those obsessed by their cholesterol count. But what about the thousands of serious American carnivores for whom an exceptional piece of Prime represents something rare, exciting, and unique? Will they be forced into the same disgraceful compromise they now tolerate peering down at rows of uniformly frozen vegetables or at mounds of sickeningly pale, artificially ripened tomatoes?

Although this possibility definitely exists, there are still enough problems to be resolved within the industry to safeguard consumers—at least for the time being—against standardized beef. Before such a product can be marketed exclusively, even more regulations governing inspection and grading will have to be enacted. The various mechanical and chemical methods of tenderizing meat continue to inspire heated debate, while the touchy and mysterious subjects of hormone additives, antibiotics, and preservatives are constantly being investigated by both the USDA and the FDA.

While the industry is in the process of trying to produce its perfect steak, consumers should make even greater demands regarding what is presently available. But before they can make demands, they would be wise to learn exactly what they're looking for in the way of quality meat. All too many people take their normal stand in front of the meat counter or staring at a menu, unaware of what they're buying or ordering and usually baffled by the confusing array of steak names. Few take the time to ask questions about the mind-boggling descriptions of cuts, opting simply to grab what looks cherry red and lean or listening to some waiter waxing ecstatically about a restaurant's steaks being the greatest in America. If these are your habits, you're headed in the wrong direction for superior beef.

The first step is learning to identify the various cuts of steak without depending on the radically diverse nomenclature printed on labels, butchers' stickers, and menus. Why there is no more uniformity throughout the nation in the names of cuts is beyond me. If the industry is so interested in standardization, it might begin with its terminology. Is there anything, for example, to distinguish a rib steak from a rib-eye steak? Why is it that the steak cut from the rib end of the short loin is called a Delmonico in one section of the country and a club in another? What is the difference between a T-bone and a porterhouse; a New York strip, Kansas City strip, and shell steak; a rump steak and a silver tip; a round-bone (double-bone) sirloin and a pinbone (wedge bone) sirloin; a fillet and a tournedos? And exactly what is the hanger steak that is currently so chic to order in restaurants? For the time being at least, you should familiarize yourself with these cuts and names by studying a good meat book.

Once you're adept at identifying cuts, you're in the position to evaluate the grade and quality of steak. Prime is the finest beef available, but outside the Midwest, you're likely to find this grade only in the most reputable and expensive butcher shops and steak houses in large metropolitan areas. Ideally, this exquisite meat appears almost violet in color from proper dry aging. Dry aging is a lengthy, costly process whereby whole sides of beef are kept in constant dry refrigeration at thirty-four to thirty-six degrees for up to thirty days to break down the tissues and make the meat more flavorful and tender. Every day the beef loses water and about 1 percent of its weight, an explanation of why Prime carcasses you might see in butcher shops or the windows of serious steak houses appear more shriveled and downright unsightly than regular beef and why well-aged meat is more expensive. The lean of the best steak is well marbled but not overwhelmed by fat, the outer layer of fat thick and almost pure white, and the bone (if any) not yellowed. As to taste and texture, it is mellow, juicy, and tender, with a minimum of connective tissue.

Most Prime is either shipped to better hotels and restaurants or distributed within the local region where it is processed. Rarely will you find it in ordinary supermarkets, and even in those that boast of a specialty meat department, I'm very wary of bright red, poorly marbled steaks advertised as Prime. For reasons I've already discussed, true Prime is becoming more and more scarce, and even if you happen to live in Kansas City, Omaha, Denver, or Chicago and don't know your butcher personally, chances are you'll get a quality of beef that is closer to Choice and still pay a pretty penny for it. I have serious doubts about paying serious money for meat that has traveled ten days, or that is perhaps watered with preservative, or that risks exposure during transport from distributor to retail dealer. As much as I admire this noble grade of beef, I have become as skeptical of purchasing it outside the Midwest as I am of investing in a case of fine burgundy shipped overseas from France.

Despite the fact that sophisticated palates demand the perfection of dry-aged Prime, the vast majority of steaks sold at respectable markets and restaurants is of Choice grade. Generally this is excellent, reasonably priced beef, but, again, your knowledgeable eye can determine the difference between a memorable meal and an ordinary one. Unfortunately the tendency of most consumers is to search for under-aged (thus probably tenderized), bright-red steaks that are all but devoid of fat. If you choose this type of beef, your steak will most likely be full of connective tissue and flavorless. Should you try to economize by accepting any grade less than Choice, you're asking for real trouble. If you see no inspection stamp, insist that the butcher show you beef that does bear a grade. Select grade meat is suitable for slow-roasting or braising, but not for grilling or pan-searing.

Predictably, any steak lover must exercise the keenest precaution in even the fanciest restaurants. A few states require that the grade of beef be indicated on their menus, but more often than not the customer has little idea as to the quality of steak he's ordering. First, if you happen to be from out of town, you should make every effort to solicit local opinions regarding the overall reputation of any establishment. Also, when calling for reservations (even at the most popular upscale chains), don't hesitate to confirm not only what grade of meat is served but which cuts are available. (Better restaurants always offer at least one cut of sirloin and a fillet.) Second, if you are determined to enjoy outstanding steak when dining out, you must demand to see the raw product before it is cooked. Any restaurant that refuses you this privilege does not deserve your patronage.

One important final question is how to cook steak properly. Some people (myself included) crave the added flavor of charcoal, others prefer their steak simply broiled, while a growing minority is adopting the European method of pan-searing steak and using the deglazed juices as part of a sauce. Any technique is completely satisfactory so long as you handle it correctly and do not overcook the meat. (A great steak should never be cooked more than medium-rare.) If you intend to use charcoal, the meat should be grilled close enough to the gray coals to assure a crusty exterior and a juicy pink-red interior. (Personally, I'd never uses a gas grill for steaks, since, contrary to all the hype, I've yet to find one that provides the same intensity of open fire as the cheap charcoal model I use regularly.) In broiling, the oven should be preheated to five hundred degrees and the steak (preferably about one and one-half inches thick) cooked four inches from the heat for approximately three minutes on each side. To pan-broil, heat a heavy frying pan until very hot, add a little oil (unless the meat is Prime), and sear both sides for one minute. Reduce the heat, continue cooking, turning once, from seven to ten minutes; remove the steak from the pan, discard the oil and fat, then prepare a sauce by sautéing a few chopped shallots in a tablespoon of butter and deglazing the pan with a little good red wine.

Despite all the overinflated phobias about fats and cholesterol and triglycerides and what have you, steak is not only here to stay as part of the twenty-first-century American diet but skyrocketing in popularity (and price) like never before in our history. How long true Prime beef remains available in our swankiest butcher shops and restaurants is a scary question, but what worries me most is what obsessed enthusiasts like myself would do if tiny, remote, half-century-old operations like Snow's ceased to exist in the Midwest and the possibility of never again sinking teeth into a rare, ideal, quintessential American steak became a tragic reality. For the present, I refuse to dwell on it. Besides, I'm way overdue for another quick excursion to Kansas City.

THE MYSTERY
OF *LACTOBACILLUS*
SANFRANCISCO

A T 9:00 A.M. ON ANY GIVEN SATURDAY MORNING IN BERKELEY, California, across the bay from San Francisco, a long line of people has already begun to snake its way into a crowded parking lot on San Pablo Avenue. In the lot are a magnificent two-tone brown Rolls-Royce, a sprinkling of sleek Mercedes, and a contingent of more modest vehicles. Standing patiently behind a couple decked out in jogging attire are a dignified middle-aged lady and gentleman straight out of Pacific Heights or Hillsborough, and squatting behind them are three latter-day hippies sipping Starbucks coffee. First impressions suggest that this disparate group is waiting for the opening of an auction gallery or a new video shop. Wrong. What these eclectic individuals share is a passion for genuine sourdough bread, and the reason they've shown up one hour before the Acme Bread Company unlocks its door is because they know that what is reputedly the greatest sourdough in the entire country will be sold out by noon. To face the weekend without a couple of Acme's sourdough baguettes or *bâtards* or *pain au levain* or whole-wheat walnut is a lamentable prospect not one cares to contemplate.

New Yorkers swoon over their hot pastrami, natives of Dallas would wage war to preserve the integrity of their barbecued brisket, and New Orleanians never cease extolling their gumbos and remoulades, but no oral obsession is quite so serious, so profound, so intense as that of a San Franciscan for sourdough bread. And rightly so, since there's unquestionably no other bread in the United States—none!—that can hold a candle to the crusty, pungent loaf that has been a San Francisco staple for well over a century. Today, an increasing number of professional and amateur chefs (as well as commercial bakeries) are experimenting more and more with sourdough as a medium not just for standard bread but also for pancakes, muffins, biscuits, waffles, rolls, bagels, even cakes. Often the results are impressive; but as one who has traveled repeatedly to that beautiful city by the bay partly to study and sample sourdough, and who has baked and consumed enough sourdough products to fill a cable car, I must agree with the ardent locals that no sourdough made elsewhere can equal the loaves produced in San Francisco. Period.

So what is San Francisco sourdough? How did the city develop into America's sourdough capital? And why is the bread so special? Contrary to what you may think, sourdough was not created in the early bakeries of San Francisco. The dough, in fact, can be traced back over four thousand years to the Egyptians, most likely the first people to learn that when a mixture of wheat and water was allowed to ferment in a warm place, the "raised" bread it made, riddled with tiny air pockets, was much lighter and more flavorful than standard unleavened cakes. It was also discovered that the mysterious agent later identified as active yeast could be passed on to other loaves by saving small quantities of dough and using them as "starters" for new batches of bread.

The wild yeasts that inoculated the starters of the ancients were probably derived from some form of beer, but eventually it was learned that virtually any grain or starchy vegetable, when left to ferment, could produce the yeast (or acetic acid) necessary for successful bread starters. Until commercial yeast was first developed in the nineteenth century, all the great leavened breads of Germany, France, and the rest of the civilized world were made from natural starters, and even today, a truly serious baker, like Poîlane in Paris (considered by many the overall finest in the world), would never think of fouling its sourdough bread by adding a grain of commercial yeast to the starter.

Everyone has a theory as to where the original San Francisco starters came from. The most popular (and romantic) notion is that, during the westward migration in the nineteenth century, trail cooks, or "sourdoughs," as they were called, carried their lively and valuable starters with them, protecting the fermenting pots with all resources possible and often sleeping with them so that body warmth would assure another day's batch of sourdough bread, biscuits, and flapjacks. Some historians link San Francisco sourdough with the Gold Rush and the forty-niners, not a few of whom (like Isadore Boudin, whose name is still synonymous with great sourdough) were accomplished European bakers seeking their fortunes in the California mines. Others find a connection between the French refugees of the Mexican "Pastry War" of 1838, when, after a political brouhaha, a French pastry chef was awarded a large sum in compensation for the destruction of his shop by disrespectful Mexican soldiers. And still others insist that sourdough was introduced to San Francisco by Alaskan pioneers returning from Klondike gold-mining camps.

Sourdough lore is rich in colorful anecdotes, but, as one adventurer described the preparation of biscuits, it's for sure that every facet of sourdough baking was taken seriously: "You add milk in the morning to the sourdough pot; then, to stiffen it, you add flour and thoroughly work it till you get a good thick batter. Then you set it behind the stove, where it will keep warm for five or six hours . . . let it rise and sour. When you are ready to make your biscuits, you add salt and soda and some fresh flour, pinch off your big fat biscuits, roll them in melted lard, and let them set fifteen or twenty minutes to make their chemical change, then put them in the hot oven to bake. There's no biscuit worth bothering about when you've been used to sourdough."

If the exact origins of San Francisco sourdough remain obscure, the scientific reasons for the bread's superiority are even more elusive and complex. Over a period of time, I must have asked two dozen professional bakers and chefs in and around the city what they felt contributed most to the bread's unique qualities, and rarely were any two explanations the same. It is no secret, of course, that San Francisco, perched on the edge of the Pacific Ocean, has always boasted a special microclimate. Even the finest bread baked only ten miles from the Golden Gate can have an altogether different taste and texture. But is it a question of the moderate temperature, or the humidity, or the water, or some strange spore in the salt air from the Pacific, or a combination of these and other natural phenomena?

After scientists at University of California, Los Angeles and the University of California, Davis had made attempts and failed to isolate any microorganism that might explain the special properties of San Francisco sourdough, one specialist from the Bay Area, Leo Kline, discovered in the late sixties not only a particular strain of yeast in five different starters but also the specific bacterium, *Lactobacillus sanfrancisco,* that is now considered responsible for the dough's basic character. Important no doubt, but detractors (especially those striving for a legal appellation that would restrict the term "San Francisco sourdough" to products baked only in San Francisco) still argue that there's a great deal more to sourdough than a single yeast or bacterial organism, perhaps dozens and dozens of criteria that will never be understood but must be considered in any analysis of why the dough is indigenous.

Nothing is more important to San Francisco bakers than safeguarding the secret of their precious starters (or "sponges," as some professionals call them). Even during the Gold Rush, efforts to preserve a prized starter were almost as intense as the frenzy to find gold, and legends abound about how such early bakeries as Larraburu, Boudin, Parisian, Toscana, and Colombo were so protective of their original starters that they kept them under lock and key. Today, security is no less tight. When Boudin, for example, opened its first outlet in San Diego and had to transport a mound of starter to mother a new generation of bread, the company president secured the starter in a strongbox, insured it for one million dollars, carried it in a first-class airplane seat, and delivered it to the bakery in an armored car. The owner of Acme Bread Company couldn't have been more helpful and hospitable while conducting a short tour of the famous bakery, but when I asked him if I might peek into a large container of sponge kept in a stainless-steel cold locker (he estimated that his original starter dated back at least a decade), he became visibly nervous. At the highly respected Patisserie Française in the Castro district, the most the owner there would tell about her mother dough was that it had been developed from fermented raisins, and even up at the Model Bakery as St. Helena in the Napa Valley (where I sampled the best sourdough outside San Francisco), the folks were adamant in refusing to sell me even a tablespoon of starter.

Although it is unlikely that even the most ingenious baker outside the Bay Area will ever manage to produce genuine San Francisco sourdough, this doesn't necessarily mean that you can't turn out delicious baked goods that at least approximate the real McCoy and that far surpass in savor and texture the vast majority of bland, innocuous breads to which we're normally exposed. Some West Coasters would have you believe that you can't make sourdough bread unless you either transport a live starter from San Francisco or begin the process by activating a little commercial dry starter processed right in the city and available by mail in small containers.

Nonsense. Since some of the best sourdough bread I've tasted is served at Fournou's Ovens at the Renaissance Stanford Court hotel in San Francisco (a pastry chef there told me she not only used fermented grapes to "reinforce" her sponge but placed it on the hotel roof to expose it to fog!), I eventually coaxed management to part with a cup of their sacred starter and raced back East to bake bread on the eastern end of Long Island.

At the same time, I decided not only to use a dry San Francisco starter but to create my own, mixing equal amounts of plain white flour and East Hampton tap water, covering the bowl with cheesecloth, and allowing it to ferment and collect whatever bacteria might be in the air for five days. When I carefully baked three loaves of bread, each with a totally different starter, I—and others—could detect few major distinctions. The bread was definitely not the true San Francisco sourdough I'd gotten to know so well, but it was nevertheless tangy, delectably aromatic and chewy, and beautifully crusted—in other words, and for whatever chemical or biological reasons, very good Eastern sourdough bread.

I am convinced, therefore, that all it takes to enjoy memorable sourdough products is patience, patience, patience. It is important to remember that any live starter must be "fed" periodically with equal amounts of flour and liquid (plain warm water, even white wine); that at least one cup of the original starter or of sponge (the mixture of starter, flour, and liquid used to actually make the dough) must always be preserved in a loosely closed glass jar and stored in the refrigerator; that if the liquid that rises to the top of the starter is pinkish instead of clear, the spoiled starter should be discarded and another begun; and that the starter should always be returned to room temperature before being used.

But the main secret to sourdough baking is that you never rush things. To begin a natural starter without the addition of commercial yeast, for example, requires four to five days of fermentation, depending on temperature (the ideal is about eighty-five degrees); for one with yeast (which can yield a slightly different flavor), the time is usually reduced to about three days, or till the starter is bubbly. To attain a pleasant sour flavor and a light, chewy texture in any sourdough product, the longer the dough stands in the sponge stage (once again, the sponge being the mixture of starter and part of the liquid and flour called for in a recipe), the better the results—and this can mean up to twenty-four hours. When a recipe directs that sourdough should be allowed to rise until doubled in bulk, and the dough is still unresponsive even after two or three hours, don't be impatient; most likely your room area is too chilly or drafty, a problem easily rectified by placing the dough in a closed oven with the light on.

I've heard even the most seasoned San Francisco bakers complain repeatedly about the inconsistent performance of sourdough: how one day the flavor is perfectly robust, the next day insipid; how during so-so weather the crust is ideal or weak; how an entire batch of bread must be thrown out since the interiors refused to honeycomb properly.

"Why don't I bake sourdough?" asks one of the city's most famous chefs, Bradley Ogden. "Because I just can't trust it; just too unpredictable."

Yes, dealing with any sourdough can be tricky business; and, yes, there may be some failures. But it is, after all, this mysterious quality that makes the dough so special and the experience so exciting, and I, for one, would never dream of abandoning the challenge and depriving myself of one of America's true culinary glories. I mean, what am I supposed to nourish myself on: Wonder Bread?

Natural Sourdough Starter

MAKES ABOUT 3 CUPS OF STARTER

2 cups unbleached white flour
2 cups warm water

In a pottery or glass bowl, combine half the flour and half the water; stir till smooth. Cover the bowl securely with cheesecloth and let stand in a warm area (about 85°F) 24 hours, or till bubbly.

Add the remaining flour and water, stir well, recover, and let stand 4 days. (Discard and begin again if liquid that rises to the top takes on a pinkish color.)

Stir well and store the starter in the refrigerator in a large glass jar. Return to room temperature before using. When not used for 2 weeks, discard half the starter, "feed" it 1 cup of flour and 1 cup of warm water, stir well, and store as before.

Foolproof Sourdough Starter

MAKES ABOUT 3 CUPS OF STARTER

2 cups warm water
1 envelope (¼ ounce) active dry yeast
2 cups unbleached white flour

In a pottery or glass bowl, combine ¼ cup of the water and the yeast, stir, and let proof 10 minutes. Add the remaining water and the flour, stir well till smooth, cover securely with cheesecloth, and let stand in a warm area (about 85°F) 3 to 4 days.

Stir well and store in the refrigerator in a large lidded glass jar. Return the starter to room temperature before using. When not used for 2 weeks, discard half the starter, "feed" it 1 cup of flour and 1 cup of warm water, stir well, and store as before.

My San Francisco Sourdough Bread

MAKES 2 LOAVES

2 cups sourdough starter (page 82 or above), at room temperature
2 cups warm water
6–6½ cups bread flour
1 envelope (¼ ounce) active dry yeast
1 tablespoon salt

To make the sponge, combine the starter, 1 cup of the warm water, and 2 cups of the bread flour in a large pottery or glass bowl. Stir till well blended and smooth, cover with plastic wrap, and let stand in a warm area at least 12 hours, or till the sponge is bubbly and tangy smelling.

When ready to make bread, return 1 cup of the sponge to the starter container. Combine the yeast and remaining water in a small bowl and let proof 10 minutes. Add to the sourdough mixture along with the salt and stir till smooth. Gradually add the remaining flour 1 cup at a time, stirring with a wooden spoon till the dough is firm but still slightly sticky.

Turn the dough out onto a lightly floured surface, knead about 10 minutes, place in a large greased bowl, cover with plastic wrap, and let rise in a warm area about 2 hours, or till double in bulk.

Punch down the dough, return to the floured surface, and knead about

1 minute. Cut the dough into 2 pieces and form each piece into a round or oval loaf, tucking the edges under the bottom and pinching them together. Place pinched sides down on a large, heavy, greased baking sheet, cover with a clean towel, and let rise about 30 minutes, or till puffy.

Preheat the oven to 450°F.

Cut slashes on the tops of the loaves with a razor blade. Spray the tops with water using a plant mister and bake 5 minutes. Spray again, bake 5 minutes longer, and spray once more. Reduce the heat to 350°F and bake 25 minutes, or till the bread is golden brown, crusty, and sounds hollow when thumped. Let cool completely on a wire rack.

PUMPKIN POWER

"IF IT WEREN'T FOR JACK-O'-LANTERNS, WE WOULD HARDLY EVER see a pumpkin," rages food writer John Thorne. "Pies are about the only thing we do with them, and many people make theirs out of a can."

Thorne is mostly right in his conviction, and all I can add is that our present indifference toward this most noble of squashes is nothing less than a national disgrace. Never mind that the term *pumpkin* derives from *pepon,* the ancient Greek word for a large melon, or that the Elizabethans relished their *pompions,* or that the gourd has been popular everywhere from France and Italy to the Balkans for centuries. What matters is that the pumpkin is—or should be—as much a part of our culinary heritage as pecans and maple syrup. The vegetable (technically a fruit) not only helped to nourish our Native American and Colonial ancestors (including a pie served at the Pilgrims' second Thanksgiving in 1623) but in more enlightened times played a major role in the kitchens of Thomas Jefferson, Fannie Farmer, and James Beard.

Today, pumpkin lovers constitute a very rare breed in America, but when you encounter a true enthusiast, the experience can be both enlightening and encouraging. There's one very wealthy lady I know down in Dallas, Texas, for example, who has such a passion for pumpkins that she has compiled and privately published *The Compleat Pumpkin Eater,* composed of over four hundred pumpkin recipes. She even named her family's air charter service Pumpkin Air. (The plane was once used to transport a bumper crop of pumpkins from her garden on the Texas coast back to Dallas.) Caroline Hunt Schoellkopf will tell you that, botanically speaking, the pumpkin is not a vegetable but a berry formed from a single pistil of the flower. She can explain the differences between such pumpkin varieties as Big Max, Triple Delight, and Naked Seeded. She can go on for hours about the advantages of using Early Sugar Sweets or Winter Luxurys for pies, the ways that seeds of Lady Godivas are particularly suited to toasting, and the reasons small gardens should be planted with Cinderellas and Spirits. And she has recipes for stuffed pumpkin blossoms, peanut butter pumpkin soup, pumpkin ambrosia, pumpkin lasagne, and pumpkin marmalade tarts.

While I might not be quite as obsessed with pumpkin as Mrs. Schoellkopf, it is a gourd that I, unlike most of my fellow countrymen, take very seriously. One of the real dramas of every fall season for me is the boastful appearance of shiny pumpkins ripening amid their coarse, heart-shaped leaves in the fields not far from my house on eastern Long Island. There they stretch as far as the eye can see, some small and round as honeydew melons, others lopsided and almost scary looking, and still others so mammoth that only a forklift could budge them from their silty beds. To me, they're all beautiful and evocative of youth, and home, and festive holiday meals. I love to thump them, feel their sunny warmth, caress their smooth skins, and reflect on the versatile role they've always played in world gastronomy.

Pumpkins are native to the Americas and one of the oldest members of the cucurbit family of squashes, cucumbers, and melons to grow in the Western Hemisphere. (They were totally unknown to the Old World before Columbus.) Fossilized rinds and seeds found in the Peruvian Andes date back thousands of years B.C., and we know from remains at pre-Columbian burial sites that ancient Indian tribes of South America used pumpkins for everything from food to cooking vessels to carved ceremonial masks. In the seventeenth century, Spanish conquistadors carried pumpkin seeds back to Europe, but a hundred years earlier, Jacques Cartier had reported from the St. Lawrence region on the *gros melons* cooked by the Indians.

History records that the first Pilgrims were given corn and pumpkin seeds by the Indians, and that by the second Thanksgiving in 1623, the pumpkin was being baked, boiled, fried in cakes, fermented into a crude ale, and incorporated in a pie with maple syrup. "We had pumpkins in the morning and pumpkins at noon," rhymed one colonist, "and if it were not for pumpkins, we'd be undone soon."

From Europe, pumpkin seeds found their way to the Middle East, Africa, and Asia, and today the vegetable enjoys universal popularity in numerous cuisines. In Israel, it is stuffed with various ground meats; in Sri Lanka, curried; in Greece, fried in oil; in France, pureed into soups. In the Caribbean, it is made into many varieties of bread; in China, turned into delicate dumplings; and in Russia, boiled slowly with rice to form a thick breakfast porridge.

But in the United States? I'm the first to admit that nothing is more delicious than our spicy, silky-smooth pumpkin pie or a steaming bowl of pumpkin soup flavored with smoky bacon or ham, but I'm afraid that so far not even our most innovative chefs have ventured widely into the exciting realm of pumpkin cookery. And the possibilities are limitless. Pumpkins can be cut into strips and fried like French fries; mixed with other vegetables and either baked or glazed to a golden finish; incorporated into hearty stews; used as a base for subtle sauces; turned into an elegant soufflé; and even made into an unusual ice cream. I often add a little pumpkin puree to the batter for waffles, muffins, blinis, and pancakes; it deepens the flavor and lightens the texture. And what could be more appealing than a small baked pumpkin stuffed with spicy chopped lamb and vegetables, or a compote of cooked pumpkin, apples, and onions, or thick pumpkin and apricot preserves? That pumpkin tends to be bland and needs the help of other flavors only heightens the culinary challenge.

Although pumpkins can measure up to a couple of feet in diameter and weigh well over a hundred pounds, it is the small, less fibrous varieties that are best for cooking. Look for pumpkins six to eight inches in diameter that are bright orange and firm, with unblemished rinds and without cracks or soft spots. When stored in a cool, dry area (never touching one another), small pumpkins will keep well for two to three weeks, while larger ones with tough rinds (used for jack-o'-lanterns) can be held for two months without deterioration. Pumpkin that is cut, wrapped in plastic, and refrigerated maintains its savor and texture for about five days. Cooked fresh pumpkin puree (which I prefer to the commercial canned product) freezes well for up to a year. And remember: don't throw away the pumpkin seeds, which are rich in iron, have significant amounts of B vitamins, and can be toasted, salted, and served with cocktails or used to enhance a multitude of dishes.

Today, hardly a month passes without one trendy exotic fruit or vegetable being touted as the putative salvation of gastronomy: ramps, purple potatoes, tropical rambutans and longans, heirloom radishes and tomatoes, starfruit, microgreens, and numerous organic "baby" items that I wish would become at least teenagers. I say that's all fine and good if it makes cooking more exciting for some, but I also insist that before we explore the exotic with often ephemeral results, we exploit in more imaginative ways such wistful bounty as the noble pumpkin that has been absurdly neglected in this country and deserves new attention in the kitchen.

Fresh Pumpkin Puree

MAKES ABOUT 5 CUPS

Preheat the oven to 350°F.

Cut the stem from a 6- to 7-pound pumpkin and discard. Cut the pumpkin into quarters and remove the seeds and membranes, reserving the seeds for toasting at another time.

Wrap each quarter of the pumpkin tightly in foil, place on a large, heavy baking sheet, and bake about 1 hour, or till the pulp is tender.

Scoop the pulp from the shells and cut into cubes. Puree in a food processor or force through the fine disk of a food mill. Store the puree in an airtight container in the refrigerator up to 5 days, or freeze up to 1 year.

Toasted Pumpkin Seeds

MAKES ABOUT 2 CUPS

2 cups pumpkin seeds (membranes removed)
4 tablespoons butter, melted
Salt to taste

Preheat the oven to 350°F.

Place the pumpkin seeds in a strainer and rinse under cold running water till they no longer feel slick. Dry the seeds well with paper towels and spread them out on a baking sheet. Drizzle the melted butter evenly over the seeds.

Toast 15 to 20 minutes, or till golden brown, shaking the baking sheet from time to time. Drain on paper towels. Season with salt and serve with cocktails or use in other dishes. Store in an airtight container at room temperature up to 2 weeks.

Gratin of Pumpkin and Wild Mushrooms

SERVES 6

1½ ounces dried cèpes,
   chanterelles, or shiitakes
One 4-pound pumpkin
5 tablespoons butter
1 small onion, minced

1 garlic clove, minced
3 tablespoons heavy cream
Pinch of ground mace or nutmeg
Salt and freshly ground pepper to
   taste

In a bowl, soak the mushrooms in 1¼ cups of warm water about 20 minutes to soften. Pick over for grit, rinse, chop coarsely, and pat dry with paper towels. Strain the mushroom liquor through a triple layer of cheese-cloth and set aside.

Remove the seeds and membranes from the pumpkin and peel off the outermost skin with a sharp knife or vegetable peeler. Cut pumpkin into ¼-inch-thick slices.

Preheat the oven to 425°F.

In a small skillet, melt 3 tablespoons of the butter over moderate heat. Add the onion, garlic, and chopped mushrooms. Cook, stirring occasionally, 3 minutes. Add the cream, mace, ½ cup of the reserved mushroom liquor, and salt and pepper. Simmer 3 minutes longer.

Arrange a layer of sliced pumpkin in a buttered 9-inch square baking dish, salt lightly, and spoon on some of the mushroom mixture. Continue layering the pumpkin and mushroom mixture, ending with a layer of pumpkin. Dot the top with the remaining 2 tablespoons butter and bake till the top is slightly browned, about 20 minutes. Serve hot.

Pumpkin and Bean Stew with Country Ham

SERVES 6 TO 8

2 cups dried Great Northern white beans

3 tablespoons butter

½ cup olive oil

2 large onions, coarsely chopped

2 garlic cloves, minced

1 small dried hot pepper, seeded and coarsely chopped

1 green bell pepper, seeded and coarsely chopped

2 large ripe tomatoes, peeled, seeded, and coarsely chopped

½ pound lean cured country ham, cut into large dice

2 cups chicken broth

½ teaspoon dried thyme, crumbled

½ teaspoon dried summer savory, crumbled

Salt and freshly ground pepper to taste

One 4-pound pumpkin

Place the beans in a large bowl, add enough cold water to cover by 2 inches, and let soak overnight. Pick over to remove any grit and drain in a colander.

In a large, heavy casserole, heat the butter and oil over moderate heat, add the onions, garlic, hot pepper, and bell pepper, and cook, stirring often, till the vegetables soften, about 5 minutes.

Add the beans to the casserole. Add the tomatoes, ham, broth, thyme, summer savory, and pepper; stir well. Bring the liquid to a boil, reduce the heat to low, cover, and simmer about 2 hours, or till the beans are tender.

Cut open the pumpkin and remove the seeds and membranes. Trim off the outermost skin with a sharp knife or vegetable peeler. Cut the flesh into 1-inch chunks and stir into the beans. Add more broth or water if the stew seems too thick, cover, and continue simmering about 30 minutes, or till the pumpkin is tender. Taste for salt and pepper and serve the stew piping hot in an earthenware vessel.

Turkey Scallops with Pumpkin Seed Sauce

SERVES 4 TO 6

½ large uncooked turkey breast, about 1 pound
Salt and freshly ground pepper
4 tablespoons butter
1 tablespoon vegetable oil
1 small onion, minced
1 garlic clove, minced
1 cup fresh pumpkin puree (see recipe, p. 88) or canned pumpkin puree
½ cup crushed toasted pumpkin seeds (see recipe, p.88)
1 cup heavy cream
Pinch of grated nutmeg
Snipped fresh chives, for garnish

Skin the turkey breast, slice on the diagonal against the grain into ¼-inch scallops, place on waxed paper, and season lightly with salt and pepper.

In a large skillet, heat 2 tablespoons of the butter and ½ tablespoon of the oil over moderately low heat. Add half the turkey scallops, sauté 3 minutes on each side, and transfer to a large serving platter; cover to keep warm. Repeat with the remaining butter, oil, and turkey, keeping sautéed scallops warm.

Add the onion and garlic to the skillet and cook, stirring, 2 minutes, until softened. Increase the heat slightly, add the pumpkin puree and seeds, and stir well. Stir in the cream and season with the nutmeg and salt and pepper to taste. Cook till the sauce thickens slightly, 2 to 3 minutes. Pour the sauce over the scallops and sprinkle chives over the top.

Pumpkin Ice Cream

MAKES ABOUT 1¾ QUARTS

1 cup sugar

2 teaspoons cornstarch

1 quart milk

3 large eggs, separated

1 teaspoon pure vanilla extract

2 teaspoons grated orange zest

2 teaspoons lemon zest

2 cups fresh pumpkin puree (see recipe, p. 88) or canned pumpkin puree

1 cup heavy cream, whipped

In the top of a double boiler, combine the sugar and cornstarch and stir in the milk till well blended. Add the egg yolks and beat with an electric mixer till frothy. Set the custard over simmering water and cook, stirring often, for 10 minutes. Beat with the mixer for 1 minute and remove from the heat. Let cool to room temperature.

Stir the vanilla and orange and lemon zest into the custard. Transfer to a stainless-steel bowl, fold in the pumpkin puree, and stir till well blended. Wash and dry the mixer blades.

In another bowl, beat the egg whites with the mixer till they start to stiffen. Fold gently but thoroughly into the pumpkin custard. Place in the freezer till it becomes mushy. Remove, beat with the mixer till fluffy, then beat in the whipped cream till well blended. Return to the freezer till the ice cream is firm.

CHOWDER CHOW DOWN

ONE OF THE MOST MEMORABLE WINTER MEALS I EVER prepared for guests at my house on eastern Long Island was an emergency lunch that highlighted a tureen of piping-hot shrimp and corn chowder. The forecast the night before had announced the possibility of light snow the following day, a delightful enough prospect had we not been confronted the next morning with about two feet of white fluff with more coming down. No way could we drive almost fifteen miles to what had promised to be a stylish lunch hosted by a close friend. No way could I make even minimal rounds of the markets to collect fresh meats, fresh produce, fresh anything. And no way was I going to substitute for lunch the regal saddle of lamb I planned to roast for dinner. I knew I had to pull off something clever if I wanted to avoid opening canned goods or serving omelettes and bacon.

Quickly I rummaged through my freezer. There were beautiful shrimp frozen in water; flat sealed bags of summer corn kernels that had been cut from the cobs within hours of picking; several containers of chicken stock I'm never without; and a couple of baguettes I'd baked some weeks before. In the fridge were some red-tipped lettuce and Belgian endives, still in fine condition from the previous weekend, and, in the cellar, plenty of chardonnay. By the time the snow was an inch higher, I had a shrimp and corn chowder simmering on the stove; and by the time all action outside had stopped, we were all perched around my big pine table before a roaring fire, having spent two wonderful hours lunching on hot chowder, salad, chewy bread, chilled wine, and wedges of homemade fruitcake I always have mellowing in tins. If I had planned the simple lunch a month ahead, it couldn't have come off better.

I've loved a good, honest chowder ever since my childhood in the South, and especially since this distinctive potage has evolved into a speciality that is as all-American as crab cakes and apple pie, I find it sad that more home cooks and restaurant chefs don't take the dish more seriously. Today, most people identify chowders as thick seafood soups associated with the Northeast, the most popular of which are the creamy New England and the tomatoey Manhattan clam chowders. But the story of chowder is much more complex.

Most historians trace the origins of chowder back to the French *chaudière*, a large pot into which early Breton fishermen would toss part of their catch to make wholesome fish stew. Supposedly the custom was carried by French sailors to Newfoundland and Nova Scotia during the seventeenth century, only to manifest itself the following century in the many forms of water-based fish chowder found throughout New England.

I choose to believe, instead, that the name of the dish is more sensibly linked with the old Devonshire word *jowter,* meaning a fish merchant, and that it, like so many English dishes that helped compose our early culinary repertory, was introduced by settlers not only in New England but throughout all the original colonies. Sources indicate, after all, that the words *chowter* and *chowder* were in full usage in both Devonshire and Cornwall as early as the sixteenth century; indeed, by the mid-eighteenth century, chowder had already been codified in one of England's most famous cookbooks, Hannah Glasse's *The Art of Cookery.*

Whatever the origins, it is clear that by 1800, when Amelia Simmons published the first American recipe for chowder in her *American Cookery,* the basic ingredients of fish, onions, salt pork, crackers (or "biscuits"), and water (with potatoes on the side) had been well established. By the 1830s, clam chowder (with milk or cream added to the water) had gained favor in Boston, and by the 1840s, it seems that potatoes were added, becoming a primary thickener in numerous Yankee chowders.

No doubt seafood chowder flourished as a staple primarily in New England, each region proffering its own interpretation, while cooks took the liberty (often to the outrage of others) of enhancing their creamy white soups with onions, tomatoes or tomato ketchup, herbs, spices, wine, and other embellishments.

Every encomium imaginable was paid to various chowders of the period, but surely none was recorded with greater gusto than Ishmael's description of a classic example in Melville's *Moby Dick:* "Oh, sweet friends! hearken to me. It was made of small juicy clams, scarcely bigger than hazelnuts, mixed with pounded ship biscuits, and salted pork cut up into little flakes; the whole enriched with butter, and plentifully seasoned with pepper and salt. . . . Chowder for breakfast, and chowder for dinner, and chowder for supper, till you began to look for fishbones coming through your clothes."

By 1875, the inhabitants of Nantucket were modifying the concept of chowder by preparing it with veal and chicken, while down in Pennsylvania, Virginia, and the Carolinas chowders were being made with catfish, shrimp, fowl, country ham, corn, root vegetables, and various types of beans. The expansion westward produced chowders containing green peas, okra, chili peppers, razor clams, abalone, and exotic species of Pacific fish, while back in New York, there appeared the chowder that almost inspired New Englanders to take up arms and that continues to this day to be the subject of heated argument and ridicule.

As opposed to the relatively austere, milk-based New England clam chowder, Manhattan clam chowder not only boasted tomatoes as its distinctive component but also included such unorthodox ingredients as bell peppers, carrots, Worcestershire sauce, cloves, allspice, and heaven knows what else. The first appearance of this audacious concoction is not recorded—nor did the original Yankee detractors care to acknowledge that ketchup was used to thicken the earliest Colonial chowders or that Rhode Island cooks often added tomatoes to their chowders—and there is still not one shred of evidence that the chowder was created in Manhattan. It might have been first served in the late nineteenth century at Coney Island stands or at the legendary Delmonico's restaurant; or it may have been a speciality at the Fulton Fish Market in the early 1900s; or it could have evolved as "Manhattan" clam chowder only in the 1930s, as the descendant of an earlier, tomatoey "New York" clam chowder referred to in certain cookbooks.

Personally, I have no quarrel with a well-made Manhattan chowder, but many do. "A terrible pink mixture," growls Eleanor Early in her *New England Sampler.* "Tomatoes and clams have no more affinity than ice cream and horseradish." And James Beard once referred to "that rather horrendous soup called Manhattan clam chowder . . . which resembles a vegetable soup that accidentally had some clams dumped into it." Suffice it that this particular chowder war will no doubt be waged for decades to come.

As anyone knows who ever tasted Jasper White's utterly sublime lobster and corn chowder at one of his restaurants in Boston, chowder has come a long way since the days when sailors and settlers simmered fish, salt pork, and crackers in a cauldron of water. Today, however, as interest in our culinary past intensifies and our gustatory sophistication assumes new dimensions, chowder is indeed another splendid dish just waiting to be rediscovered and possibly reinterpreted by adventurous cooks.

I'm the first to admit that a perfect New England clam chowder (like those served at Locke-Ober's in Boston and Gosman's Dock in Montauk, Long Island) represents a glorious peak in American gastronomy. But I'm also the first to insist that chowder is a fascinating regional concoction that lends itself to endless experimentation. As long as you remember that the texture should be roughly between that of a thin soup and a modest stew (thick bisque or bean soup is not chowder, nor is cioppino or gumbo), you should feel free to utilize all types of meats, fowl, vegetables, mushrooms, cheeses, legumes, and, of course, seafood. To get the initial "feel" of what a genuine chowder should taste and look like, try first preparing either the classic New England clam chowder or my shrimp and corn chowder.

In a country increasingly plagued by tortured concoctions—like daikon ravioli in lobster consommé with salsify, quince, and fermented beer broth, or stratified coconut milk and chicken soup—it's comforting to remember that there are still many solidly American chowders that not only defy shoddy innovations but link us to one of our proudest culinary traditions. All we have to do is reexplore the regions, renew our grasp on a few time-proven techniques, grab a big pot, and use a little sensible imagination.

Traditional New England Clam Chowder

1 large boiling potato, peeled and
cut into ½-inch dice
8 tablespoons (1 stick) butter
2 tablespoons salt pork, cut into
½-inch pieces
1 medium onion, chopped
⅓ cup all-purpose flour
4 cups bottled clam juice

1 pound fresh clam meat, coarsely
chopped
1 cup half-and-half
½ cup heavy cream
Salt and freshly ground pepper to
taste
Oyster crackers

In a saucepan, combine the potato with enough water to cover, bring to
a boil, reduce the heat to low, and simmer about 5 minutes, or till cooked
but still firm. Plunge into cold water, drain, and set aside.

In another large, heavy saucepan, melt the butter over medium-low
heat. Add the salt pork and cook 5 to 7 minutes, or till it turns light brown.
Add the onion and continue cooking about 5 minutes, or till the onion is
translucent.

Sprinkle the flour on top, stir, and cook 3 to 5 minutes, stirring and taking care not to let it color. Increase the heat to moderate, gradually stir in
the clam juice, and bring to a boil, stirring till the mixture is smooth.

Add the clams and cook 5 minutes. Add the half-and-half, cream, and
salt and pepper. Reduce the heat to low and simmer the chowder 15 minutes, stirring occasionally and adding a little more clam juice if a thinner
chowder is desired. Ladle the chowder into heated soup plates or bowls and
serve with oyster crackers.

Long Island Shrimp and Corn Chowder

SERVES 6

4 slices bacon
2 tablespoons butter
1 medium onion, minced
2 celery ribs, minced
2 tablespoons minced green bell
   pepper
6 cups chicken broth
2 pounds fresh medium shrimp
½ lemon, seeded

2 cups fresh or thawed frozen corn
   kernels
Salt, freshly ground pepper, and
   Tabasco to taste
1 cup heavy cream
2 small carrots, scraped and sliced
   paper thin
½ red bell pepper, finely sliced

In a skillet, fry the bacon till crisp; drain on paper towels. Pour off all but 2 tablespoons of grease from the skillet and crumble the bacon.

Heat the reserved bacon grease and the butter over moderately low heat. Add the onion, celery, and green pepper, and sauté about 5 minutes, or till the vegetables are soft. Set aside.

In a large saucepan, combine half the chicken broth and the shrimp. Squeeze the lemon juice into the pot and add the lemon half. Bring to a boil, remove from the heat, cover, and let stand 3 minutes. Drain the shrimp in a colander, set over another large, heavy saucepan to catch the stock.

When cool enough to handle, shell and devein the shrimp. Reserve 12 shrimp for garnish; put the remainder in a blender or food processor with the remaining cold chicken broth and puree until smooth. Stir the liquified shrimp into the hot stock.

Add the corn to the shrimp stock and cook over moderate heat 2 minutes, stirring. Add the reserved sautéed vegetables to the chowder, bring to a brisk boil, reduce the heat, and cook 2 minutes. Remove from the heat and season with salt, pepper, and Tabasco. Cover and let stand 30 minutes.

When ready to serve, bring the chowder almost to a boil. Stir in the cream, carrots, and red pepper. Taste for seasoning. Ladle the chowder into heated soup plates and garnish each portion with 2 whole reserved shrimp plus a sprinkling of the crumbled bacon.

Florida Red Snapper Chowder

SERVES 6

2 medium fillets of red snapper (or other firm-fleshed white fish), about 1 pound total
1 cup dry white wine
4 tablespoons butter
1 medium onion, chopped
1 celery rib (leaves included), chopped
1 carrot, scraped and chopped
2 tablespoons all-purpose flour
1 teaspoon dried oregano, crumbled
1 bay leaf
4 canned Italian plum tomatoes, drained and chopped
3 cups fish stock or bottled clam juice
Salt and freshly ground pepper to taste

Place the snapper fillets in a large nonreactive skillet, add the wine and enough water to just cover, and poach for about 15 minutes, or till the fish begins to flake. With a slotted spatula, transfer the fillets to a platter and flake in large pieces; reserve the cooking liquid.

In a large saucepan, melt the butter over moderate heat, add the onion, celery, and carrot, and cook, stirring, 5 minutes. Stir in the flour and add the oregano, bay leaf, tomatoes, stock, and 1 cup of the reserved cooking liquid. Bring to a boil, reduce the heat to low, cover, and simmer for 30 minutes, stirring from time to time.

Press the soup through a fine sieve or food mill into another large saucepan. Add the flaked snapper, season with salt and pepper, and heat thoroughly. Ladle the chowder into heated soup plates.

California Crab and Scallop Chowder

SERVES 6

4 tablespoons butter

2 scallions (white part only), finely chopped

3 cups milk

3 cups half-and-half

1 tablespoon Worcestershire sauce

2 teaspoons prepared white horseradish

¼ teaspoon finely crushed fennel seeds

Salt and freshly ground pepper to taste

1 pound fresh sea scallops, quartered

½ pound fresh claw crabmeat, picked over to remove any shell or cartilage

2 tablespoons dry sherry

2 tablespoons minced fresh chives

In a small skillet, melt 1 tablespoon of the butter over low heat, add the scallions, and cook 2 minutes.

In a large, heavy saucepan, combine the milk, half-and-half, Worcestershire, horseradish, fennel, salt, pepper, and remaining 3 tablespoons butter. Warm gradually over moderate heat, stirring, till very hot but not boiling.

Add the scallops, crabmeat, and sherry. Reduce the heat to low and simmer the chowder about 5 minutes, stirring. Ladle the chowder into heated soup plates and garnish each portion with a pinch of chives.

Michigan Wild Mushroom and Parsnip Chowder

SERVES 6

4 slices of bacon, finely diced
1 medium onion, finely chopped
2 cups coarsely chopped fresh
  oyster or chanterelle wild
  mushrooms
2 cups coarsely chopped peeled
  parsnips

1½ cups milk
1½ cups half-and-half
4 tablespoons butter
½ cup cracker crumbs
Salt and freshly ground pepper to
  taste

In a large, heavy saucepan, fry the bacon over moderate heat till almost crisp, add the onion and mushrooms, reduce the heat to low, and cook, stirring, 5 to 8 minutes, or till the vegetables are soft.

Add the parsnips and enough water to cover. Bring to a boil, reduce the heat to moderate, and cook about 15 minutes, or till the parsnips are soft.

Stir in the milk and half-and-half. Add the butter, cracker crumbs, and salt and pepper. Stir till the soup is well blended and the butter melted. Ladle the chowder into heated soup plates.

Southern Chicken and Ham Chowder

6 slices of bacon, cut into 1-inch
    pieces
One 3½-pound chicken, cut up
1 small meaty ham hock, tough
    skin removed
1 large onion, studded with 3
    cloves
3 celery ribs (leaves included),
    broken in half
½ teaspoon dried tarragon,
    crumbled

½ teaspoon dried thyme, crumbled
Salt and freshly ground pepper to
    taste
3 quarts cold water
2 medium red potatoes, peeled and
    diced
1 red bell pepper, cored, seeded,
    and finely diced

In a large, heavy skillet, fry the bacon till cooked but not crisp; drain on paper towels. Add the chicken pieces to the bacon grease in the skillet and brown on all sides over moderate heat.

Meanwhile, in a large, heavy pot, combine the ham hock, onion, celery, tarragon, thyme, salt and pepper, and water and bring to a boil. When the chicken has browned, add it to the pot along with the bacon. Return the mixture to a boil, reduce the heat to low, cover, and simmer 1 hour.

With a slotted spoon, remove the chicken to a plate and continue simmering the stock about 45 minutes longer. When cool enough to handle, skin the chicken breasts and wings, remove the meat from the bones, and cut into small dice; reserve the dark meat from the other pieces for hash and salads.

Transfer the ham hock to a cutting board. Strain the stock through a fine sieve into another large pot and discard all the solids. Shred the ham finely and add to the stock. Add the potatoes and bell pepper. If the soup is too thick, add more water. Bring to a simmer and cook about 15 minutes, or till the potatoes are just tender. Add the chicken, stir well, taste for salt and pepper, and ladle the chowder into heated soup plates.

WILD IN THE WOODS

JUST THE NAMES THEMSELVES ARE ENOUGH TO TITILLATE THE imagination: fairy ring, shaggy mane, king bolete, cèpe, chicken-of-the-woods, blewit, mo-er. In the markets, some can't help but catch the eye: orangish, trumpet-headed, ribbed chanterelles; golden, gnarly oysters; brown, beefy, smooth portobellos the size of coffee saucers; black, deeply crenellated morels; brilliant red, brittle russulas that crumble almost at the touch; bright, long enokis that resemble thick white hairpins; and many others of every size, strange shape, texture, and hue imaginable. Place them in the context of certain classic foreign dishes with which they've been associated for centuries and watch the mouths of serious gastronomes water: *morilles à la crème, cèpes à la bordelaise, risotto con funghi, porcini stufati, Rehschnitzel mit Steinpilzen,* crystal shrimp with cloud ears.

Throughout Europe and the Orient, wild mushrooms have not only always been prized as one of nature's great gustatory delicacies but also have been incorporated into enough dishes to constitute a veritable wild mushroom cuisine. The French sauté their meaty cèpes with shallots in oil, add fragile blewits (*mousserons*) to their omelettes and scrambled eggs, flavor sauces with their noble *morilles,* and highlight any number of soups, stews, gratins, and stuffings with trumpet-shaped chanterelles, *girolles, pleurotes,* and *oronges.*

In Italy, earthy porcini are chopped into pasta, risotto, and polenta, stuffed into squid and potatoes, braised with sausages and pork, smothered with herbs and tomatoes, and simply sautéed in butter before being adorned with shavings of fresh white truffle. Germans love nothing more than venison cutlets cloaked in a juniper and wild mushroom sauce or a hearty stew of tongue, sweetbreads, and woody *Waldegerlingen,* while in Hungary any number of fungi are turned into fritters, packed into strudel, and even used to make puddings.

Who could imagine authentic Japanese cuisine without its shiitake, enoki, and *nameko* mushrooms? And what would Chinese cookery be without its incredible variety of dishes featuring dried black mushrooms, cloud ears, thin straw mushrooms, and swollen, crunchy mo-ers?

Americans are not exactly ignorant of wild mushrooms in cooking, not when increasing quantities of fresh shiitakes, porcini, and chanterelles are now widely available in speciality food shops and some supermarkets, and when grilled meaty portobellos and various pastas and sauces with wild fungi are showing up on more and more restaurant menus. But the notion that exotic mushrooms have assumed a leading role in the normal American diet is little more than wishful thinking on the part of professional foodies who blindly equate the culinary practices of innovative restaurant chefs with those of the general public. That it's taking so long for wild mushrooms to catch on in the home kitchen is lamentable, but it's fully understandable.

Unlike millions of Europeans and Asians who, for generations, have been educated from childhood to recognize and collect edible species, Americans are taught simply to stay clear of all wild mushrooms as prevention against possible "toadstool" toxicity. And make no mistake: certain wild mushrooms are indeed very dangerous to eat, and amateurs with no mycological training should never venture out even to forage, much less consume, any—repeat *any*—species that has not been certified as safe by experts.

On the other hand, you really don't know what you're missing by not at least trying some of the many eligible fresh, dried, and canned varieties that are now available and that can literally transform the way you cook. To compare the rich flavor of most wild mushrooms with that of the cultivated, overbred, characterless white agarics—the common button mushrooms you find in every supermarket—is like comparing the savors of sturgeon and lumpfish caviar. "Pure mold, mere toys for chefs," quips one famous French food writer about the bland button mushrooms tossed in so many salads and stuck on shish kebab skewers.

The gastronomic popularity of mushrooms can be traced at least as far back as ancient Egypt, where they were considered plants of immortality and reserved for tables of the pharaohs. The Greek and Roman patricians thought mushrooms were endowed with magical healing properties, and throughout the Middle Ages it was believed that these strange fungi, created by fairies and sown by elves, had the ability to impart supernatural powers.

The Japanese succeeded in cultivating their famous shiitake well over two thousand years ago, but it was not till the seventeenth century (when mushrooms began to assume their indispensable role in most cuisines of Western Europe) that Olivier de Serres, agronomist to France's King Louis XIV, made the first attempt to cultivate the same agaric (or *champignon de Paris*) with which we're so familiar in this country. (So far, most wild mushrooms defy cultivation.)

Today, some two thousand different species of wild mushrooms are eaten throughout the world, the largest markets being France, Italy, Poland, Finland, the Ukraine, and East Asia. (On the first Saturday of every November at St. Bonnet-le-Froid in the upper Loire region of France, there is even an official Mushroom Fair, where restaurateurs, hoteliers, a few three-star chefs, and ordinary enthusiasts flock to purchase the finest *girolles, morilles,* cèpes, and dozens of other fresh and dried varieties.) Virtually every major species found in Europe and Asia grows somewhere in the United States, yet by contrast the overwhelming majority of the 500 million pounds of mushrooms marketed in this country are still agarics.

My own memories of eating wild mushrooms abroad are rich: a luscious tomato and *girolle* tart created by Fredy Giradet at his legendary restaurant in Switzerland; André Daguin's smooth puree of cèpes with roast goose and Michel Guérard's frogs' legs and *mousserons* in puff pastry in southwest France; an unforgettable gratin of duck and chanterelles at Die Ente vom Lehel in Wiesbaden, Germany; a large bowl of polenta enriched with porcini at the Cipriani in Venice; and Gordon Ramsey's inimitable pigs' trotters with mixed chanterelles and morels at Aubergine in London.

Equally impressive, however, are certain dishes at trend-setting restaurants around the United States. At Chez Panisse in Berkeley, California, Alice Waters incorporates various wild mushrooms in her cornbread stuffing for roast duckling, her potato gratin, and a savory ragout, while up at the French Laundry in Napa Valley, Thomas Keller's monkfish with braised oxtails, salsify, and cèpes is nothing less than phenomenal. A few years ago, I tasted my first gigantic, garlicky grilled portobello at Tony's in Houston, and today I'd return just to order the shiitake and celeriac salad with anchovy dressing on a bed of radicchio. In New York, I've marveled over crunchy panini sandwiches stuffed with hen-of-the-woods mushrooms and tâleggio cheese at Craftbar; Michael Romano's exquisite roast leg of veal with goat cheese and shiitake sauce at Union Square Café; and, most recently, Jonathan Waxman's Madeira-glazed sweetbreads with aromatic, chewy morels at Washington Park. Even Emeril Lagasse in New Orleans has transformed part of Creole cookery by incorporating oyster mushrooms and chanterelles in a delectable crab cheesecake with scallion sauce. So there is some important action with wild mushrooms in the United States, though it's only the tip of the iceberg.

What I have come to realize while scouting wild mushrooms in America is, much as I love eating and cooking with fresh varieties when they're in pristine condition, both the dried and canned products can be as exciting or even more so if dealt with properly. Stocked by the ounce in better food shops throughout the country, or by the half-kilo and kilo at speciality food importers, dried mushrooms can actually taste better than fresh for the simple reason that dehydration intensifies flavors. It's true that dried mushrooms can be very expensive (morels easily run as high as one hundred dollars a pound), but remember that since two ounces of dried mushrooms equal a pound of fresh, a little can go a long way.

Remember also that a few wild mushrooms added to white agarics can virtually transform an otherwise prosaic dish into something really special, and that so much as a pinch of powdered dried mushrooms (pulverized in the blender or food processor) contributes a delightful pungency to sauces, soups, and stews. Stored in airtight containers, dried mushrooms keep indefinitely. (I still have about a half-pound of dried cèpes I acquired a year ago and keep very well, thank you, in a large, tightly sealed dog biscuit jar.) The only mushroom I must have fresh or canned is the chanterelle, which tends to become leathery when dried and reconstituted.

Other than not having to be cleaned, canned mushrooms are used as if they were fresh, while dried must be reconstituted in warm water about twenty or thirty minutes, picked over for grit, and rinsed thoroughly in fresh running water. I consider it nothing less than criminal to throw out the mushroom liquid, which, once strained through a triple thickness of cheesecloth or coffee filter paper, can be used to enhance any number of sauces or braised meat, poultry, and vegetable dishes. Mushrooms have many minerals, vitamins, and plenty of proteins, but since their carbohydrate content is primarily in the form of indigestible cellulose, all but the cultivated varieties should be cooked at least fifteen minutes before eating.

With gastronomy in the United States still in the throes of (confused) revolution and evolution, it seems only natural that wild mushrooms are destined to play an increasingly prominent role both in our cutting-edge restaurants and our home kitchens. Already, mycological societies from the Pacific Northwest to New Jersey are shipping the yields of their foraging to food shops, restaurants, and supermarkets and teaching potential enthusiasts the necessary skills required to gather edible species. Professional chefs are lining up reliable private sources to provide them with steady deliveries of fresh chanterelles, fairy rings, boletes, black trumpets, morels, and *suillus*. Biologists in California are reporting even greater success at raising shiitakes, enokis, *namekos*, phoenix tail clusters, and other exotic Oriental varieties under controlled conditions. And even the least pretentious food emporiums stock all sorts of interesting canned and dried mushrooms.

Folded into omelettes, scrambled eggs, and soufflés; added to sauces, stews, soups, and savory pies; stuffed into roasts and vegetables; or simply sautéed with herbs in butter or oil, woodland mushrooms are indeed one of the most versatile and appealing ingredients in the vast realm of comestibles.

Of course, this is not news to chef Jack Czarnecki, who, after operating the legendary wild mushroom restaurant Joe's in Reading, Pennsylvania, for many years, took over the Joel Palmer House in Dayton, Oregon, not long ago and continues to confront America's fears and innocence by incorporating up to thirty different types of mushrooms in practically every dish served. Trained to forage in Pennsylvania by his father, Joe, before formally studying bacteriology and restaurant management, Jack (along with his family) now not only gathers his own mushrooms from the Oregon countryside but also scientifically identities, classifies, cleans, and dries them in his private laboratory.

At his restaurant, there is a thick wild mushroom soup with a mushroom design traced on top in cream; crab cakes with portobellos and mustard vinaigrette; quenelles of halibut with wild mushroom and pinot gris sauce; snails with black chanterelles, garlic, and parsley; wild Oregon salmon with curried couscous and porcini duxelles; roast duck with russula mushrooms; and all sorts of handsome mushrooms used as stuffing and garnish for meat, fowl, and game. Needless to say, Jack Czarnecki takes his wild mushrooms very seriously, as do his customers.

"People seem to be more and more fascinated by my mushroom dishes," he says confidently, "and I think the reason is simple. Today, Americans are receptive to almost any innovative idea that pertains to food, and wild mushrooms offer a challenging new flavor and ever-changing new taste experience as more and more varieties become available. In the past, folks in this country might have refused to even give them a try; but now they're discovering that, when handled properly, these fungi can be still another facet of the wonderful magic of eating well."

Bourbon Burgers Stuffed with Dried Cèpes

SERVES 4

1 ounce dried cèpes
8 tablespoons (1 stick) butter
2 slices of white bread, crusts
   removed
3 tablespoons milk
3 medium onions, finely chopped
1 garlic clove, minced
1½ pounds ground beef sirloin or
   round

2 large eggs
Salt and freshly ground pepper to
   taste
½ cup bread crumbs
2 medium ripe tomatoes, peeled,
   seeded, and chopped
3 tablespoons bourbon
Pinch of dried thyme
Tabasco

In a small bowl, soak the dried mushrooms in 1 cup of warm water for 30 minutes. Pick them over for grit, rinse well, pat dry, and chop coarsely. Strain the mushroom liquor through a triple layer of cheesecloth into a bowl and set aside.

In a heavy skillet, melt 2 tablespoons of the butter over moderate heat, add the mushrooms, sauté about 10 minutes, and transfer to a plate. In a large bowl, combine the bread and milk and let stand to soften. Melt another tablespoon of the butter in the same skillet, add one-third of the onions and all the garlic, and cook, stirring, 3 minutes, then mix into the softened bread.

Add the beef, 1 egg (beaten), and salt and pepper, and mix thoroughly. Divide the meat into 4 balls, make a hole in the center of each, fill with equal amounts of the mushrooms, fold meat down carefully over the stuffing, and press the meat down into oval burgers about 1½ inches thick. In a small bowl, beat the second egg with 1 teaspoon of water, brush the glaze over each burger, and coat the burgers with the bread crumbs.

Melt another 2 tablespoons of butter in the skillet, add the remaining onions, the tomatoes, bourbon, thyme, 2 dashes of Tabasco, and 3 tablespoons of the reserved mushroom liquor. Cook over moderate heat, stirring often, till only a little liquid remains. Keep the sauce hot.

In another large, heavy skillet, melt the remaining butter over moderate heat, add the burgers, and sauté on both sides till the crusts are golden brown and the interiors are medium-rare, about 5 minutes on the first side and 3 minutes on the second. Transfer the burgers to a hot serving platter and top with the sauce.

Jeremiah Tower's Polenta with Wild Mushroom Ragout

THE RAGOUT
2 tablespoons mixed fresh herbs,
    finely chopped
1 cup sour cream
4 tablespoons butter
2 pounds combined fresh cèpe,
    shiitake, and chanterelle
    mushrooms, sliced
1 garlic clove, finely chopped

Salt and freshly ground pepper to
    taste
½ cup chicken broth
2 tablespoons chopped fresh
    parsley leaves

THE POLENTA
2 to 3 cups water
1 cup coarse cornmeal
4 tablespoons butter

To begin the ragout, combine the herbs and sour cream in a bowl and let stand overnight or up to several days in the refrigerator.

To make the polenta, bring 2 cups of the water to a rolling boil in a heavy saucepan. Very gradually add the cornmeal in a steady stream, whisking vigorously till all the cornmeal is incorporated and there are no lumps. Now using a wooden spoon, stir constantly, scraping around the bottom corners of the pan where the polenta will try to stick and burn. Reduce the heat to moderately low, and stir slowly and constantly for 45 minutes, till the mixture is very smooth and nicely thickened. Stir in the butter till well incorporated, and keep the polenta hot in a double boiler till ready to use.

To make the ragout, melt 2 tablespoons of the butter in a large, heavy skillet. Add the mushrooms and garlic and season with salt and pepper. Cook over moderate heat, stirring often, 5 minutes. Add the broth and continue to cook till the mushrooms are soft and tender, 5 to 10 minutes. Add the remaining 2 tablespoons butter and stir till incorporated. Taste for salt and pepper.

To serve, spoon equal amounts of the herb cream in the center of 4 plates, spoon equal amounts of the polenta over the cream, then spoon equal amounts of the ragout over the polenta. Sprinkle the tops with parsley and serve immediately.

Poached Halibut with Shrimp and Oyster Mushrooms

6 tablespoons olive oil

1½ pounds small fresh shrimp in the shell, rinsed

1 small onion, chopped

1 small carrot, scraped and finely diced

1 celery rib, finely diced

2 garlic cloves, minced

3 ounces brandy

3 ounces dry white wine

4 medium ripe tomatoes, peeled, seeded, and finely diced

3 ounces tomato puree

1 quart chicken broth

6 whole black peppercorns

Pinch of dried thyme

4 fresh halibut fillets, 6 ounces each (or other white fish)

Salt and freshly ground pepper to taste

½ pound fresh oyster mushrooms, sliced

2 ounces fresh spinach or watercress, chopped (about ¼ cup)

In a large, heavy skillet, heat the oil till very hot, add the shrimp, reduce the heat to moderate, and sauté till the shells turn pink, 2 to 3 minutes. Add the onion, carrot, celery, and garlic. Cook, stirring, 3 minutes, pour off the oil, and transfer to a plate.

Add the brandy and wine to the skillet. Add three-fourths of the tomatoes and all the tomato puree and cook down almost to a paste. Add the broth, peppercorns, and thyme, bring to a boil, reduce heat to a simmer, and cook till reduced by one-third, skimming as foam rises. Strain the broth through cheesecloth into a bowl. Shell and devein the shrimp and keep warm.

Season the fish fillets with salt and pepper, and arrange in a large, deep skillet. Ladle the shrimp broth over the fillets, bring to a boil, reduce heat to a simmer, and poach the fish 3 minutes. Transfer to a large serving platter, top with the shelled shrimp, and cover with foil to keep warm.

Strain the broth into another small skillet, add the mushrooms, and cook over moderate heat 10 minutes. Add the spinach and remaining tomatoes, simmer about 2 minutes longer, and ladle over the fish and shrimp. Serve immediately.

Sautéed Chicken and Chanterelles

One 3½-pound chicken, cut up
5 tablespoons butter
½ pound fresh chanterelle
  mushrooms, sliced
Salt and freshly ground pepper to
  taste
¼ cup all-purpose flour

1 tablespoon vegetable oil
15 very small white onions, peeled
Pinch of dried tarragon
1 bay leaf
½ cup dry red wine
½ cup heavy cream

Rinse the chicken and pat dry.

In a medium skillet, melt 2 tablespoons of the butter over moderate heat. Add the chanterelles, sauté 3 minutes, stirring, and set aside.

Season the chicken pieces with salt and pepper and dredge lightly in the flour. In a large, heavy skillet, heat the remaining butter and the oil over moderate heat and brown the chicken on all sides, beginning with the dark pieces. Transfer to a large plate.

Add the onions to the skillet and sauté, rolling, until browned lightly all over, about 8 minutes. Return chicken to the skillet and add the mushrooms, tarragon, bay leaf, and white wine. Cover tightly, reduce the heat to low, and cook till the chicken is tender, 35 to 45 minutes.

With a slotted spoon, transfer contents of the skillet to a hot platter. Skim the fat from the cooking liquid, add the cream, and boil, stirring, about 3 minutes, or till the sauce thickens slightly. Taste for seasoning and pour the sauce over the chicken and mushrooms.

CHICKEN SALAD CHIC

IN MY YOUNGER, OVERINDULGENT DAYS, NOTHING GAVE ME MORE pleasure than the simple, solitary copious chicken salad lunch I treated myself to every Wednesday in the splendid confines of the Oak Bar at the Plaza Hotel in New York. In that era, the Oak Bar at noon was virtually an all-male club, a discreet and sophisticated bastion where many of the financial, political, and social shakers of New York parlayed over platters of fat Blue Point oysters and crusty corned-beef hash. Nobody had ever heard of seared tuna steaks and bastardized cocktails like the cosmopolitan, a pallid incarnation of a martini.

My weekly ritual never varied. Arriving at exactly twelve-thirty (with a reservation and wearing the required jacket and tie), I would first perch at the massive bar, exchange gossip with Teddy the bartender as he deftly mixed the first of two ice-cold, very dry gin martinis, and gaze pensively at Everett Shinn's nostalgic mural of Manhattan life, allowing the gin and dignified surroundings to work their magic on my soul.

At a quarter past one, Martin, the starched-collared maître d'hôtel, would show me to a table overlooking Central Park, aware, as always, that I would be ordering the chicken salad plus a stein of tepid English ale on draft. I loved the crisp linen napkin, the heavy silver, the crystal water goblet, the fresh sesame bread sticks and sweet butter, and the quiet, civilised crowd around me. But what this innocent occasion was really all about was that sumptuous salad of large, poached chicken chunks, diced avocado, chopped boiled eggs with slightly soft yolks, crumbled bacon, a mixture of shredded chicory, romaine, and red cabbage, and a velvety Roquefort dressing.

Today, I know that, in principle, it was actually the Plaza's version of the Cobb salad, that blissful concoction created by Robert Cobb back in 1936 at his legendary Brown Derby restaurant in Hollywood. But then, I couldn't have cared less about the salad's origins as I consumed the first sensuous forkful, admired the textural contrasts of chicken, avocado and egg, crunchy bacon and chicory, and savored the after-bite of the noble Roquefort. Never did that salad contain anything but the finest ingredients, never was it blended till the moment it was to be served, and never was a single component allowed to overwhelm the perfect balance of flavors. For others the occasion might have had no real meaning, but for me, this relaxed, eminently satisfying lunch was a ceremony that always managed to make me feel a bit more confident about the confused world rushing around outside.

Of course, there have been radical changes in the Oak Bar over the past decades: a more relaxed dress code, stupid mobile phones, and even a steady contingent of shady ladies on the prowl. But the fact that today you can still order approximately the same delectable chicken salad I cherished so many years ago seems to testify to the durability and popularity of this all-American dish. And who doesn't love a good chicken salad, our top professional chefs included.

"There's really nothing like it when I don't feel up to major cooking and yet want to serve something at home I'm sure all my friends will enjoy," says Lidia Shire, new owner of Boston's venerable Locke-Ober's restaurant.

"One of our most beloved dishes at lunch is my chicken, green bean, pancetta, and arugula salad," confides chef Michael Romano at Union Square Café in New York.

At Commander's Palace in New Orleans, the onion-crusted fried chicken salad with blue cheese dressing is nothing less than beguiling, and I'd return to Fearrington House in Chapel Hill, North Carolina, if for no other reason than to dive into the glorious chicken, orange, and grape salad topped with toasted almonds. David Page's spicy roasted chicken, apple, and blue cheese salad at Home in Manhattan gives subtle new dimension to the old favorite. And leave it to former owner of Stars in San Francisco and current television personality Jeremiah Tower, not only to come up with a highly innovative warm chicken, sweetbread, black bean, and pepper coleslaw salad but to wax nostalgic about the salad he got hooked on during the sixties.

"When traveling about the country as a youngster, I'd literally go out of my way to have one of those thick, chunky chicken salads with celery and fresh mayonnaise you always found in the old diners. Chicken salad is the only truly great dish to come out of that era of ladies' country-club lunches and afternoon teas, and today I'd be content with a crispy Chinese chicken salad and Champagne for lunch every day of the year. I never tire of experimenting with chicken salad, since its possibilities are endless."

While it's still hard to beat a classic American chicken salad composed of tender chunks of poached breast, diced celery, perhaps a few chopped scallions or olives, salt and pepper, and top-quality mayonnaise, I couldn't agree more with Tower that no dish lends itself better to fascinating new interpretations and approaches: different cooking and marinating techniques for the chicken; ingredient combinations that provide unusual flavors and textures while still enhancing the taste of the chicken; and numerous interesting dressings. Chicken that is grilled, baked, roasted, fried, or smoked, for instance, can make for salads just as delicious as those in which the chicken is poached, so long as it's not overcooked. And although white breast is still the preferred chicken part, flavorful dark meat, liver, and giblets can also be used with tasty results. Do note that a whole slab of chicken perched on greens is *not* chicken salad.

The most readily available foundation of chicken salad remains a combination of the standard lettuces found in supermarkets—romaine, Boston, bibb, curly endive, red-tipped leaf—but if you really want to add new flair to the dish the way our more adventurous chefs are doing, try substituting colorful radicchio, *mâche,* savoy cabbage, shredded fresh sorrel leaves, nasturtium flowers, squash blossoms, or boiled rice noodles. When added to the salad in discreet amounts, boiled fava beans or chickpeas, sugar snap peas, blistered chile peppers, capers, and virtually any types of nut make enticing components. And some of my best salads owe much of their distinction to minced bell pepper, wild mushrooms, diced lemon or lime zest, shredded ginger, fresh herbs, and such compatible fruits as melons, mangoes, fresh pineapple, blood oranges, guavas, and silky-sweet cherimoya. I know one chef who swears by edible rose petals in his chicken salad, but I haven't tried those yet.

Whatever you decide to include, be mindful that chicken salad is only as good as the amount and quality of the dressing used to bind the ingredients or add the finishing touch. A dry salad is virtually inedible; one that is overdressed can be appalling. For years, when preparing to toss a salad with mayonnaise, I would never have dreamed of binding it with anything but the homemade variety; now I don't hesitate to use Hellmann's when I don't feel like making fresh.

For a lighter, smoother mayonnaise dressing, try combining the mayo with a little yogurt, sour cream, or crème fraîche. For a subtly flavored mayonnaise, add timid amounts of curry powder, minced garlic or chile peppers, finely crumbled hard cheeses, or any variety of chopped fresh herbs. Chicken salad that includes smoked or marinated chicken, assertive spices, or other ingredients with distinct flavors is often best when dressed with a simple vinaigrette. For a basically bland salad, you might consider various nut oils, as well as flavored or well-aged vinegars.

Finally, do beware of overcooking a chicken intended for salad. In general, the chicken is done when the interior juices run clear, but since so many chicken salads are made with poached chicken, let's consider that procedure. First, I always use unboned chicken breasts since the bones add flavor to the meat during the cooking process and are easily removed afterward. Second, the tenderest, juiciest chicken is accomplished by gentle poaching—not boiling—at the barest simmer, a process that allows the meat to cook through while maintaining most of its natural moisture. Third, time your preparations so the chicken can cool in its cooking liquid, an extra step guaranteeing meat that is fully moist and almost silky in texture.

Although perfect timing naturally depends on the size of the breasts, the best rule of thumb is that the chicken is cooked completely after about twenty minutes of poaching or when slightly springy to the touch. For chicken that will be left to cool in its broth, about fifteen minutes of actual poaching is usually adequate. As for those restaurant chefs today who somehow find virtue in serving rare, undercooked chicken, I think they should have their heads examined. I resolutely refuse to eat any salad (or other preparation) in which the chicken is not adequately cooked. Undercooked chicken is tough, unsafe, and repulsive.

Contrary to public opinion, you can no more produce great chicken salad by simply throwing together whatever leftovers and dressing you might find in the refrigerator than you can make memorable potato salad with old potatoes and other components far past their prime. And why even try, given that the most elaborate fresh chicken salads normally require a minimum of time and effort. It's still a dish that's basically inexpensive to produce and fun to make, and while I'm sure I'll always love and respect an old-fashioned salad like the one I relished so many years ago at the Plaza, with the exotic array of new secondary ingredients now flooding the markets, there's really no reason why this classic shouldn't be allowed to evolve in global ways that can only enhance its enjoyment.

Cobb Salad: The King

SERVES 6 TO 8

2 whole chicken breasts, split
2 scallions (white and 2 inches of green)
1 celery rib, cut in half
1 bay leaf
6 peppercorns
4 cups chicken broth
Salt and freshly ground pepper to taste
1 bunch watercress, tough stems removed, rinsed, dried, and chilled
½ small head chicory, rinsed, dried, and chilled
½ medium head romaine, rinsed, dried, and chilled

4 large hard-boiled eggs, coarsely chopped
1 ripe avocado, peeled, pitted, diced, and sprinkled with lemon juice
2 medium ripe tomatoes, peeled, seeded, and coarsely chopped
6 strips crisply fried bacon, crumbled
2 ounces Roquefort or blue cheese, crumbled
3 tablespoons chopped fresh chives
½ cup wine vinegar
1 teaspoon dry mustard
1 teaspoon Worcestershire sauce
1 cup olive oil

Arrange the chicken breasts in a large, deep skillet or medium baking pan. Add the scallions, celery, bay leaf, peppercorns, broth, salt and pepper, and just enough water to cover, if necessary. Bring to a boil, reduce the heat to low, and poach the chicken at the barest simmer for 15 minutes. Remove from the heat and let cool in the broth.

With a slotted spoon, transfer the chicken to a work surface. Discard the skin and bones, cut the meat into ½-inch cubes, and place in a large mixing bowl. Pull or shred the greens into bite-size pieces and add to the chicken. Add the eggs, avocado, tomatoes, bacon, cheese, and chives and toss till well blended.

In a small bowl, whisk together the vinegar, mustard, Worcestershire, and salt and pepper to taste. Whisk in the oil till thoroughly incorporated, pour dressing over the salad, and toss till the ingredients are well coated.

To serve, mound the salad across a serving platter or divide equally among individual serving plates.

Asian Fried Chicken Salad

One 3-pound chicken, cut up
1 medium onion, peeled and
  studded with 4 cloves
1 celery rib (leaves included), cut
  in half
½ cup cornstarch
½ cup peanut oil, plus more for
  frying
2 teaspoons dry Chinese mustard
2 teaspoons Chinese 5-spice
  powder

1 small fresh hot red pepper,
  seeded and minced
1 teaspoon salt
½ teaspoon Asian sesame oil
1 head iceberg lettuce, shredded
2 tablespoons chopped cilantro
3 scallions (white part only),
  shredded
1 cup chopped cashew nuts
¼ cup toasted sesame seeds
Boiled rice noodles, at room
  temperature

Place the chicken, onion, and celery in a kettle with enough water to cover. Bring to a boil, reduce the heat to medium-low, cover, and simmer for 15 minutes (the chicken will finish cooking when it is fried). Using a slotted spoon, transfer the chicken to a work surface and, when cool enough to handle, dust the pieces with the cornstarch, rubbing it in by hand.

Heat 1½ inches of peanut oil in a large, heavy skillet. Add the chicken in two batches, fry 10 minutes over moderate heat, turning once, and drain on paper towels. Place the chicken on a cutting board, remove and discard the skin and bones, and shred the meat.

In a large bowl, combine the ½ cup peanut oil, mustard, 5-spice powder, hot pepper, and salt and whisk briskly. Add the shredded chicken and toss. Add the sesame oil, lettuce, cilantro, scallions, nuts, and sesame seeds and toss till the ingredients are well coated. Line a platter with rice noodles and mound the chicken salad in the center.

Tropical Chicken Salad in Radicchio

3 whole chicken breasts, split
1 medium onion, cut in half
1 celery rib, cut in half
3 whole cloves
2 ripe mangoes, peeled and cut into ½-inch cubes
2 cups fresh pineapple cubes (½-inch)
1 cup seedless green grapes
3 scallions (white part only), minced
½ cup coarsely chopped toasted almonds
1 tablespoon minced peeled fresh ginger
1 tablespoon minced fresh cilantro
1 tablespoon minced fresh mint leaves
1 tablespoon finely diced lime zest
Salt and freshly ground pepper to taste
1 cup mayonnaise
½ cup sour cream
1 tablespoon fresh lime juice
6 to 8 large radicchio leaves

Arrange the chicken breasts in a large, deep skillet or medium baking pan and add the onion, celery, cloves, and just enough salted water to cover. Bring to a boil, reduce the heat to low, and poach the chicken at the barest simmer for 15 minutes; let cool in its broth.

With a slotted spoon, transfer the chicken to a work surface. Remove and discard the skin and bones and cut the meat into ½-inch cubes; place in a large bowl. Add the mangoes, pineapple, grapes, scallions, almonds, ginger, cilantro, mint, lime zest, and salt and pepper. Toss lightly. Cover and refrigerate 1 hour.

In a small bowl, combine the mayonnaise, sour cream, and lime juice; stir well. Pour the dressing over the salad and toss gently till well coated. Arrange the radicchio leaves on individual serving plates or on a serving platter and mound the chicken salad in the center of each leaf.

Curried Chicken Salad with Raisins and Peanuts

1 medium onion, halved
1 celery rib, cut in half
1 carrot, scraped and quartered
3 sprigs parsley
1 bay leaf
6 peppercorns
4 cups chicken broth
3 whole chicken breasts, split
1 medium cucumber, peeled, seeded, and diced

1 cup roasted peanuts
½ cup seedless golden raisins
½ cup mayonnaise
½ cup plain yogurt
2 tablespoons medium-hot curry powder
Salt and freshly ground pepper to taste
Fresh sorrel leaves or watercress

In a large, deep skillet or medium baking pan, combine the onion, celery, carrot, parsley, bay leaf, peppercorns, stock, and enough water to cover. Bring to a boil, reduce the heat to low, and simmer the court bouillon 15 minutes. Add the chicken breasts and poach at the barest simmer for 20 minutes; let the chicken cool in the bouillon.

With a slotted spoon, transfer the chicken to a work surface. Remove and discard the skin and bones and cut the meat into ¾-inch chunks or cubes. Place the chicken in a large bowl; add the cucumber, peanuts, and raisins, and toss.

In a small bowl, combine the mayonnaise, yogurt, curry powder, and salt and pepper; stir well. Pour the dressing over the chicken and mix gently till well coated. Line the edges of a platter with sorrel leaves or watercress and mound the chicken salad in the middle.

Grilled Marinated Chicken Salad with Broccoli and Pine Nuts

½ cup dry sherry
½ cup soy sauce
1 teaspoon dry mustard
1 garlic clove, minced
1 tablespoon finely chopped fresh
  ginger
Salt and freshly ground pepper to
  taste
3 whole chicken breasts, split
½ head fresh broccoli, florets
removed and blanched (about
  2 cups)
1 cup toasted pine nuts
2 tablespoons chopped fresh
  tarragon, or ½ teaspoon dried
2 teaspoons Dijon mustard
1 tablespoon balsamic vinegar
½ cup mayonnaise
½ cup sour cream
Belgian endive leaves

In a small bowl, whisk together the sherry, soy sauce, dry mustard, garlic, ginger, and salt and pepper till the marinade is well blended. Arrange the chicken breasts in a large, shallow baking dish, pour the marinade over the top, cover with plastic wrap, and marinate in the refrigerator 2 to 3 hours.

Grill the chicken 4 inches over hot charcoal for 20 to 25 minutes, turning once. When cool enough to handle, skin and bone the chicken, cut the meat into ½-inch cubes, and place in a large mixing bowl. Add the broccoli, pine nuts, and tarragon; toss.

In a small bowl, whisk together the mustard and balsamic vinegar till well blended. Add the mayonnaise, sour cream, and salt and pepper to taste, and blend well again. Pour the dressing over the chicken and broccoli and toss gently till well coated. Line a platter with endive leaves and mound the chicken salad in the center.

COMFORT ME WITH MEAT LOAF

MEAT LOAF MANIA

MOST SERIOUS FOODOPHILES IN THE UNITED STATES ARE closet eaters when they're not indulging in all the fancy stuff. I've watched Julia Child demolish an entire bag of Pepperidge Farm Goldfish in less than an hour. Nobody can knock off a fat cheeseburger faster (and with greater relish) than Jacques Pépin. Paula Wolfert is addicted to Fritos throughout the day, even while testing her latest complex Moroccan or Sardinian recipe. Jeffrey Steingarten, I'm convinced, literally couldn't exist without a bottle of ketchup within immediate reach. And Jeremiah Tower's inordinate love of fresh beluga caviar is surpassed only by his spiritual need of greasy fish and chips and Häagen-Dazs ice cream. As for yours truly, I won't touch commercial cookies, cakes, or jams, but I'll kill for a heaping tablespoon of peanut butter (crunchy) or wedge of thick-crusted, gooey pepperoni pizza.

No doubt these disparate, furtive gratifications are as sensual to present-day *becs-fins* as spaghetti and meatballs was to Craig Claiborne, but if I had to name a single gustatory passion that unites all foodists but stubbornly remains on the back shelf of respectability, it would have to be all-American meat loaf. When Mimi Sheraton, for instance, gave up reviewing restaurants for the *New York Times,* the first thing she announced ecstatically was how she was now free to slip over to a favorite hideaway in the bowels of Brooklyn for all the meat loaf with gravy she wanted. Wander into the unfashionable 72 Market Street Oyster Bar & Grill in Los Angeles any late night of the week, and you're likely to see at least a couple of the city's most cutting-edge chefs doing full justice to the hefty meat loaf and mash. One surveyor for the Zagat Guide to Chicago restaurants raves about the "classic" meat loaf at Ed Debevic's Short Orders Deluxe, but adds timidly that "loving this place is one of my guilty secrets." When I asked Georgia's star cooking teacher and television personality Natalie Dupree to recommend a restaurant in Atlanta where I could find some no-nonsense American food, she almost whispered that the veal meat loaf with celery mashed potatoes at the Buckhead Diner was not to be missed. And I'm never in Dallas that one savvy hostess, who normally entertains on a grand scale at the chichi Mansion on Turtle Creek, doesn't quietly suggest that one evening we steal over to the Dixie House for what has been pegged Mom's Meat Loaf for as long as anybody can remember.

It's not that the food snobs are exactly embarrassed over their craving for putatively humble meat loaf; the problem is that they've yet to perceive the dish as worthy of the same serious critical analysis, messianic discussion, and concerted experimentation as, say, pickled pigs' cheeks or braised monkfish liver. As a result, most simply don't understand meat loaf, and, as a result of this benign ignorance or indifference, most are not too fastidious about the loaves they ingest with such blissful abandon. Yes, a few professional chefs have had the courage and curiosity to include some imaginative version of meat loaf on their trendy menus, but more often than not, the concoction is so contrived that the whole idea of recreating their secret dream dish is utterly defeated—like transcribing a classic Bach fugue into a rap mode to such a radical degree that the integrity of the glorious original music is lost completely.

And here I part company with my peers, since I have nothing but unadulterated respect and concern for meat loaf and am proud to tout its lofty social status loudly and clearly whenever the dish warrants praise. Needless to say, there is meat loaf, and there is meat loaf, and the horror stories I could relate about meat loaf meals in cafeterias, highway diners and third-rate coffee shops, friends' houses, and a few snazzy restaurants are hairy. In a nutshell, for every Platonic meat loaf I've encountered, there are at least five that were best relegated to my beagle's bowl. And there's absolutely no excuse in this, none whatsoever. Any fool should be capable of turning out a superlative meat loaf, one that is so sublime, so special, and so personal that those at the table will leave wondering how in heaven's name the dish ever acquired its questionable reputation and why it isn't featured in even the smartest American restaurants.

This by no means implies that you must search desperately for some exotic ingredient, since there are no exotic ingredients in a great meat loaf.

Nor does it require purchasing any fancy equipment or practicing a certain cooking technique, since even a novice is fully capable of producing superior meat loaf with a minimum of expense and bother. Never in the annals of gastronomy has a dish demanded so little to be so good, and never has there been a preparation whose success depends so much more on love and respect than it does on culinary expertise.

Although there are not—and should never be—many rigid rules for making meat loaf, serious meat loafers like myself do agree on a few essential points that can make the difference between a mediocre loaf and one that truly stuns. First and foremost, a great meat loaf is moist and succulent, even when the surface is delectably crusty from being baked free-form in an uncovered shallow pan. Moisture is supplied and maintained mainly by an ample amount of fat in the ground meats used, so if you have a phobia about cholesterol, you might as well discount from the start the possibility of turning out a memorable loaf. Too much fat, on the other hand, can result in a soggy, unappealing loaf, which is one reason I personally prefer leaner cuts of meat with a little bulk sausage added for moisture (as well as for extra flavor). Other acceptable sources of moisture are small amounts of beef stock, tomato sauce or ketchup, chopped fresh vegetables, milk, and Worcestershire sauce. I've also discovered that bread crumbs soaked in heavy cream or half-and-half can provide an almost unctuous quality to the finished product.

Some fanatics like meat loaf made exclusively with beef. I don't, for the simple reason that such a loaf tastes more like well-seasoned hamburger than the more complex dish that great meat loaf should be. For my palate, an equal combination of ground beef, pork, and veal yields the ideal loaf in flavor and texture. I must say, however, that when ground veal (whose gelatinous properties add juiciness and enhance texture) has been difficult to obtain, I've turned out some pretty impressive examples with only beef, pork, and that sneaky sausage. I do know about meat loaves prepared with chicken, chicken livers, ham, tongue, lamb, and heaven knows what else, but as far as I'm concerned, that's more like some fancy pâté or terrine than meat loaf—and I won't hear of it.

Nor does authentic meat loaf contain such frivolous additions as curry, apples, anchovies, walnuts, cloves, horseradish, or other alien items that certain zealous young chefs might somehow feel add "character." Nonsense. Experimenting with various classic components (onions, mushrooms, bell peppers, Worcestershire and Tabasco, garlic, herbs, etc.) is one thing; changing the identity of the loaf beyond recognition is another. Forget also about trying to make a loaf that contains no filler or eggs unless, again, you want to end up with a heavy pâté. Small amounts of bread crumbs, crushed soda crackers, rolled oats, or the like help balance the texture, while eggs at once lighten the loaf and bind it for easy slicing.

There's one way, and one way only, to mix a meat loaf: with your hands. And don't be timid. Just dive in, blending the ingredients evenly with your fingers and scraping any stray mixture from the sides of the bowl. (But don't overmix, which will toughen the loaf.) Then, when you're satisfied with the feel, the look, and the aroma, you can always pack the mixture tightly into a loaf pan, which will yield a fairly crusty top but soft sides. On the other hand, you might prefer, as I do, to form it into a thick oval or a long rectangle or a square before positioning your creation in a wide, shallow baking vessel—for overall crustiness—and draping a few slices of smoky bacon over the top.

And, you ask, what about gravy? There is no gravy. There is no call for gravy. Great meat loaf would be utterly desecrated by gravy, just as great mashed potatoes need no gravy. Do not serve gravy.

Predictably, I think my ultimate meat loaf is indeed the best on earth, and I must say, I've had lots of compliments on it. Some overly sensitive fellow addicts, I regret to say, do not agree that my meat loaf is the finest on earth, and they've told me why. That's fine, for at least I know that their interest is genuine and that maybe they're just trying to overcome any dumb reservations over the supreme merits of a dish that should be right up there in popularity with seared fresh tuna steaks and braised rabbit legs. Besides, what I never fail to remember is that no matter how masterful I think my cooking is, no matter how high jubilant spirits may soar, and no matter how many thunderous plaudits may come my way after every delectable morsel on every plate has been devoured, I and my noble meat loaf must stand alone.

The Ultimate Meat Loaf

SERVES 8

5 tablespoons butter

½ pound large fresh mushrooms, stems finely chopped and caps reserved

1 large onion, finely chopped

½ medium green bell pepper, seeded and finely chopped

2 celery ribs, finely chopped

3 garlic cloves, minced

½ teaspoon dried thyme, crumbled

½ teaspoon dried rosemary, crumbled

1 pound ground beef round

1 pound ground pork

1 pound ground veal

½ pound bulk pork sausage

1 tablespoon Dijon mustard

½ cup tomato ketchup

3 tablespoons Worcestershire sauce

½ teaspoon Tabasco

Salt and freshly ground pepper to taste

3 large eggs, beaten

1 cup breadcrumbs soaked in ½ cup heavy cream

3 strips bacon

Stuffed green olives, cut in half

In a medium skillet, melt 3 tablespoons of the butter over moderate heat, add the mushroom stems, and stir about 5 minutes or till most of their liquid has evaporated. Add the onion, bell pepper, celery, garlic, thyme, and rosemary, reduce the heat to low, cover, and simmer about 15 minutes or till the vegetables are soft and the liquid has evaporated.

Preheat the oven to 350°F.

Place the meats in a large mixing bowl, add the sautéed vegetables, and mix lightly. Add the mustard, ketchup, Worcestershire, Tabasco, salt and pepper, eggs, and breadcrumbs and mix with your hands till blended thoroughly. Shape the mixture into a firm thick oval loaf, place in a shallow baking or gratin dish, drape bacon over the top, and bake 1 hour in upper third of the oven. Remove the bacon strips and continue baking 15 to 20 minutes longer, depending on how thick the loaf is and how crusty you want the exterior to be.

Shortly before the meat loaf is removed from the oven, melt the remaining butter in a small skillet over moderate heat, add the reserved mushroom caps, and stir about 2 minutes or till nicely glazed. Transfer the meat loaf to a large, heated platter, arrange olives over the top, and garnish the edges with the mushroom caps.

GASTRONOMIC GOO

To PUT IT BLUNTLY, PEANUT BUTTER IS ONE OF THE GREATEST foods ever created, invented, devised, or developed by man and one of America's most important contributions to civilization. I might relish and consume a good deal of such highfalutin delicacies as caviar, foie gras, and white truffles, but, if necessary, I could live without these. I couldn't survive without peanut butter. Of course, it's a very personal gustatory passion shared with no other soul but my beagle dog, who loves the stuff as much or possibly more than his addicted master. Not that there's anything necessarily clandestine about the delectable habit—except maybe eating it off a finger. It's just that peanut butter (like Cuban cigars, the savage music of Carl Orff, or sex) is one of those supreme earthly (and earthy) pleasures best savored strictly in private.

Perhaps the reason I never engage in oral discourse on peanut butter the way I would on, say, roasted goose hearts, squid risotto, or Asian sea slugs is because I'm hopelessly incapable of discriminating between styles and brands. This should make me feel ashamed, but the truth is that I've never found a really bad legitimate jar of peanut butter (more on those awful "spreads" and reduced-fat rip-offs in a moment). Jif, Planters, Skippy, Krema, Peter Pan, Reese's Deaf Smith, Smucker's, King Kullen, Waldbaum's Master Choice—I love them all as much as I loved Beech-Nut and Big Top as a child, and I don't show favoritism. The unctuous goo can be smooth or crunchy, full of stabilizers or all-natural with separated oil floating on top, sweet or salty. All that matters is price, the permitted maximum being $1.79 for a regular 18-ounce jar. Given the nonexistence of prejudice, and despite my parsimony, I'm admittedly a walking advertisement for the entire peanut butter industry.

Being hardly fastidious about the actual peanut butter ingested one way or another every single day of my life, I'm still something of a scholar when it comes to the history of the tan-colored substance, how it developed as an American staple, and who eats what and how much throughout the country. Suffice it that a century ago, a certain St. Louis physician encouraged a food company to develop a ground peanut paste as a nutritious protein substitute for people with poor teeth. At about the same time, the Kellogg brothers (of cereal fame) in Battle Creek, Michigan, began experimenting with peanut butter as a vegetarian source of protein for patients in a sanitarium. The first commercial product (along with the first all-American hot dog—I think) was introduced to the world in 1904 at the Universal Exposition in St. Louis, and four years later, Krema (the oldest company still in operation today) marketed the first brand in Columbus, Ohio. It was only a question of time before Swift & Company produced its E. K. Pond peanut butter (only to change the name in 1928 to Peter Pan), followed by Skippy in 1932 and, eventually, Big Top in 1955 and Jif in 1958.

Today, peanut butter is found in 75 percent of American homes, leading the comedian Bill Cosby to remark not long ago that "Man cannot live by bread alone; he must also have peanut butter." Made primarily from ground roasted runner peanuts grown in the South, plus various hydrogenated oils, optional sweeteners, and salt, real peanut butter must contain by law a minimum of 90 percent peanuts, no more than 55 percent fat, and absolutely no artificial colorings or preservatives. If the peanut content is less than 90 percent, the product must be called peanut *spread*—and they're all dreadful.

Stabilizers are usually added to keep the oil from separating and to improve shelf life, but there are some finicky aficionados who wouldn't dream of eating anything but all-natural brands like Smucker's and those found in health-food shops, all of which, unless kept refrigerated, must have the surface oil continually stirred back into the paste. As for that new, hatefully dry, wretched reduced-fat style of peanut butter designed for health fanatics who have no right to be eating peanut butter in the first place, when even my dog refused a glob spread on a biscuit, I tossed the entire jar into the garbage. The production of this muck should be banned.

Jif, which churns out a whopping 250,000 jars of peanut butter every day, is the largest producer, followed by Skippy and Peter Pan. Hawaii and Alaska (believe it or not) lead the country in peanut butter consumption. And we seem to prefer smooth to crunchy by almost three to one. Likewise, stabilized styles far outsell the all-natural products except, predictably, in the health-obsessed state of California. Peanut butter is rich in protein, fat, and other nutrients necessary for sound child growth, but adults now actually eat more of it than children. If you don't like peanut butter, it can only be because you suffer from arachibutrophobia (the fear of getting it stuck to the roof of the mouth).

As to exactly how much peanut butter is consumed in my home each month, let's just say that I'm never without at least two jars in the house and that one of those puny 12-ounce containers wouldn't last a week. For years, I settled for the standard 18-ounce jars of Peter Pan, Reese's, or whatever brands happened to be on sale, then, to save time and even more money, I progressed to the sensible 28-ounce jars. Now that Jif, King Kullen, and a few other companies are producing heroic 40-ounce containers at greatly reduced cost—not to mention the two-packed 20-ounce jars of Skippy at Sam's Club for a mere pittance—I no longer ever worry about running out of peanut butter. Of course, total ecstasy is when my mother in the South sends up a one- or two-pound bag of those extra-large, roasted and salted, utterly delectable Virginia goobers and I make my own peanut butter in a blender or food processor (1½ tablespoons of peanut oil run through with every cup of peanuts).

I've seen a few jars of peanut butter outside the United States, but never *once* met a foreigner who really likes the stuff—which figures. As a result, to avoid the panic of deprivation aboard planes and ships, at hotels, and in food shops, no trip is ever undertaken without a full 18-ounce jar of peanut butter and a small plastic knife so I can indulge in furtive gluttony in even the most unlikely places. Heads do turn when, in the air, I refuse to eat the mess placed before me, unscrew the top of my trusty container, and spread luscious, odoriferous goo over whatever bread or crackers are proffered; but more often than not, the glances are more peeks of envy than ridicule. Feeling peckish on trains, I might well wipe a finger in the jar for a restorative jolt. The ritual of ordering an elaborate Club sandwich from room service in a luxury London hotel is never complete unless the potato chips are adorned with a little PB. And nothing is more consoling after days of haute cuisine in Paris restaurants or aboard the *QE2* than a quiet, solitary respite of two fresh whole wheat slices, a small pot of jam, and plenty of you know what—washed down with a Pepsi.

Although I've never gone so far as to desecrate precious fresh beluga caviar or Scotch smoked salmon with anything more than a few squeezes of lemon juice, the number of toothsome dishes that can be either made with or enhanced by peanut butter are almost limitless. I have recipes for peanut butter cakes, pies, breads, cookies, muffins, coffee cakes, soups, quiches, dips, milkshakes, brownies, candies, sauces, and salad dressings, and then there's peanut butter–glazed ham, and chicken kebabs, and spicy noodles, and braised pork cutlets, and tostadas, and turkey croquettes, and . . . the list is endless. Needless to say, peanut butter sandwiches comprise a whole separate category: on plain white, whole wheat, or rye bread, on toast, on buns or biscuits, on pita or giant crackers with everything from cheap grape jelly to sumptuous homemade preserves, bacon to bananas, coconut to pickles, cream cheese to shaved chocolate. The urgent peanut butter appetite has no limits. A manual laborer I know tells me about a peanut butter and coleslaw burger on a hard sesame-seed roll that he and his buddies order with coffee every morning for breakfast at the local deli. I plan to try that soon.

Now, should the topic of peanut butter be broached around most people, religiously the first sobbing comment is, "Oooh, it's so faaaattening!" Well, so is sausage, and lasagne, and chocolate cake, and all those other wonderful things that the Good Lord intended man to eat. At least peanut butter has not a trace of cholesterol, but even if it did, the dietetic kill-joys who love to flaunt masochistic self-denial would still drive me to distraction.

The truth is that two tablespoons of genuine, unadulterated peanut butter—enough for a decent sandwich or four or five crackers—contain about 190 calories, while a single avocado has about 380; a tiny can of sardines, 260, and an ounce of Limburger cheese, 200. The question is whether you'd prefer an avocado, sardines, or Limburger to a yummy PB on white toast, the answer to which I know as well as the next fiend.

I can report that, even with the addiction, my own weight has remained pretty constant for the past twenty years and that my health is remarkably sound. Perhaps more important is the fact that Bedford Beagle has just entered his fifth year on this earth, weighs a slim twenty pounds, and, salivating with tail wagging, continues to watch impatiently when I reach for the sacred jar and prepare his routine fix.

Noodles with Peanut Butter–Garlic Sauce

SERVES 2

1 teaspoon sugar
2 tablespoons soy sauce
1½ tablespoons wine vinegar
1 tablespoon Asian sesame oil
1 teaspoon chili oil
1½ teaspoons smooth peanut

butter blended with 2
tablespoons water
1 tablespoon minced scallion
¼ teaspoon grated fresh ginger
¼ teaspoon minced garlic
½ pound fine egg noodles

In a large mixing bowl, blend all the ingredients except the noodles, stir vigorously, and set aside. (If the sauce separates, it can be reintegrated by adding 1 or 2 drops of boiling water and stirring lightly.)

In a kettle, bring 3 quarts of salted water to a boil, add the noodles, and cook till desired tenderness is achieved. Drain the noodles in a colander, run under cold running water, drain thoroughly, and transfer to a large serving bowl. Pour the sauce over the noodles, toss, and serve lukewarm or cold.

Peanut Butter Pound Cake

SERVES 12

2½ sticks (10 ounces) butter,
  softened
2 cups sugar
6 large eggs

½ cup smooth peanut butter
2 cups all-purpose flour
½ cup crushed roasted peanuts

Preheat the oven to 350°F. Grease a 10 x 5–inch loaf pan and set aside.

In a large mixing bowl, cream the butter with an electric mixer, add the sugar gradually, and beat till fluffy. Add the eggs one at a time, beating after each addition. Blend in the peanut butter with a wooden spoon. Add the flour 1 cup at a time and mix till well blended and smooth.

Scrape the batter into the prepared pan and bake for 15 minutes. Remove the pan from the oven, sprinkle the crushed peanuts over the batter, and continue baking till a skewer inserted in the middle comes out clean, about 1 hour longer.

Let the cake cool slightly, then unmold onto a large serving plate.

Peanut Butter–Chocolate Chip Cookies

MAKES ABOUT 50 COOKIES

½ cup chunky peanut butter
8 tablespoons (1 stick) butter,
    softened
½ cup granulated sugar
½ cup firmly packed light brown
    sugar
2 large eggs

1 teaspoon pure vanilla extract
1¼ cups all-purpose flour
½ teaspoon baking soda
½ teaspoon salt
6 ounces chocolate chips
½ cup peanuts, coarsely chopped
    in a food processor

Preheat the oven to 350°F.

In a large mixing bowl, cream the peanut butter and butter with an electric mixer till soft. Add the granulated and brown sugar and continue creaming till the mixture is well blended. Add the eggs and vanilla, and beat till light and fluffy.

In a small bowl, combine the flour, baking soda, and salt; stir till well blended. Add the dry ingredients to the butter mixture and blend well. Add the chocolate chips and peanuts and stir with a wooden spoon till evenly mixed.

Drop the batter by teaspoons 2 inches apart onto an ungreased cookie sheet and bake till browned, about 12 minutes.

Crunchy Peanut Butter Ice Cream

MAKES ABOUT 1 GALLON ICE CREAM; SERVES AT LEAST 15

1½ cups crunchy peanut butter
Two 15-ounce cans sweetened condensed milk
Two 13-ounce cans evaporated milk
2 tablespoons pure vanilla extract

In the top of a double boiler, melt the peanut butter over briskly simmering—not boiling—water and remove from the heat.

In a large mixing bowl, combine the condensed milk, evaporated milk, and vanilla; stir till well blended. Add the melted peanut butter and stir till well blended and smooth. Scrape the mixture into the container of an electric ice cream freezer and freeze according to the manufacturer's directions.

When the ice cream is frozen, remove the dasher, cover the container, pack more ice and ice cream salt around the container, and let the ice cream mellow for 2 to 3 hours before serving.

ODE ON A CAN OF TUNA

I MAKE ABSOLUTELY NO APOLOGIES FOR MY LIFELONG AND INTENSE love affair with canned tuna. In fact, I find it utterly appalling that this delectable staple has been disparaged by food snobs who have somehow come to the fatuous conclusion that only the fresh fish is worthy of human consumption. Despite what the parvenus think, canned tuna is and always will be one of the world's great delicacies, and the very idea of using anything else to make a sumptuous tuna melt, a classic *salade niçoise,* an intelligent tuna-and-noodle casserole, or, above all, a sublime tuna salad is absurd.

As for fresh tuna itself, which is probably the most wildly popular item on any trendy restaurant menu in America, I've been trying to analyze why I resolutely refuse to eat the stuff in this country. It could be because of the tiny, squiggling, repulsive white worm I noticed in a fashionably under-seared piece of yellowfin served some time ago at a chic bistro in San Francisco. Perhaps I'm convinced that most professional chefs—not to mention home cooks—simply don't know the first thing about preparing fresh tuna correctly (that is, slowly baked) the way they do around the Mediterranean. It might have something to do with the glitzy, status-conscious, gullible crowd that perceives the fish as a healthful, thinning substitute for meat. But the more I reflect, the more I'm apt to believe it's just because my fancy for canned tuna is so strong that I have a mental block against those dry, bland, grilled slabs and all the raw fish used in tartares and sushi. No doubt there are many who would classify me as a gastronomic philistine, but I couldn't care less.

Although my devotion to canned tuna is rather wanton, it's a passion over which I have little control. At the moment, for instance, there are about thirty cans of various weights and grades of the fish on my kitchen shelf.

Each was acquired compulsively either at a price club, at the supermarket (on sale, of course), or during my foreign travels. Each contains tuna packed in vegetable oil, canola oil, olive oil, or brine (I wouldn't touch that flavorless product canned in water); and each is intended for specific preparations.

When I'm forced to fly, I'm never without at least two three-ounce, flip-top tins of solid white albacore that's easy to eat with a plastic fork. Europeans (like the Japanese) take their tuna very seriously, and in central London, I know exactly which Italian delis make the best tuna-and-corn salad. In Paris, I head for shops such as Raffi and Hédiard that stock the exquisite white tunny (*le germon*) of Brittany and the firm, unctuous *thonine* of the Riviera, packed flat in olive oil like sardines. On trips to Italy, I search for cans of the highly prized, expensive, creamy-pink belly cut of bluefin called *ventresca*. And when my primal instincts are turned loose in restaurants and cafés anywhere along the Mediterranean, I sniff out everything from Catalan *xató* (tuna and salt cod salad) to Greek tuna with chickpeas to fried Tunisian *briks* stuffed with tuna, capers, and tomatoes to that glorious French tuna, onion, and bell pepper sandwich known as *pan bagna*—all prepared traditionally with the region's superior canned bluefin, albacore, or yellowfin.

I do enjoy all those exotic products and dishes, but, after all is said and done, the truth is that there's still nothing on earth that can equal a really good, all-American tuna fish salad sandwich made with the generally high-quality Pacific tuna preserved in California and readily available in all our markets. I've never met anybody (foreigners included) who didn't like our old-fashioned tuna fish salad sandwich, and all I can say about those pretentious phonies who think they're elevating the classic salad's pedigree by making it with grilled and flaked fresh tuna steaks instead of the tender, full-flavored canned fish is that they really should seek medical help.

I wish I could provide a definitive recipe for the quintessential tuna salad sandwich, but since the distinctive fish lends itself to so many delectable interpretations, the best I can do is offer a few basic guidelines and make suggestions. While I do prefer any major brand of choice "solid white" albacore packed in oil, I certainly don't object to the lower-graded (and less expensive) "chunk light" varieties of yellowfin, skipjack, and bluefin. I do, however, avoid cheap supermarket house brands, which tend to be a flaky mush of the lowest grade tuna and may even contain some artificially flavored agents.

Tuna salad almost demands a little finely chopped celery and sweet pickle, plus black pepper, but beyond these three essentials, the possibilities might include discreet amounts of chopped stuffed olives, hard-boiled egg, bell pepper, red onion or chives, fresh dill, avocado, or capers. The trick is not to overwhelm the delicate tuna with any supplementary ingredient. Great tuna salad can never, repeat *never,* be bound with that hideous "lite," low-calorie mayonnaise. I use only Hellmann's—about one heaping tablespoon per six-ounce can of tuna—and since the mayo contains enough sodium for my taste, I add no salt. I mix my salad lightly but thoroughly, and I may or may not add a crisp leaf of iceberg lettuce to the sandwich.

Oh yes, the type of bread: I pile my tuna on soft, plain white, high enough so that part of the salad can ooze out the sides of the sandwich onto the plate and be eaten with the fingers. And I dare anybody to tell me that's not wonderful eating.

ICEBERG AHEAD

I HATE TO MAKE A FUSS, BUT IT'S MY MORAL DUTY TO DEFEND THE integrity and try to rectify the tattered reputation of one of the most maligned victuals of the American kitchen, namely iceberg lettuce. I usually keep quiet when some rube makes malicious remarks about the maraschino cherry in my bourbon manhattan. I tolerate nasty comments about cocktail peanuts, canned tuna, and nonvirgin olive oil. But I have absolutely no patience with those who pompously proclaim iceberg lettuce to be mundane, tasteless, and uncouth. In my view, they'd just as soon be mocking the Constitution or burning the flag.

One of my most heated arguments about iceberg used to be with none other than Craig Claiborne, who, despite all his other wisdom, viciously classified the lettuce as "commonplace" and "very low on the scale of salad greens." Food writer and iron-handed restaurant critic Mimi Sheraton has always loathed iceberg in any form or shape. Cautious cookbook editors cringe at the very idea of recipes that might include the green. And trendy hotshot chefs all over the country blindly denounce the head as if it were fit only for feeding livestock. I could suggest that such prejudice stems from a basic misunderstanding of what iceberg is all about, but I'm afraid that what it really betrays is nothing but unadulterated snobbery.

Don't get me wrong. It so happens that my summer garden teems with tender bibb and Boston lettuce, peppery arugula and bitter radicchio, romaine, mâche, and often coppery leaf lettuce, each of which has its appropriate place on my dinner table. It's also true, however, that I'm never, ever without an inexpensive, crispy, and, yes, flavorful head of iceberg in the fridge, and that I handle and use it with the same respect accorded the fanciest greens costing exhorbitant prices in markets.

Those who act uppity about iceberg would do well to learn that its ancestor, "Tennis Ball" lettuce, was not only cultivated but highly prized by none other than Thomas Jefferson. The variety we know today was introduced just over a hundred years ago in Warminster, Pennsylvania, by the well-known seed experts W. Atlee & Company, and demand was such that by the 1920s the sapid head was a staple in virtually every American kitchen. Restaurants prided themselves on wedges of succulent, sweet-and-bitter hearts of iceberg doused with Thousand Island or blue-cheese dressing; James Beard applauded the lettuce's subtle flavor and wonderful texture; and mothers across the nation knew exactly what was indispensable for a genuine BLT or Club sandwich. Only when gustatory artifice reared its arrogant head in the 1970s did respectable iceberg begin its ignominious fall from grace.

I suppose what galls me most is the way so many classic and delicious dishes risk utter distortion all because cooks are fatuously embarrassed to use the one lettuce that helps make the preparations so distinctive. What savvy California chef, by contrast, would dream of composing an authentic Cobb salad, crab Louis, or chiffonade seafood salad that contains no crunchy iceberg for ideal textural contrast? Tex-Mex tacos and enchiladas, Southwestern tortilla salad and *posole,* and Midwestern layered salad would simply lose most of their character without shredded iceberg. And to make Chinese-American minced chicken or squab in lettuce cups or a Carolina wilted salad with anything but zesty leaves of iceberg almost defeats the purpose. Paul Prudhomme would deem substituting something like shredded romaine or escarole for iceberg as a bed for New Orleans shrimp remoulade sheer heresy, and as for those BLT and Club sandwiches, what do the posturing foodies really expect a mom to use? Radicchio?

I shop for iceberg as carefully as I pick out perfect green beans or fondle mangoes for ripeness. First, I refuse to pay more than seventy-nine cents a head, which is why I usually have two heads found on sale. No matter how inexpensive, on the other hand, I reject any iceberg that is not firm when pressed, since compactness guarantees both crisper leaves and longer storage life. I also pass on any head with a badly rusted stem and even a trace of mottling of the lower leaves.

To prepare a good head of iceberg, I discard any limp outer leaves and cut off (with a stainless steel knife) about two inches of stem to greatly retard eventual oxidation at the base. Quite frankly, I haven't washed iceberg for years, but if you're finicky, rinse under cold water and dry *not* the entire head (which only expedites rusting and discoloration) but the individual leaves or wedges as they're used. To safeguard its quality, iceberg should be kept only slightly moist, so I wrap the head loosely in a double thickness of paper towels, then store it in a plastic bag in the bottom drawer of the refrigerator. Mine stays in near-perfect condition at least a week—which is more than I can say for leaf lettuce and arugula.

Since America seems to be on the verge of finally shedding its dubious mantle of culinary pretense and returning to the sanity of its grass roots, I predict that iceberg lettuce will soon resurface to claim its rightful and proud place of honor in every household and restaurant. I forecast further that the much-slandered iceberg wedges of yesteryear will inspire perceptive professional chefs to create not only sensible variations, but exciting new dressings—and that there won't be a snicker to be heard. Just recently, in fact, *New York* magazine restaurant critic Gael Greene praised the crunchy Gorgonzola salad at a place in the Hamptons, adding "you'll rediscover why Americans were content for years with nothing but iceberg." Testing various lettuces for the perfect classic Greek salad, *Cook's Illustrated* editor Christopher Kimball was "taken aback" by the ideal texture of iceberg. And I myself, while scouting the plush Peninsula Grill in Charleston, South Carolina, couldn't have been more pleasantly surprised to notice on chef Robert Carter's eclectic menu a chilled wedge of iceberg with buttermilk dressing and small cubes of smoked bacon jerky. Somebody once made the snide remark that maybe someday there would regrettably be an organization called "Friends of Iceberg Lettuce." All I can say is that if such a society were ever founded, I'd be more than happy to nominate myself as president.

Crab Louis

1½ cups mayonnaise
¼ cup bottled chili sauce
2 scallions (white and 2 inches of green), minced
½ small green bell pepper, seeded and minced
1 tablespoon fresh lemon juice
1 teaspoon Worcestershire sauce
Tabasco to taste
½ teaspoon salt

1½ pounds lump crabmeat, picked over for shells
1 firm head iceberg lettuce, shredded and chilled
3 large ripe avocados, halved, pitted, and peeled
2 medium ripe tomatoes, cored and cut into 6 wedges
3 large hard-boiled eggs, cut lengthwise into quarters

In a large mixing bowl, combine the mayonnaise, chili sauce, scallions, bell pepper, lemon juice, Worcestershire, Tabasco, and salt, and whisk till well blended. Add the crabmeat and toss gently till well coated with the dressing.

Make a bed of lettuce on each of 6 salad plates. Mound equal amounts of the crab mixture into the 6 avocado cavities, center the halves on the lettuce beds, and garnish the edges with tomatoes and eggs.

Shrimp Remoulade

½ cup ketchup

3 tablespoons Creole mustard

2 tablespoons distilled white vinegar

2 large eggs

Juice of 1 lemon

1 cup finely chopped scallions
(white and 2 inches of green)

½ cup finely chopped celery

½ cup finely chopped parsley

1 garlic clove, minced

1 tablespoon prepared white
horseradish

¼ teaspoon cayenne

1 teaspoon salt

Dash of Tabasco

1⅓ cups vegetable oil

1½ pounds fresh medium shrimp

2 lemons, cut in half and seeded

1 firm medium head iceberg
lettuce, chopped

In a blender or food processor, combine the ketchup, mustard, vinegar, eggs, lemon juice, scallions, celery, parsley, garlic, horseradish, cayenne, salt, and Tabasco. Blend to a smooth consistency. In a slow, steady stream, add the oil and blend till nicely thickened. Transfer the sauce to a large bowl, cover with plastic wrap, and set the remoulade dressing aside.

In a large saucepan, combine the shrimp with enough water to cover, squeeze the lemon halves into the water, and drop in the halves. Bring to a boil, remove from the heat, cover, and let stand for 2 minutes or until the shrimp are pink and curled. Drain the shrimp and, when cool enough to handle, shell and devein them.

Add the shrimp to the remoulade dressing, toss well, cover with plastic wrap, and chill for about 30 minutes.

To serve, make a bed of chopped lettuce on each of 6 salad plates and arrange equal amounts of shrimp on top of each bed.

Chicken Soong

1 firm head iceberg lettuce
1 large skinned and boned chicken breast (about 12 ounces), finely diced
1 large egg white
1 tablespoon cornstarch
½ teaspoon salt
1 cup peanut oil
1 celery rib, finely chopped
1 small carrot, scraped and finely chopped
2 scallions, finely chopped

1 garlic clove, minced
1 teaspoon finely chopped fresh ginger
2 small fresh hot green peppers, seeded and finely chopped
10 water chestnuts, chopped
2 tablespoons dry sherry
1½ teaspoons soy sauce
1 teaspoon sugar
½ teaspoon Asian sesame oil

Core the lettuce, separate the crisper leaves into cups, and set aside. In a large mixing bowl, combine the chicken, egg white, cornstarch, and salt; stir till well blended.

In a wok or large, heavy skillet, heat the peanut oil over moderately high heat, add the chicken, and cook about 2 minutes, stirring constantly. With a slotted spoon, transfer the chicken to a plate.

Add the celery, carrot, scallions, garlic, ginger, hot peppers, and water chestnuts to the skillet and cook, stirring, about 2 minutes. Return the chicken to the skillet. Add the sherry, soy sauce, sugar, and sesame oil. Stir till well blended and piping hot and transfer the mixture to a large plate. Let cool slightly.

Spoon equal amounts of the chicken mixture into lettuce cups and serve at room temperature.

Texas Tortilla Salad

1 tablespoon corn oil
½ pound ground beef round
One 16-ounce can pinto beans,
  drained
½ teaspoon ground cumin
Salt and pepper to taste
1 medium head iceberg lettuce,
  torn into bits
1 medium Spanish or white onion,
  chopped
1 ripe avocado, pitted, peeled, and
cubed
½ pound extra-sharp cheddar
  cheese, grated
1 large ripe tomato, roughly
  chopped
2 cups mayonnaise
¼ cup bottled taco sauce
1 teaspoon chili powder
Toasted corn tortillas (or Dorito
  chips) broken into small pieces,
  to taste

In a large skillet, heat the corn oil over moderate heat. Break up the beef into the oil and cook, stirring often, till browned, about 5 minutes. Add the beans, cumin, and salt and pepper. Stir till well blended and remove from the heat.

In a large salad bowl, combine the lettuce, onion, avocado, cheese, and tomato. Add the warm beef and beans and toss till well blended.

In a small bowl, combine the mayonnaise, taco sauce, and chili powder and stir till well blended. Add the dressing to the salad and toss to mix. Add the tortilla pieces, toss the salad gently again, and serve as a main-course salad.

JOIN THE CLUB

'M GOING TO BE SO BOLD AS TO SUGGEST THAT THE QUINTES-
sential American dish—the one that combines old-fashioned Yankee
ingenuity and a striking economy of means—is not fried chicken or chili or
apple pie but the handsome, delectable, nutritious, forever-comforting creation called the Club sandwich. I'd like to go one step further and insist that
I have never met a single hungry, honest American (or Englishman or
Frenchman or German) who, when asked to reflect on the joy of savoring
silky poached chicken breast and smoky bacon and juicy ripe tomato and
crisp lettuce layered between two or three slices of toasted bread smeared
with fresh mayonnaise, would not admit to loving a classic Club sandwich.
It's an item that most of us instinctively take for granted, to such an extent
that, in spite of its ability to arouse strong passions, we tend not to talk
much about the sandwich, not to take it quite as seriously as we should.

Well, I'm very proud to say that I've not only spent a good many years
thinking and talking about Club sandwiches and eating enough to warrant
extra doses of Prevacid; I've also spent an inordinate amount of time scouring
the planet for both classic and innovative examples of what can now only be
classified as an international favorite. Some people intimate that I should be
a little embarrassed over my obsession with the Club, that, after all, nobody
should be that serious about . . . a sandwich. I'm not in the least embarrassed.

I still drool, for instance, over memories of Anne Rosensweig's extrava-
gant lobster Club on brioche at Arcadia restaurant in New York, and a double-decker of moist roast turkey, thick bacon, and Gruyère on toasted Sally
Lund bread at the Hotel Bel-Air in Los Angeles. A Club of lamb, lobster,
and wild mushrooms on a sesame baguette at the Hotel Nassauer Hof in
Wiesbaden, Germany, may be a bit daunting but nevertheless makes me

salivate. The oblong wonder spread with fresh Thousand Island dressing served with a heavy silver knife and fork and crisp linen napkin at the Cipriani in Venice is an elegant lunch in itself that I relish. And even when I'm not staying at the Drake in Chicago, I break neck getting to the cozy Coq d'Or bar at least once for the greatest Club in America on toasted whole-grain bread.

Now, please, I beg you, don't ask about the origins of the Club or exactly why it has so readily been adapted by hotels around the world, for, much to my eternal frustration, the name and evolution of the sandwich—unlike those of the Reuben, hoagy, Denver, hot dog, and hamburger—are destined to remain shrouded in mystery. All evidence points to the fact that the Club (or Clubhouse) sandwich definitely existed in the United States by the late nineteenth century, but any answers as to who first created it, and how or why, are strictly hypothetical.

For a while, it was believed that the first mention of the Club was in Ray L. McCardell's *Conversations of a Chorus Girl,* in 1903, and that the sandwich was then included in the 1906 edition of Fannie Farmer's *Boston Cooking School Cookbook* and in Maria Willett Howard's *Lowney's Cook Book* of 1908. Then, in a book entitled *New York: A Guide to the Empire State,* published in 1962, a big case was made for the sandwich's having first appeared in 1894 at Richard Canfield's famous Saratoga Club in Saratoga, New York (where, supposedly, the Saratoga chip—otherwise known as the potato chip—was also born).

After none other than the provocative, free-wheeling journalist of the fifties Mr. Lucius Beebe once suggested to me that the sandwich surely came about on the double-decker "club cars" of our early trains, I myself promulgated this theory until a certain train historian I contacted sent me a few old club-car menus listing a "Three-Decker Club House" sandwich. Utterly baffled, I decided then and there to give up my inquiries into the sandwich's history.

As to the problem of what does or does not constitute a genuine Club sandwich, again there are no definitive answers. The late, great James Beard, who loved a well-made Club as much as the next gourmand, remembered the "original" sandwich as having only two pieces of buttered white toast. He considered the double-decker with three slices a "horror" and balked at the idea that turkey breast could be substituted for chicken. Other aficionados, however, point out that a single-decker (often referred to as a junior Club) is no more than a BLT with chicken added. And as for including such components as cheese, ham, tongue, hard-boiled egg, or cucumbers and substituting turkey for chicken or Thousand Island dressing for mayo, suffice it that numerous American cookbooks published early in the twentieth century describe combinations that would shock even today's boldest young chefs.

Personally, I am both conservative and liberal when it comes to the Club sandwich. If, for example, I'm craving what I consider to be a classic Club, nothing will satisfy but a double-decker of thinly sliced poached chicken breast and juicy ripe tomato, semicrisp, lean bacon, and iceberg lettuce carefully layered between thin pieces of white toast spread with mayonnaise, either fresh or Hellmann's. I want salt and plenty of pepper on my sandwich. I want the sandwich to be quartered diagonally, each quarter secured with frilled toothpicks. And I must also have plain potato chips, sweet pickles, a few large green or black olives, and a Coke.

On the other hand, I don't reject certain major (often radical) variations on the Club, so long as its basic principles are respected and the sandwich is of a manageable size. A "king Club" of rare roast beef, raw onion rings, and lettuce on toasted cracked wheat bread spread with creamy blue cheese can be celestial, as can an Italian single-decker of mozzarella, salami, bell peppers, and anchovies on sliced homemade Italian bread or focaccia. For a "deli Club," combine liverwurst, red onion rings, and sour pickles between thin slices of pumpernickel moistened with mustard or Russian dressing; for an elegant "opera Club," try smoked salmon or baby shrimp, dilled cucumbers, and salmon caviar, neatly layered between three slices of buttered rye; and for what West Coasters call an "alligator Club," pile flaked canned or seared fresh tuna, tiny sardines, and slices of ripe avocado on yeasty sourdough drizzled with Green Goddess dressing.

At a National Restaurant Association conference held in Washington, D.C., not long ago, participants appeared a bit incredulous at the revelation that, in a sampling of fifty menus from all over the country, the frequency with which the Club sandwich is offered has increased a startling 150 percent over just the past six years. I, of course, was thrilled to hear the news, and I look forward to observing how our more creative chefs will continue to quietly reinterpret the same aristocrat that Wallis Simpson took such pride in preparing for King Edward VIII and his fellow blue bloods at Balmoral before blind passion put an end to both kingship and homey Club sandwiches. In the meantime, let me record what I consider the correct way to compose a classic Club—a sandwich so simple, so perfect in its textural contrasts, and so addictively delicious that, once you've mastered the technique and taken the first bite, you might well regard any further tampering as sacrilege.

The Quintessential Club Sandwich

For one sandwich, toast three square, untrimmed quarter-inch-thick pieces of white bread till just golden. Spread a liberal layer of mayonnaise—fresh or Hellmann's—on both sides of one piece and one side of the other two and place the bread on a cutting board. On the first piece of half-dressed toast, arrange over the mayonnaise two pieces of lean bacon, fried until almost crisp, drained, and broken in half; add two thin slices of ripe tomato, unpeeled; season to taste with salt and freshly ground pepper; and top with a piece of toast dressed on both sides. On this center piece of toast, arrange a neat double of moist, thinly sliced poached or boiled (*not* grilled) chicken breast; add one perfect, crisp leaf of iceberg (*not* bibb or Boston) lettuce; and top with the remaining piece of toast, dressed side down. (For ideal flavor and texture, it is essential that the ingredients be layered in this exact order.)

Securing the sandwich lightly but carefully with the fingertips, quickly draw a very sharp chef's knife across it on the diagonal, cutting the sandwich in one steady stroke. Repeat the procedure across the other diagonal, thus quartering the sandwich. Secure each quarter by stabbing it down the middle with a round toothpick (preferably frilled), transfer the quarters neatly onto a large serving plate, and reassemble them in their original configuration. Garnish the sides of the Club sandwich with potato chips, sweet pickles, and large unpitted olives (to be slowly gnawed and sucked on). Serve with Coke—or Pepsi.

REDRESSING THE SPUD

 IN THIS FRIVOLOUS AGE DEVOTED MORE TO FUSION CONFUSION
than to redefining and refining dozens of classic dishes that for ages have
served as the valid foundation of our eating traditions and habits, who really
gives a damn about something so supposedly banal as potato salad? I do,
that's who, and, from what I've observed while scavenging the more judi-
cious tables of the world, I'm by no means alone in indulging this particular passion. Of course, when I speak of potato salad, I'm not necessarily
referring to the standard American archetype, which even our more pretentious chefs secretly relish with hamburgers and fried chicken and all those
other consoling staples. Actually, if my periodic craving for great potato
salad depended on the dull, careless concoctions you generally find in
restaurants and delis, on buffet tables, and at picnics, I'd have the most frus-
trated appetite on earth.

The point is that those who were weaned on soothing potato salad composed of cubed boiled potatoes, chopped celery, onions, hard-boiled eggs,
maybe a little diced sweet pickle, mustard, and mayonnaise are perhaps
unaware that in other countries potato salad can take on an entirely different character. In Scandinavia, for instance, I've been served an incredible
combination of tiny, sliced new potatoes, strips of smoked salmon, minced
onions, capers, fresh dill, and red caviar, all bound together by a tangy sour
cream dressing. Accompanying a few slices of spicy cold lamb one warm
afternoon on the Greek island of Aegina was a delectable salad of thinly
sliced potatoes and cucumbers marinated in aromatic olive oil with oregano
and mint, chunks of assertive feta cheese, briny black olives, and ripe tomato wedges. And often in my wanderings about Germany's Black Forest I've
made a lunch of vinegary, lukewarm potato salad enriched with sliced wurst,

beets, and wild mushrooms, crusty black bread, and consumed with steins of frothy lager. In Spain, there was a memorable mixture of crunchy fried potatoes, spicy chorizo sausage, and fava beans; in Belgium, a sumptuous *salade liégeoise* made with diced potatoes, tiny green beans, crisp slab bacon, and hot vinegar dressing; and in Mexico, a spicy potato salad chock-full of tender cactus leaves, chick peas, hard-boiled eggs, and poblano chile peppers.

The French, of course, have probably done more than most to elevate the social status of potato salad, as anyone knows who's ever tasted a properly made *salade niçoise* on the Riviera, a chilled potato and mussel salad in Brittany or the Charente, a *salade de boeuf à la parisienne* (herby cold beef, leek, fresh horseradish, and potato salad vinaigrette) in an old-fashioned brasserie, and those wonderfully unctuous *pommes à l'huile* (warm sliced potatoes tossed with white wine, bouillon, and vinaigrette dressing) that are served with virtually all sausage dishes.

Obviously, I do like a good deal of diversity in my potato salads, including the more familiar American ones. Quite often, for example, I'll add such seasonings as curry powder, any number of fresh herbs and spices, different varieties of nuts, and such condiments as capers, sesame seeds, and crumbled bacon. I transform what is considered to be a side dish into a delicious main course by incorporating cubed brisket of beef, sautéed chicken livers, marinated artichoke hearts, or braised tongue. Blanched vegetables mixed with sliced or diced potatoes and an imaginative dressing can make for a very satisfying and healthy luncheon dish; and when you add to well-dressed potatoes such delectables as fresh grilled sardines, marinated herring, braised duck legs, venison sausage, shredded daikon, zesty chili peppers, or even a little truffle oil, the resulting flavor and texture can be not only ethereal but eminently contemporary.

On the negative side, it's true that even the most exotic ingredients cannot redeem a salad that's not prepared properly from the start. Those who make potato salad from potatoes that are weeks, possibly months old little realize that no matter how one cooks and prepares such spuds, there's no way they're going to have decent taste and texture. Throughout the summer months, I'm usually lucky enough to get exquisite new potatoes that are harvested on eastern Long Island almost every day and that I prepare with their flavorful skins left on, but when I'm forced to depend on the supermarket's supply, I'm almost always disappointed with the pickings. If the potatoes are not firm, with tight, fresh-looking skins, I don't make potato salad. Nor do I ever buy many more potatoes than the number I plan to use in a day or so since, contrary to what you read and hear, potatoes *do* wrinkle, sprout, and wither in no time.

As to the exact type of potato I use for a salad . . . ah, there's the touchy question. Most cookbooks state that the correct potato for potato salad is the classic red "boiling" potato. For salad, I generally prefer red potatoes (especially new Red Pontiacs), fingerlings, and creamy Yukon golds to the drier, more starchy russets that are so ideal for baking. But this isn't to say that I'd ever choose a soft, wrinkled red or Yukon over a russet or "all-purpose" white in prime condition. I've had wretched potato salads made from obviously inferior red potatoes, and some of the best salads I've produced were prepared with fresh, moist russets from Long Island and Maine. In a recent blind tasting conducted by a leading food magazine to determine which potato varieties were best suited to certain preparations, a baking potato took first place in the potato-salad category. Like any fresh fruit or vegetable, of course, the flavor and texture of a potato is the product of such variables as soil, climate, growing conditions, harvesting methods, and shipping procedures, meaning that no matter how perfect any "new" potato is supposed to be for a given dish, if that potato is over the hill, its inherent qualities are meaningless.

Never is precision in cooking so all-important as when boiling potatoes for potato salad, and never do home cooks commit greater folly than serving a salad made with mushy, overcooked potatoes that literally fall apart when tossed. Unfortunately, since the age and texture of potatoes can vary so widely, specific timing directions can never—repeat, *never*—be trusted when you're cooking potatoes for salad. Whether you're boiling whole, quartered, or cubed potatoes, the cardinal rule is: cook only till they are tender but still firm—or, more precisely, till they are just pierceable. It's easy to say that a whole, medium-size red boiling potato should be cooked about twenty minutes, or that cubed fingerlings are done after about eight minutes, or that small new potatoes require no more than ten minutes. But when I boil potatoes, I stand over the pot with fork or knife in hand, piercing gently and steadily. Also, remember that unless the potatoes are doused immediately with cold water (which I prefer not to do since rinsing tends to remove flavor along with starch), they will cook a few minutes more after being drained.

There are two schools of thought about when to dress boiled potatoes for salad. Some chefs insist that for ultimate flavor, potatoes should always be allowed to absorb a good portion of the dressing while they are still hot.

I agree, so long as the other ingredients are not adversely affected and the salad is to be served within the hour either warm or at room temperature (as in the case of *pommes à l'huile* or any classic version of German potato salad); but I definitely disagree when simple mayonnaise is used and the salad is intended to be chilled. Nothing is more unappetizing than a potato salad in which all the ingredients have been allowed to soften while coated with dressing, which is why I find leftover potato salad so disgusting. If I do decide to chill my salad (again, depending on the other ingredients), I never leave it in the refrigerator more than one hour before serving.

Never has the time been more propitious to not only finally address the wealth of intriguing potato salads that exist around the globe, but also apply the same ingenuity to this dish as we have to so many others—within reason, of course. Every year, there seems to be still another potato variety on the American market. The number of new compatible ingredients now available—fresh wild mushrooms, arctic char and all sorts of wonderful shellfish, heirloom tomatoes and delicate eggplants, pork and clam bellies, amazing sausages and cheeses, and so on—is almost limitless. And the array of flavored vinegars and mustards, olive, nut, chile, and truffle oils, and complex creams can give altogether different dimension to dressings.

Moreover, unlike traditional American potato salad, which is always served as a trivial side dish, these unusual salads can easily be conceived as main courses, possibly prefaced by a simple soup and served with no more than good bread and wine or microbrew. They're all easy to prepare, they're packed full of tempting flavors and textures, and, indeed, they couldn't be more comforting in a quietly sophisticated way.

French Curried Potato and Mussel Salad
with Sugar Snap Peas

In French coastal villages of Picardie, Brittany, and Normandy, I guess I've eaten every form of potato salad made with fish, spiny lobster, sweet scallops, tiny shrimp, and even periwinkles imaginable. None is more fixed in memory than one prepared with curried mussels at a small family restaurant in the Charente-Maritime called Le Soubise, just south of La Rochelle. (It's also here that I've had the best *mouclade*—hot curried creamed mussels—I've ever tasted.) I've updated the original recipe by substituting sugar snap peas for ordinary green peas and balsamic vinegar for red wine vinegar, but even with these modifications, I can eat this salad, close my eyes, and see Mme. Benoît tossing all the ingredients in a big glass bowl.

3 pounds red potatoes, peeled and cut into 1-inch cubes	½ tablespoon lemon juice
2 quarts mussels, scrubbed well	1 garlic clove, minced
1 cup dry white wine	1 tablespoon minced fresh chives
2 ounces sugar snap peas, strings removed	½ to 1 teaspoon curry powder, to taste
1½ cups mayonnaise	Salt and freshly ground pepper to taste
½ tablespoon balsamic vinegar	1 tablespoon capers, rinsed

Place the potatoes in a large saucepan with enough salted water to cover. Bring to a boil, reduce the heat to moderate, cover, and cook about 8 minutes, or till just pierceable with a fork. Drain the potatoes, place in a large salad bowl, and let cool.

Place the mussels in a large, heavy pot with the wine. Bring to a boil, reduce the heat to moderate, cover, and steam about 5 minutes, or till they open; discard any that do not. Let the mussels cool; then shell and debeard them and add them to the potatoes.

Bring a small saucepan of salted water to a boil, add the sugar snap peas, and blanch them about 3 minutes, or till just tender. Drain and add them to the potatoes and mussels.

In a bowl, combine the mayonnaise, vinegar, and lemon juice; mix till well blended. Add the garlic, chives, curry powder, and salt and pepper and blend well. Add the dressing and capers to the salad and toss till the ingredients are well coated. Cover the salad and chill 1 hour before serving.

Swedish Potato, Halibut, and Caviar Salad

Actually, I was introduced to this fairly elegant salad not in Sweden but by a portly, red-cheeked Swedish woman who did the cooking at a sauna retreat that some friends and I visited in Turku, Finland, while researching cloud-berries, reindeer meat, *juusto* cheese, a grated parsley root garnish for soup called *finnlendskaia,* and a few other unusual Finnish specialties. It's still a bit embarrassing to remember that I ate the salad dressed in only a towel around my waist, but I was faint from overexposure in the sauna and was told stern-ly by the matronly cook that I should take nourishment and drink plenty of neat, iced vodka as quickly as possible to restore my energy. Ladies in the group wore more discreet bathing suits, and we polished off the delicious salad and God knows how much vodka as if it were our last meal.

3 pounds fingerling potatoes, unpeeled

2 pounds halibut (or codfish) steaks

2 cups full-bodied lager or ale

1½ cups sour cream

½ cup distilled white vinegar

1 small onion, finely chopped

¼ cup finely chopped fresh dill

1 teaspoon salt

Freshly ground pepper to taste

2 to 3 ounces red salmon caviar (preferably fresh)

Leaves of curly endive

Scrub the potatoes lightly and place in a saucepan with enough salted water to cover. Bring to a boil, reduce the heat to moderate, cover, and cook about 10 minutes, or till just pierceable with a fork. Drain the potatoes, cut in half or into quarters, depending on size, and place in a large bowl.

Meanwhile, place the fish steaks in a large skillet or roasting pan and add the beer plus enough water to just cover. Bring to a boil, reduce the heat to moderate, and poach about 5 minutes, or till the halibut steaks are just beginning to flake. Drain the fish on paper towels, break into chunks, and add to the potatoes.

In a small bowl, combine the sour cream, vinegar, onion, dill, salt, and pepper; blend well. Pour the dressing over the potatoes and fish and toss gently till well coated. Add half the caviar and fold in gently. Line the sides of a large salad bowl with the endive, mound the salad in the middle, and scatter the remaining caviar over the top.

Greek Potato Salad with Olives and Feta Cheese

Nothing would do but for two chums and me to take a small boat from Piraeus to the small Greek island of Aegina, then ride smelly donkeys up to a taverna known for its lamb fed partly on wild herbs and pignoli nuts, stuffed with rice and spices, and spit-roasted in a wood-burning oven. We were disappointed to learn that the hot lamb was served only for dinner, but after tasting leftover meat served with this memorable potato salad, we began to understand why the Greeks relish their cold roasted lamb and goat dishes as much as the hot.

3 pounds very small new red potatoes
4 scallions (white and 2 inches of green), coarsely chopped
½ green bell pepper, coarsely chopped
½ medium cucumber, peeled and cut into thin rounds
12 brine-cured Greek olives
1 tablespoon capers, rinsed
½ pound Greek feta cheese
2 tablespoons minced fresh mint
1 tablespoon chopped fresh oregano, or ½ teaspoon dried, crumbled
Freshly ground pepper to taste
½ cup extra-virgin Greek or Italian olive oil
Juice of 1 lemon
Frisée lettuce
12 cherry tomatoes

Scrub the potatoes lightly and place in a saucepan with enough salted water to cover. Bring to a boil, reduce the heat to moderate, cover, and cook about 10 minutes, or till just pierceable with a fork. Drain the potatoes, cut in half or in slices, place in a large mixing bowl, and let cool. Add the scallions, bell pepper, cucumber, olives, capers, feta cheese, mint, oregano, and pepper and toss lightly.

In a small bowl, whisk the olive oil and lemon juice till well blended. Pour over the salad and toss gently but thoroughly to coat the ingredients. Arrange the lettuce leaves around the edges of a large salad bowl, mound the salad in the middle, and arrange the tomatoes along the side.

German Potato, Brisket, and Wild Mushroom Salad with Herb Dressing

SERVES 6

I was again at the Brenners-Park Hotel in Baden-Baden, Germany, to undergo my periodic stress cure and cell therapy and to knock off a few pounds, but after the third day I was starving and couldn't stand it one minute longer. In utter desperation, I headed for an old-fashioned *Stube* I knew in the center of town. All around people were devouring fat wursts, rich *Gulaschsuppe,* and *Kalbskeule,* but when I noticed the mouth-watering potato and meat salad overflowing with fresh *Pfifferlingen* mushrooms at the next table, I anxiously pointed a finger when the waitress arrived and soon commenced to wreck my diet with gusto. Brisket is ideal in this salad, but any cooked beef produces sumptuous results—aided, of course, by plenty of sturdy lager.

3 pounds red potatoes, peeled and cubed

2 cups leftover boiled beef brisket cut into 1-inch cubes

1 cup thinly sliced fresh chanterelle or morel mushrooms

1 large red onion, rings separated

¼ cup chopped fresh parsley leaves

1 tablespoon prepared white horseradish

Salt and freshly ground pepper to taste

¼ cup red wine vinegar

1 tablespoon spicy brown mustard

¾ cup walnut oil

2 tablespoons minced fresh dill, tarragon, and basil

1 tablespoon minced chives

1 small celery root, peeled and cut into matchstick strips

Place the potatoes in a saucepan with enough salted water to cover and bring to a boil. Reduce the heat to moderate, cover, and cook the potatoes about 8 minutes, or till just pierceable with a fork. Drain, place in a large mixing bowl, and let cool. Add the brisket, mushrooms, onion, parsley, and horseradish and toss lightly.

In a small bowl, whisk together the vinegar and mustard till well blended, add the oil, and whisk till well blended. Stir in the mixed herbs and chives. Pour the dressing over the salad and toss thoroughly to coat the ingredients. Arrange the celery root sticks around the edges of a large serving platter and mound the salad in the middle.

Spanish Fried-Potato Salad with Chorizo Sausage and Fava Beans

SERVES 6

In Jerez de la Frontera on Spain's west coast to learn firsthand all about sherry, I was served this hefty salad one day for lunch at the opulent home of a major producer. Fried-potato salad was a first for me, but what really caught my attention were the spicy chorizo sausages and fresh fava beans, both virtually unknown in the United States at the time but now readily available in many markets. If you can't find some variety of waxy yellow potatoes resembling the dense, flavor-packed *patatas* of Spain used in all types of salad and for *tapas,* use either fresh new potatoes or thin-skinned California Long Whites (often called White Roses).

3 pounds waxy yellow potatoes, peeled and thinly sliced

4 tablespoons butter

2 tablespoons Spanish or Italian olive oil

6 to 7 chorizo sausages

1½ cups boiled shelled fava beans

1 red onion, finely chopped

4 pimentos, coarsely chopped

¼ cup sherry vinegar

¼ cup dry white wine

1 tablespoon Dijon mustard

½ cup extra-virgin olive oil

¼ cup finely chopped parsley leaves

Salt and freshly ground pepper to taste

Place the potatoes in a saucepan with enough salted water to cover. Bring to a boil, reduce the heat to moderate, cover, and cook about 5 minutes, or till just tender. Drain the potatoes and pat dry with paper towels.

In a large, heavy skillet, heat the butter and olive oil over moderate heat. Add the potatoes and fry 10 to 15 minutes, or till crusty brown, turning constantly. Transfer the potatoes to paper towels to drain and cool.

Prick the sausages with a steel skewer or small paring knife, place them in a small skillet with enough water to reach halfway up the sides, and bring the water to a steady simmer. Cover and cook the sausages 20 minutes. Drain on paper towels, transfer to a cutting board, and cut into ¼-inch slices.

In a large salad bowl, combine the potatoes, sausage slices, favas, red onion, and pimentos and toss lightly. In a small bowl, whisk together the vinegar, white wine, and mustard. Add the olive oil, parsley, and salt and pepper and whisk till well blended. Pour the dressing over the salad, toss till the ingredients are well coated, and serve either slightly chilled or at room temperature.

Summer Vegetable and Daikon Salad
with Creole Mustard Dressing

SERVES 6

I'm nuts about daikon, a large Japanese radish with crisp, juicy white flesh that's increasingly available in our markets and, shredded or grated raw, is an intriguing complement to any potato and summer vegetable salad. Daikons can be small or enormous with white or black skins that must be peeled. I think the smaller varieties are sweeter and more tender, but what matters most is that the vegetable is firm and unwrinkled. For this salad, I almost demand the creamy texture of Yukon gold potatoes and utterly fresh corn from the field.

3 pounds small Yukon gold potatoes, peeled and cubed

2 to 3 ears fresh corn

1 medium zucchini, scrubbed and cut into thin half rounds

½ cup peeled and shredded raw daikon

12 small ripe cherry tomatoes

4 scallions (white and 2 inches of green), coarsely chopped

1 cup coarsely chopped fresh basil

2 tablespoons red wine vinegar

1½ tablespoons Creole mustard

1 cup hazelnut oil

Salt and freshly ground pepper to taste

Place the potatoes in a saucepan with enough salted water to cover, bring to a boil, reduce the heat to moderate, cover, and cook about 8 minutes, or till just pierceable with a fork. Drain the potatoes and place in a large salad bowl.

Place the corn in a pot with enough water to cover, bring to a boil, remove pot from the heat, cover, and let stand 1 minute. Drain the corn, cut the kernels from the cobs, and add to the potatoes. Add the zucchini, daikon, tomatoes, scallions, and basil and mix lightly.

In a small bowl, combine the vinegar and mustard and whisk till well blended. Add the hazelnut oil and salt and pepper. Whisk till well blended, pour the dressing over the salad, and toss well.

PART FOUR

FOREIGN FORAGING

THE GRATE ONE

ARRIVING BACK FROM THE DAIRY LOCATED ON HIS 625-ACRE estate northwest of Parma, Il Principe Diofebo Meli Lupi de Soragna—astride a sleek, black, custom-made, supercharged motorcycle—roars into the sunny courtyard of his 150-room, fifteenth-century castle, removes his helmet before tightening the knot of his silk necktie, and shaking his aristocratic head in frustration, relates the most recent problems with his two hundred cows. Wandering down the long corridors through the vast chambers of this feudal *rocca* that the prince calls home, I am stunned by the rich wall fabrics and ceiling frescoes, the priceless antique furniture and silver and chandeliers, the Renaissance weapons and armor, and the small private chapel where generations of Meli Lupis are buried. What the *principe* has on his mind, however, is the well-being of his Holstein heifers, the fiber and protein content of the fodder they consume, and the quality of the day's milk supply used in the production of his valuable cheese.

Down in Modena, some forty miles southwest, Marchese Claudio Rangoni Machiavelli, a direct descendant of the notorious Renaissance political author, climbs into his Volvo, opens the massive iron gates of his eighteenth-century palazzo with an electronic hand device, and proceeds to his 600-acre Spilamberto estate, complete with a large manor house, fruit groves, pigpens, and, of course, a cheese dairy. A well-tailored bank administrator, the *marchese,* as is true of the *principe,* is a very serious gentleman farmer who, like his father and grandfather before him, is deeply involved in cheese making. On this particular morning, he is concerned about a computer report indicating that Cow #286 did not consume her ideal quotient of grain overnight. But his real worry is whether a shipment of semen from a prized Canadian bull will arrive in time for certain heifers to be artificially inseminated.

Back on the outskirts of Parma, at a comfortable but unpretentious nineteenth-century villa situated in the middle of a 1,750-acre farm, the Marchesa Anna Maria del Bono Serra busies herself at a stove in the spacious kitchen while we await the arrival of Marchese Gian Domenico Serra, home from a long meeting with cattle breeders. Later on at their dairy, I'm introduced to two of the noble couple's children: thirty-one-year-old son Giovanni, who is assuming some management duties, and thirty-year-old daughter Antonietta, a licensed veterinarian who tends and pampers the two hundred cows. Later, in the cheese house, I meet Daniele Fachhini, the muscular cheese maker who, with the help of an apprentice, lifts from a giant copper cauldron and collects in a hemp sieve cloth a massive white curd, ready to be molded and gradually transformed into cheese.

What these and many other Italian blue bloods in and about Parma have in common with hundreds of more ordinary local inhabitants is the ancient art of producing one of the oldest, finest, and most expensive cheeses in the world: Parmigiano-Reggiano. To compare this genuine, mellow, fragrant, firm, and utterly addictive original with the strong, generic, commercial imitations marketed everywhere as "Parmesan" cheese is no less absurd than equating fresh beluga caviar with processed lumpfish roe. And to witness the glorious cheese's production on venerable estates and modest farms alike is to understand not only what a centuries-old tradition, passed down from father to son, is all about but also why those in all social classes who make the cheese constitute a closely knit regional family whose commercial success is dependent on mutual respect, dedication, and utmost cooperation.

Over the centuries, Parmigiano has been relished by everyone from Boccaccio to Thomas Jefferson. Why the clamor over a cheese that, more often than not, is simply grated or shaved as a seasoning or condiment for soups, pastas, vegetables, sauces, and any number of exotic dishes? First and foremost, Parmigiano-Reggiano is still fully natural and handmade in virtually the same manner and location as it has been since A.D. 1300.

In 1934, producers and dairymen established an official consortium to regulate standards and protect the cheese's integrity, and today real Parmigiano can be made legally only in the provinces of Parma, Reggio-Emilia, and Modena, in small parts of Bologna and Mantua (the Zona Tipica), and only from the region's exceptional milk, fermented whey, rennet, and salt. It cannot be made with additives, preservatives, antifermentation agents, artificial temperature controls, or high-tech automated machinery—

just the designated natural ingredients and the artisan's ancient skills. Over the years, attempts have been made to duplicate Parmigiano-Reggiano with milk from outside the official zone, but it has simply been impossible to produce a cheese that manifests the mystery of the original.

The complexity of Parmigiano-Reggiano reveals its magnitude at the cheese dairy of Marchese Machiavelli 365 days of the year. ("The cows don't stop giving milk just because it's Christmas," he quips.) At 5:30 P.M., thoroughbred Holsteins are herded steadily from feeding stalls to a circular wooden platform in the dairy and are quickly milked. The milk is immediately transported to the cheese house (*casello*), poured into large trays, and left overnight to separate naturally.

Exactly twelve hours later, the cows are milked again while cream from the previous evening's milk is skimmed off for butter. The morning's whole milk is then added to the skimmed milk, after which it is channeled into four huge copper kettles that resemble inverted church bells. Next, fermenting whey is added, heated, and slowly stirred. When the heat is turned off, rennet (a stomach extract from calves) is added. Once the milk in each kettle coagulates into a mammoth curd, it is broken by a large balloonlike whisk into pieces the size of wheat grains. After another heating and stirring, the cooked curds are allowed to settle to the bottom of the cauldron, where they once again compact into a large curd. Then the master cheese maker and his apprentice pull up the curd from the whey with a wooden paddle, wrap it in cheesecloth, and suspend it from a heavy pole to drip. After this mass is cut in half, each section is placed in a large, round wooden mold and left overnight to be repeatedly stenciled "Parmigiano-Reggiano" by a special matrix inserted between the curd and the mold. This stamp also indicates the month and year of production as well as the producer's registered vat number.

The nascent wheels are then transferred to a metal mold for two days to solidify fully before spending the next month suspended in a brine bath. Finally, the cheeses are placed on wooden shelves in a spacious fresh-air storehouse, where they will age for two years or longer, being dusted and turned a few times each month. After the first year, inspectors from the consortium tap each cylindrical seventy-five-pound wheel with a small hammer to detect imperfections (usually holes in the interior). The cheeses that are approved are branded on their vertical sides with the consortium's oval seal and can be legally classified as Parmigiano-Reggiano. Those that are suspect are either rejected altogether (in which case the name is crossed out from the rind) or allowed to be sold strictly for eating, not grating. Wheels intended for export—only cheeses of the best quality—also carry an "Export" brand marking, an assurance that the cheese has been twice tested for quality.

The ingredients, environment, and all the strict regulations are of utmost importance in the production of Parmigiano, but in the long run, what accounts most for the integrity of the cheese are the instincts and skill of the cheese maker. To become a master cheese maker traditionally requires an apprenticeship of at least ten years, after which the artisan can expect to practice the craft literally every day of every year until retirement. Confronted with ever-changing variables in the milk's acid, fat, and protein content, the cheese maker is constantly challenged to match wits with nature, applying principles that both guarantee optimum quality and give each batch of cheese its own distinction.

So prized is a master cheese maker to such producers as Prince Meli Lupi and Marchese Serra that the artisan and his family receive not only a hefty salary, but also a home on the estate, all the butter from the skimmed cream they can sell, and an allotment of pigs fattened on whey and destined to be transformed into prosciutto and the region's other pork delicacies. "No matter how perfect the fodder, the breed of cow, and the milk," emphasizes Marchese Machiavelli, "Parmigiano simply could not exist without our great cheese makers."

Today, there are more than 800 small cheese producers on every social level in the Zona Tipica, representing some 14,000 small dairy farmers. Together they turn out approximately 210 million of those seventy-five-pound wheels of cheese each year. Although such wealthier landowners as Marchese Machiavelli, Senatore Giampaoplo Mora (who represents the province of Parma), Il Principe Corrado Gonzaga di Fontanellato, and Marchese Serra use only the milk from their own dairies to make cheese, most Parmigiano-Reggiano is made by cooperatives, whereby a regulated number of dairymen provide certain cheese makers with a steady supply.

The larger cooperatives are capable of turning out up to thirty wheels per day, while at the smaller, private enterprises, the number rarely exceeds seven or eight. Because it takes two gallons of milk to make one pound of cheese—never mind the enormous cost of aging the giant cylinders for at least two years—profit making from Parmigiano might seem like an exercise in wheel spinning. However, a single wheel of the precious product fetches about $800 on the world market, and, indeed, Parmigiano inventories valued at six and seven figures are often secured in installations managed by banking firms and used as collateral for loans.

Nowhere is the gastronomical value of genuine Parmigiano more apparent than at the homes and restaurants in and about the splendid, and often overlooked, city for which the cheese is named. There, it is grated or shaved over every imaginable soup, vegetable, risotto, and pasta; incorporated into sapid sauces for meats, poultry, vegetables, and even desserts; and used to complement tortes, tarts, stews, stuffings, and truffle dishes. I sample it all, but on no occasion am I so taken as when one homely producer serves simple, perfect pieces of her cheese anointed with a few drops of homemade, thirty-year-old balsamic vinegar, accompanied by fresh, ripe figs and lambrusco, the local sparkling red wine. Only then do I experience the full drama of Parmigiano-Reggiano: its sensual smoothness, its piquant raciness counteracted by the subtly sweet taste of vinegar, its utmost elegance. It is true that small pieces of Parmigiano served plain with apéritifs or cocktails can be eminently appealing, but if you've never savored this sumptuous cheese either with fresh fruit or doused with a little well-aged *aceto balsamico,* you've missed one of the unique pleasures of the Italian table.

As the more health-conscious will happily point out, Parmigiano, made in part from skimmed milk, is among the lowest in cholesterol and saturated fats of all natural cheeses. And because it is so quickly digested and easily assimilated, it is often recommended for children and the elderly, not to mention, of course, those obsessed with their diets. I have no quarrel with that, but, like the noble producers themselves, I hardly need any dietetic justification for indulging when it comes to this cheese.

Since no more than 5 percent of all Parmigiano is exported, Americans can pay perhaps the highest price in the world for this cheese—up to twenty dollars a pound. What, then, should you look for when investing in a chunk, and how is it used to its best advantage?

First, do not purchase those tiny, anemic, usually dried-out wedges of Parmigiano wrapped in plastic and found in most supermarkets, and stay away from cartons of unidentified "imported" cheese that has already been grated. Shop instead at reputable speciality food markets, most of which carry whole or half wheels, and, to safeguard the cheese's flavor and moisture, cut it only when the time comes to fill an order. Be sure that

"Parmigiano-Reggiano" is stenciled in several places on the rind; I try to see if a sectional wheel contains the branded oval "Export," as well as the consortium's mark and the exact vat number of the cheese maker. I also hope to find a production date (both month and year—e.g., "NOV" and "01") indicated in separate boxes. Don't feel squeamish about seeking out this information; since U.S. imports of genuine Parmigiano are limited by law, both imitations and deliberate frauds abound.

If, as is often the case, a fully labeled cheese is not available, learn to study the chunk carefully, remembering that, contrary to what you might be told, overly aged Parmigiano is not necessarily better. Ideally, the cheese reaches its prime at a little over two years, after which it begins to dry out steadily and lose its inimitable aroma and savor. A perfect wedge of cheese has no more than about half an inch of dry area next to the rind and displays a uniform straw-colored hue, ranging from pale beige to shades of yellow. Typically, the body has a flaky structure highlighted by minutely granulated white dots, but, as is true with any artisan product, this texture can vary slightly.

Reject automatically any "Parmigiano" that has holes or other major flaws, and refuse to purchase any that is overly moist and oily, signs that the cheese has been stored at too high a temperature. Above all, don't be shy about requesting a sniff and taste. Classic Parmigiano-Reggiano has a deep, pungent but never acidly sharp aroma. The flavor is full, rich, mellow, and creamy on the tongue, with a lingering, tangy aftertaste that inspires a craving for more. Never has the expression "melts in the mouth" so aptly applied.

Although Parmigiano has a longer shelf life than most natural cheeses, it is senseless and uneconomical to buy more than you might use in a couple of weeks (unless the cheese is sold vacuum-packed). I know people who keep large quantities of Parmigiano refrigerated for months, wrapping it periodically in a moist cheesecloth to prevent excessive drying out, and thus never risk being without when it's needed. Personally, I prefer to purchase relatively small amounts whenever I spot a particularly beautiful wheel, wrapping each chunk tightly in plastic and storing it in the bottom of the refrigerator. Freezing Parmigiano (or any natural cheese) destroys both its texture and flavor, so never—repeat, *never*—commit this all-too-common sin.

Early one evening, after touring still another small dairy operated just outside town by a relatively young couple both of whose families have been cheese producers, I am treated to a "simple" six-course feast prepared by

Angela herself. Several leisurely minutes into the meal, I ask Bruno if he agrees that the nutritional value of Parmigiano is not, indeed, one of its most noteworthy virtues. Casually, he picks up another piece of the zesty cheese, savors it slowly and lovingly before popping a grape into his mouth, takes a long sip of wine, and appears to reflect deeply. "I suppose that's all true," he then mutters almost disinterestedly. "All we say here in Parma is, *'Mangiando il Parmigiano, no ci si ammala mai ne' si invecchia mai'*—you never get sick or grow old eating Parmigiano."

IN SILENCE, IN COOLNESS, AND IN SHADOW

THE PRISTINE HUE OF THE CURED FISH IS NOT EXACTLY PINK OR coral or creamy orange. The surface almost scintillates with a glossy, cool freshness, and should you choose to sniff, there is a suggestion of the crisp salt air of a seaside village on an early spring morning. You taste. The unctuous texture of the fish is like fine velvet, or perhaps satin, or a soft combination of both. The flavor, at first curiously salty and sweet, then perceptibly herbal, then faintly alcoholic, is ultimately and distinctly that of salmon. A squeeze of lemon or grind of pepper adds new depth, and a morsel dipped briefly into the sweet mustard sauce produces a sensory complexity that utterly baffles the palate. You take a bit of whole-grain or flatbread, a forkful of cucumber salad or creamed dill potatoes, a slug of ice-cold aquavit or vodka or frothy ale, then another thin curl of that incredible fish, and, once again, you realize that the unique ritual of eating gravlax remains one of life's supreme gustatory experiences.

It's no secret that the noblest of all fishes is the great salmon found in the waters of Ireland and Scotland, Norway, Nova Scotia, Alaska, and the Pacific Northwest. Today, thanks primarily to the phenomenal success of aquaculture, we can enjoy the privilege of savoring fresh poached, baked, grilled, or smoked salmon not only in restaurants everywhere but in our own homes. What does surprise me a bit, however, in view of our ever-heightening sophistication regarding all foods, is that most Americans are still basically unfamiliar with the ultimate salmon delicacy known in Scandinavia as gravlax (or *gravlaks,* or *gravad lax*).

Prepared by curing impeccably fresh salmon with a mixture of sugar, salt, white pepper, fresh dill weed, and possibly a strong spirit—aquavit or vodka—gravlax is the very essence of salmon, a dish with a pedigree equal to that of fresh beluga caviar or genuine pâté de foie gras, a culinary aristocrat that never fails to add elegance and a touch of mystery to even the most glamorous meal. To me, gravlax suggests the very soul of Scandinavia: the pinkish flesh redolent of the region's icy salt and fresh waters; the pickling salt and sugar reminders of frosty, long winters; the feathery tufts of dill indicative of the summer's brief rebirth; and the pepper and aquavit emblematic of a strong Nordic spirit that has endured for centuries. So closely identified is gravlax with its natural environment, and so respected by the people who relish it most, that certain Norwegians and Swedes are said to insist it should be prepared only "in silence, in coolness, and in shadow."

Although Swedes (like my own grandmother) have laid claim to this sublime delicacy for as long as anyone can remember, the fascinating origins of gravlax are no doubt Norwegian and can be traced back to Viking times. To preserve salmon taken at sea, ninth-century fishermen would first cure their catch, wrap it in dill for flavoring, and bury (or *grave*) the salmon (*laks*). Evidently this primitive means of refrigeration was used for centuries, and as I learned while visiting a salmon farm in the fjords north of Bergen, even today it is not unheard of for a Norwegian housewife to keep her holiday gravlax chilled beneath the snow when space is needed in the kitchen.

In Scandinavia, *gravlax* is still considered a very special, time-consuming, and costly dish, an almost ceremonial preparation to be included on only the most elaborate smorgasbords or served in small quantities on open-face sandwiches (*smörbröd*) or as a light first course in the finest cafés and restaurants. (Two of the most sumptuous gravlax presentations I've witnessed are on the stunning smorgasbords at Stockholm's Operakällen Restaurant and at the Frognerseteren restaurant overlooking Oslo.) Every serious cook, of course, has his or her secret method for success. While it would be nothing less than sacrilege to modify even slightly the age-old basic formula of sugar, salt, pepper, and dill for curing the salmon, there can nevertheless be hours of friendly argument about exactly how salty or sweet genuine gravlax should be, or whether the dill should be chopped or left whole, or why perfect texture and flavor are attained only when the fish is weighted down and marinated for one, two, or three days.

Equally controversial is the question of which other foods and what beverages best complement the luscious gravlax, not to mention how the obligatory mustard-dill sauce should be made. Purists, I discovered, insist that any accompaniment other than a piece of lemon, a few slices of bland flatbread, a thimbleful of sauce, and a shot of good aquavit (or, in Norway, *akkevit*) only destroys the natural flavor of the salmon. Others say that tradition demands that gravlax be consumed with either parslied boiled potatoes or chunky creamed dill potatoes, dark-grain bread, plenty of sauce, and full-bodied beer. More liberated enthusiasts find nothing wrong with the fish being served not only with potatoes and a variety of breads, but also with a tart cucumber salad, a small amount of *cold* scrambled eggs with chives, and both aquavit and beer (the latter to chase the former throughout the repast). And when it gets down to whether a proper mustard-dill sauce should contain one or two types of mustard, a little chopped sweet pickle, and perhaps a spoonful of cream, the discussion can indeed become heated. While in Scandinavia, I ate gravlax in every style and with every accompaniment imaginable, and I loved it all—shamelessly.

The way I choose to serve gravlax in my own home depends strictly on the nature of the meal. More often than not at a formal dinner, for instance, I much prefer to start things off with a few slices of gravlax, thin black bread, and ponies of iced aquavit or vodka than with such overworked temptations as caviar or smoked salmon. Nothing, on the other hand, makes for a more unusual and stylish spring lunch than a plate of chilled gravlax surrounded by cubes of creamed dill potatoes at room temperature, marinated cucumber salad, a few rye crisps, and mustard sauce, all to be washed down with a flinty Chablis or premium ale. And for the most casual lunch or snack with afternoon tea, many times I simply take slices of thin, buttered white or pumpernickel bread, arrange curls of gravlax on top, add lemon juice and a dollop of mustard sauce, and garnish the salmon with chopped fresh dill. Gravlax certainly lends itself to a variety of occasions, and so long as you do nothing to alter radically the unique character of the fish, guests will always know that what they're savoring is indeed something extraordinary.

My recipe for classic gravlax with mustard-dill sauce comes directly from the small island of Sotra in the fjords of western Norway. This is the way the dish has been prepared for generations in the family of Torild Misje, who, with her husband, Jostein, operates one of the largest salmon farms in the country and whose reputation as an accomplished cook is widespread.

I've never tasted finer, more authentic gravlax. Although the curing process does require turning and basting the salmon for a few days, the preparation is simplicity itself. The only unalterable rules are that you must use the freshest top-quality salmon (such as the very best disease-free Norwegian farmed fish, which are distributed with a clip on the gill marked "Superior") and fresh dill (available almost year-round at greengrocers and in better supermarkets). Tightly wrapped in plastic or foil, gravlax keeps well under refrigeration for up to a week.

As our gastronomic enthusiasm in this country assumes momentum, I have no doubt that gravlax will soon, as it should, capture the imagination of more and more professional and amateur chefs alike. In the meantime, I do suggest you waste no time seeking out a beautiful center cut of fresh salmon, then experiment a little with the curing mixture you rub lovingly into the pink flesh, let the fish marinate to mellow perfection, and indulge yourself and your family and friends in a Scandinavian delicacy that is as delectable as it is distinctive.

Gravlax with Mustard-Dill Sauce

SERVES 8

THE GRAVLAX

3 pounds center-cut fresh salmon, cleaned and scaled

3 tablespoons aquavit, cognac, or dry sherry

¼ cup coarse salt

¼ cup granulated sugar

2 tablespoons white peppercorns, crushed

1 large bunch fresh dill weed, chopped

Lemon slices and Boston lettuce for garnish

THE SAUCE

¼ cup Dijon mustard

1 teaspoon dry mustard

2 tablespoons granulated sugar

½ teaspoon salt

2 tablespoons white vinegar

¼ cup vegetable oil

1 tablespoon heavy cream

3 tablespoons finely chopped fresh dill weed

Bone the salmon to produce 2 fillets of equal size, leaving on the skin, and place the fillets skin-side down in a large, shallow glass or stainless steel baking dish. Sprinkle the aquavit evenly over the fillets. In a bowl, combine the salt, sugar, crushed peppercorns, and chopped dill and rub this mixture evenly and thoroughly into the flesh of the salmon. Position one fillet, skin-side up, on top of the other and cover with foil. Place a heavy plate on top of the salmon and weight down by balancing three or four cans of food or soup on the plate. Refrigerate for 2 to 3 days, turning the fish over twice a day, basting the interior and exterior with the accumulated liquid marinade, and replacing the weights.

When the gravlax has cured, remove the fish from its marinade, scrape away most of the curing mixture, and refrigerate till ready to serve. To serve, slice thinly on the bias, curl slices slightly on each plate, garnish plates with lemon slices and lettuce leaves, and present with the mustard-dill sauce on the side.

To make the sauce, combine the mustards, sugar, and salt in a bowl and whisk in the vinegar till well blended. Gradually add the oil, whisking, then whisk in the cream till well blended. Stir in the dill.

SEXY SOUP

TO MY MIND, THERE'S A BIG DIFFERENCE BETWEEN FOODS THAT are sensuous and those that are sexy. Foie gras, truffled eggs, sea urchins, Stilton cheese, and white peaches are indeed sensuous. Fresh morels, oysters, braised beef cheeks, roast grouse, and gumbo are definitely sexy. Some people like to go on about how sexy caviar, lobster, and smoked salmon are. I find nothing sexy about caviar, lobster, and smoked salmon. Sensuous, yes, but certainly not sexy. To be sexy, a food must awaken certain primal instincts, stimulate the id, and inspire a little recklessness. I could name a few dozen more candidates for the sexiest food on earth, but when all is said and done, none has the earthy allure, the wanton charm, and the saturnalian ability to seduce like the onion soups I've encountered in almost every corner of the Western world.

Like the bohemian lady she is, onion soup is neither trendy nor sophisticated, but she is irresistible. Dressed in her golden mantle, she is most often spotted in the dark, romantic Left Bank bistros of Paris, but wrapped in any number of other dazzling guises, she also haunts the *tascas* of Lisbon, the wood-paneled pubs of London and Copenhagen, the smoky *stuben* of Munich, and even the rutty cafés of Buenos Aires. In these places, the nocturnal courtesan is still not only greatly appreciated but respected as the fickle creature she is.

Once was the time in America when she was considered exotic, but eventually she was judged to be superannuated and nudged from her natural milieu in deference to more glamorous but less exciting parvenus. The irony is that, even though we've yet to come up with an original version of the dish, Americans—our most acclaimed chefs included—have never really forsaken onion soup and love nothing more than to benefit from her favors in privacy. Perhaps if they only understood her multifaceted talents better, this beneficent, fun-loving lady of the night could spread even more comfort and joy about this country. And maybe if, for once, they followed her a bit more closely from one locale to the next, she might reclaim her former glory and teach us a few new tricks.

Naturally, each of the provinces in France swears it has developed the ultimate *soupe à l'oignon.* Burgundy's version is topped with a poached egg; Normandy's incorporates clarified fat and calvados; the *tourin* of Bordeaux and Périgord is enriched with egg yolks or tomato purée; the *gratinée lyonnaise* calls for garlic, herbs, and wine vinegar. But I protest. Even though each can be a delectable soup in its own right, none is the authentic, soulful *gratinée* topped with toasted croutons and bubbly with Gruyère cheese. That soup belongs to Paris—to cobblestone streets and smoke-filled *boîtes,* to informal gatherings with old friends, to late-night adventure and youthful romance. It is uncomplicated and incomparable.

Having said that, I can now report that I've enjoyed some onion soups that couldn't have been more unorthodox. In Spain, the soup is often enhanced with almonds; in Portugal, with raisins and sweet wines. In eastern European and Middle Eastern countries, cooks might add such indigenous ingredients as lentils, yogurt, mint, paprika, and any number of spices. In England, soup made with onions and Stilton cheese has become a classic; in Morocco, natives have long thickened their sturdy concoctions with minced chicken or pigeon and chickpeas; and in Denmark and Germany, they add dark beer, mustard, and all types of spices. When found in the United States, most onion soups are mere imitations of the simple French *gratinée,* but move south through the Caribbean and South America, and you find the dish transformed with coconut milk, chili peppers, and exotic local cheeses.

Whether you prefer gentle white onions or more robust yellow ones, a base of white wine or stock to one of water, a soup that's thick and rich to one that's thin and light, what really matters is that the onions you use be of the best possible quality (today's prized sweet Vidalias, Mauis, and Walla Wallas are just too tame for onion soup); that the stock be fresh, the wine first-rate, and the other ingredients never compromised. Above all, when you're adding secondary ingredients and seasonings, remember who the real star is, for nothing is more wretched than an onion soup in which the onions themselves don't shine.

Given proper attention and nurture, this is a soup that prefers to stand alone, although a platter of briny fresh oysters on the half shell with a zesty shallot-and-wine vinegar sauce makes a nice prelude, and a tart green salad, rugged loaf, and lusty red wine are ideal accompaniments. Afterward, depending on your degree of satiety, a selection of cold cuts or hot sausages would be appropriate, followed by nothing more sensual than poached fruit. Simplicity is the key to the onion soup ritual, and never forget that the coquette does not like unnecessary distractions.

Parisian Gratinée

SERVES 6

4 tablespoons butter
1 tablespoon olive oil
8 medium onions (about 2 pounds), thinly sliced
1 garlic clove, minced
⅛ teaspoon sugar
Salt and freshly ground pepper to taste
3 tablespoons all-purpose flour

4 cups beef stock or broth
4 cups water
1 cup dry white wine
½ teaspoon dried thyme, crumbled
Pinch of grated nutmeg
6 toasted rounds of French bread
1 pound Gruyère or Emmenthaler cheese, grated

In a large, heavy casserole, preferably enameled cast-iron, heat the butter and oil over moderate heat. Add the onions and garlic and cook, stirring often, 5 minutes to soften. Add the sugar and salt and pepper, reduce the heat to low, and continue cooking, stirring and scraping the vessel frequently with a wooden spoon, for 20 minutes, or till the onions are slightly browned.

Add the flour, stir, and cook 2 minutes longer. Add 2 cups of the stock, bring to a boil, and stir well. Add the remaining stock, the water, wine, thyme, and nutmeg. Return to a boil, reduce the heat to low, cover, and simmer gently 45 minutes, stirring frequently.

Preheat the oven to 375°F.

Divide the soup evenly among 6 ovenproof soup bowls and place a round of toasted bread in the center of each. Top each bowl with generous sprinklings of cheese, place the bowls on a heavy baking sheet, and bake 15 minutes, or till the cheese is bubbly and beginning to brown.

English Onion and Stilton Soup

SERVES 6

4 tablespoons butter
6 medium onions (about 1½ pounds), minced
3 tablespoons all-purpose flour

5 cups chicken stock or broth
2 cups milk
½ pound Stilton cheese, crumbled
Freshly ground pepper to taste

In a large, heavy saucepan, melt the butter over low heat, add the onions, and cook about 10 minutes, stirring often.

Add the flour, stir, and cook 2 minutes. Add the stock, stir, bring to a boil, reduce the heat to low, and simmer 20 minutes longer or till the onions are very soft. Add the Stilton and stir about 5 minutes or till the cheese is melted. Add the pepper, stir, and ladle into soup bowls.

Danish Creamed Onion and Beer Soup

SERVES 6

6 tablespoons butter
8 medium onions (about 2 pounds), finely chopped
1 garlic clove, minced
1½ cups chicken stock or broth
Two 12-ounce bottles dark beer or ale

1 cup half-and-half
1 teaspoon dry mustard
½ teaspoon ground nutmeg
5 large egg yolks
Salt and freshly ground pepper to taste
Paprika

In a large, heavy saucepan, melt the butter over low heat. Add the onions and garlic and cook about 15 minutes, stirring often. Add the stock, stir, transfer the mixture in batches to a blender, puree, and return to the saucepan. Add the beer, half-and-half, mustard, and nutmeg, bring the mixture to a boil, simmer until reduced by about ½ cup, or till slightly thickened, and remove from the heat.

In a small bowl, whisk the egg yolks lightly. Gradually whisk in about ¼ cup of the hot beer mixture till well blended, then whisk the yolk mixture back into the beer mixture. Cook the soup over low heat till it has the desired consistency, never allowing it to boil. Add the salt and pepper, stir, ladle into soup bowls, and sprinkle a little paprika on top of each portion.

Yugoslavian Dilled Onion Soup

¼ cup lard or vegetable shortening
6 medium onions (about 1½ pounds), thinly sliced
1 small celery rib, minced
1 garlic clove, minced
4 cups light beef stock or broth
3 cups tomato juice

½ teaspoon caraway seeds
1 cup plain yogurt
1½ tablespoons minced fresh dill
⅛ teaspoon cayenne
Salt and freshly ground pepper to taste

In a large, heavy saucepan, melt the lard over low heat. Add the onions, celery, and garlic and cook about 15 minutes, stirring often.

Add the stock, tomato juice, and caraway seeds and bring to a boil. Reduce the heat to low, cover, and simmer 30 minutes. Add the yogurt, dill, cayenne, and salt and pepper, stir well, and ladle into soup bowls.

Portuguese Onion Soup

3 tablespoons butter
2 tablespoons olive oil
8 medium yellow onions (about 2 pounds), thinly sliced
6 whole cloves
1 teaspoon paprika
2 tablespoons golden seedless raisins or dried currants

5 cups rich beef broth
Salt and freshly ground pepper to taste
4 large egg yolks
¼ cup Madeira wine

In a large, heavy casserole, heat the butter and oil over moderate heat. Add the onions and cook about 20 minutes, stirring often, or till onions are softened and slightly browned. Add the cloves, paprika, raisins, and broth. Reduce the heat to low, cover, and simmer 1 hour. Uncover and simmer about ½ hour longer. Season with salt and pepper.

In a small bowl, whisk the egg yolks. Mix a little of the hot broth into the eggs, return mixture to the casserole, and cook about 4 minutes, stirring constantly. Add the Madeira and stir well. Ladle the soup into soup plate or bowls.

South American Onion Soup

2 tablespoons butter
2 tablespoons peanut oil
6 medium onions (about 1½
    pounds), thinly sliced
Pinch of ground allspice
Salt and freshly ground pepper to
    taste

3 tablespoons all-purpose flour
6 cups chicken stock or broth
2 cups coconut milk
Small croutons

In a large, heavy saucepan, heat the butter and oil over moderate heat. Add the onions, allspice, and salt and pepper and cook 15 minutes, stirring often. Add the flour, stir, and cook 2 minutes. Add the stock, stir, bring to a simmer, and cook about 10 minutes or till the onions are very soft.

Add the coconut milk, stir, and simmer about 5 minutes longer. Taste for salt and pepper, ladle into soup bowls, and sprinkle each portion with a few croutons.

RIVIERA SALAD

WHEN OVERWHELMED BY THE CRAVING FOR CERTAIN INDIGE-
nous regional foods that, at least to my way of thinking, can only
be fully appreciated on home territory, I've been known to literally grab a
flight to eat my fill of Dungeness crab and sourdough bread in San
Francisco, fried baby eels in Barcelona, Bresse duckling and St.-Marcellin
cheese in Lyon, and crawfish étouffé in New Orleans. As for my beloved
"composed" salads (I don't eat innocuous tossed green salads), rarely do I
have to venture too far for a decent Cobb, Caesar, or Club when I don't feel
like making them myself, but after a particularly disastrous encounter not
long ago with a so-called *salade niçoise* at a certain cutting-edge restaurant
in New York, I felt compelled to call Delta and book a flight to Nice.

Of course, I hadn't been exactly unaware of how some of our more unruly
chefs were gradually transforming *salade niçoise* into one calamity after the
next. Don't get me wrong: no salad in the world lends itself more to exciting
variations than this eponymous Riviera classic, and, over the years, I myself
have come up with some pretty eclectic versions. But, I ask you, what was I
expected to make of this hodgepodge I found myself gawking at incredulously:
a gigantic designer plate of mesclun and beet leaves topped with seared raw
fresh tuna chunks, thin slices of mushy organic parsnips and jícama, tomato
concassé, split baby ramps, a few bland California black ripe olives, and a single poached quail's egg positioned in the center? No marinated potatoes and
green beans, no scallions, no anchovies, no herbs, no salt and pepper, and I
learned only after asking that the dressing, served with precaution on the
side, was safflower oil and (cheap) balsamic vinegar. The salad was proudly
contemporary, eminently "healthy," and utterly tasteless and absurd. I took
two bites, sent it back, and ordered a burger.

About two weeks later, in contrast, I'm perched blissfully with a couple of old friends at a sunny café at Beaulieu-sur-Mer, east of Nice, overlooking the blue Mediterranean. On the table is one large glass bowl of *salade niçoise,* a baguette of chewy bread and slab of soft, sweet butter, and a bottle of chilled Malherbe rosé wine. As we chat and sip, we pick leisurely at the multicolored salad glistening with fragrant local olive oil. There are big chunks of unctuous, full-flavored canned tuna; small mounds of diced, marinated boiled potatoes with shiny red bell peppers, tender thin green beans, and slivers of crisp artichoke; sweet scallions nudged between wedges of juicy tomatoes and quarters of hard-boiled eggs; briny Niçois cured black olives along with tinned anchovies scattered around the edges; and a scattering of fresh thyme and basil leaves—all nestled in and around the most beautiful young lettuce leaves imaginable.

I toss a piece of tuna to a golden spaniel sitting patiently at my side, then stab a flaky nugget for myself, add a tomato, slice of artichoke, and basil leaf, and allow the contrasting flavors and textures to work their magic in my mouth. Another sip of iced wine, a tear of bread, and I'm ready to finger a few bright olives and gnaw them clean, try the lubricious potatoes with a couple of zesty onions, and maneuver an anchovy around an egg.

When the major components have been consumed, I finish off a few of the pristine lettuce leaves and then take a last crust of bread, swirl it around in the residual oil and juices, and savor the remaining mingled flavors in a single bite. Now time for a creamy apricot tart, then a café filtre and aromatic, delicious Gitane. If complete gustatory and emotional contentment are at all possible, this is as close as I can come to being content.

No matter how much of a cliché it may appear to pretentious foodniks, a great *salade niçoise* is one dish that never fails at once to excite and soothe, to evoke long, lazy lunches, and to transform an otherwise ordinary meal into a bright, often nostalgic, delectably insouciant occasion. What no doubt accounts for the diminished reputation of this sublime Provençal speciality is not only snobbism but the appalling culinary abuse to which the salad has been subjected in recent years. The truth is that *salade niçoise* should be one of the simplest, most appetizing creations ever to evolve in the entire French repertoire. Approach it with high regard and respect for the correct ingredients, colors, and design, and you have a spectacular and irresistible dish; but distort its basic character almost beyond recognition, and you end up with nothing more than a confused mess like what I was forced to confront in that silly New York restaurant.

Not that the salad has not met with heated controversy ever since its initial appearance. While numerous versions of what we call *salade niçoise* (or *la salade nissarda,* in Niçois dialect) have been concocted for ages along the Riviera, food historians, strangely enough, made almost no reference to the salad until well into the nineteenth century. One modern French cookbook author quaintly refers to a certain Tanta Mietta as the peasant *niçoise* who came up with the idea in the eighteenth century, but the first recognizable description of the salad is found in Alexandre Dumas *père's Grande Dictionnaire de Cuisine,* published posthumously in 1872, for what he called a "*salade assaisonnée à la Chaptal.*" By the turn of the century, Escoffier himself (who was born not far from Nice at Villeneuve-Loubet) was proclaiming the merits of a genuine *salade niçoise,* and since then the only French dishes that have inspired more spirited debate are cassoulet and bouillabaisse.

When most of us envision a classic *salade niçoise,* we see a plate or deep glass bowl lined with tender lettuce leaves and filled, in one design or another, with preserved tuna, blanched green beans, diced boiled potatoes, tomato wedges, hard-boiled eggs, black olives, some form of onion, and anchovies, all anointed with a tangy vinaigrette dressing. The ingredients can be mounded separately or arranged in various patterns, or even tossed together. But now the arguments begin.

Purists in Nice insist that an authentic *salade niçoise* is never served in a bowl but rather a round or oval dish; that it should never include green beans, potatoes, or anything cooked, other than perhaps hard-boiled eggs; that only canned tuna, whole black olives, tomato wedges, and other *raw* vegetables are legitimate components; and that the use of vinegar in the dressing is nothing less than sacrilege. Then what, one asks, do they think of their most famous citizen, Monsieur Escoffier, who added to his salad both blanched green bean and marinated potatoes, as well as capers and anchovies? And what about the region's official cookbook spokesman, Jean-Noël Escudier, who hardly considered tuna an essential ingredient, who suggested that the tomatoes and olives be sliced, and who was all for adding vinegar to the olive oil?

In his authoritative *The Food of France,* Waverly Root maintained that no decent *salade niçoise* ever has a leaf of lettuce and that the appropriate dressing is *pissala* (anchovy paste) blended with olive oil. Julia Child, once a part-time resident of Provence, cannot conceive of a salad in which each ingredient is not tossed separately with the dressing and seasonings before being added to the plate. And James Beard, who always considered *salade niçoise* "one of the most inspired salads I know," allowed for experimentation only after his five constants were observed: canned tuna, anchovies, eggs, ripe tomatoes, and cured black olives.

What these experts fail to emphasize, however, and what makes a *salade niçoise* found on the Côte d'Azur superior to even the best we can produce, is the unique distinction and quality of the ingredients. The finest Mediterranean blue-fin tuna and anchovies preserved in top-grade olive oil; local tiny golden new potatoes and fragile lettuces; impeccably fresh thin green beans and tender baby artichokes; farm eggs with rich, deep-orange yolks; small, sweet, thick-skinned tomatoes that grow almost year-round; *niçoise* olives picked right in the area and cured in a minimum of brine— little wonder that, psychological reasons aside, no *salade niçoise* ever tastes exactly like the ones concocted from St. Tropez to Menton. Yes, a few of these ingredients are indeed now available in our best markets; and yes, it's always possible to compose delicious replicas that at least approximate the genuine original. But make no mistake that a classic *salade niçoise* is as basically elusive off home ground as a real Marseille bouillabaisse.

Having eaten the salad in virtually every town on the French Riviera, I don't think there's a style, technique, or ingredient I've missed. I've seen every green from rocket to lamb's lettuce to purslane used to line the plate. I've had blanched chickpeas or fava beans substituted for the traditional green beans, diced turnips or artichoke hearts for the potatoes, and in place of colorful raw bell peppers, strips of pimento or zesty celery knob. I remember a delectable salad composed of nothing but young sorrel leaves, tuna, tomatoes, hearts of palm, radishes, and fresh anchovies. And one of the most compelling dishes at a restaurant in Cagnes-sur-Mer was a *salade niçoise* with all the standard components cushioned on a bed of *champignons à la grecque*. (The one item I've never, ever seen in an authentic *salade niçoise* is the fresh, undercooked tuna that trendsetters like Alice Waters have been using for years and that is still such a rage with so many American chefs.)

All of which is to say that there are many savory ways to produce a *salade niçoise,* so long, that is, as you respect certain principles of flavor, texture, and color and don't deny the salad its basic identity. I have no objection, for example, to highlighting other types of seafood (tinned sardines, marinated shrimp or mussels, even smoked salmon) instead of the classic canned tuna, but to go so far as to prepare this salad (as I've noticed in some of our restaurants) with diced meats or fowl is simply wrong. Likewise, it's quite conceivable to include almost any fresh summer vegetable (sweet corn kernels, marinated baby green peas or sugar snap peas, raw broccoli florets, tiny cherry tomatoes), but to add any fruit to the salad would transform it into another dish altogether. Feel free, also, to experiment with all sorts of fresh herbs in discreet amounts. Remember, though, that the only acceptable dressing for *salade niçoise* is either a plain or herb vinaigrette or simply the finest extra-virgin olive oil.

I do think it's great the way some of our more enterprising and talented chefs have added real depth to composed salads. Daniel Boulud's woodsy pheasant, wild mushroom, artichoke, and walnut salad; Charlie Trotter's squab, water chestnut, butternut squash, preserved ginger, and watercress salad; Thomas Keller's fig, roasted bell pepper, and shaved fennel salad with balsamic glaze; Jeremiah Tower's lobster, radicchio, Belgian endive, and salmon-roe salad with hazelnut oil–tarragon vinaigrette—all are splendid examples of how sophisticated this type of salad has become over the past few years and indicative of its renewed role in our gastronomy. But innovation should never be allowed to smother any worthwhile tradition, *salade niçoise* being a major case in point. Restore it to its former glory, I say. Sure, experiment with the salad sensibly the way I and thousands before me have done, but the main thing is to make it, serve it, demand it in restaurants, and let it work its timeless seduction.

Classic Salade Niçoise

¼ cup wine vinegar

1 teaspoon Dijon mustard

2 garlic cloves, minced

¾ cup extra-virgin French or
  Italian olive oil

3 tablespoons minced fresh herbs:
  tarragon, thyme, chervil,
  parsley

Salt and freshly ground pepper to
  taste

4 to 6 medium new potatoes

¾ pound young, thin green beans,
  trimmed, rinsed, and drained

1 medium head Boston or bibb
  lettuce

Two 6-ounce cans albacore tuna in
  oil, drained

4 ripe medium tomatoes,
  quartered

3 large hard-boiled eggs, quartered

6 to 8 scallions, trimmed

½ cup small cured black olives
  (preferably *niçoise*)

6 to 10 canned anchovy fillets,
  drained

6 fresh basil leaves, torn

In a small bowl, whisk together the vinegar, mustard, and garlic till well blended. Add the olive oil and minced herbs, and whisk till the dressing has emulsified. Season with salt and pepper.

Peel the potatoes, cut into 1-inch dice, and boil in salted water about 5 minutes, or till just tender. Drain well, transfer to a bowl, and toss with about ¼ cup of the dressing.

Drop the beans into boiling water for 5 minutes and drain well. Transfer to a bowl and toss with about 2 tablespoons of the dressing.

Separate, rinse, and dry the lettuce leaves, place in a bowl, and toss lightly with 2 tablespoons of the dressing.

Line the edges of a large oval platter with the lettuce leaves and arrange two mounds of tuna in the center. Mound the potatoes and beans around the tuna, then arrange the tomatoes, eggs, scallions, and olives in an attractive, colorful pattern about the platter. Lay the anchovies over the top, sprinkle on the basil leaves, and pour the remaining dressing all over the ingredients.

Serve the salad at room temperature or slightly chilled.

Salade Niçoise with Sardines, Corn, and Peas

SERVES 6

2 tablespoons wine vinegar

½ teaspoon Dijon mustard

1 garlic clove, minced

½ cup extra-virgin French or
　Italian olive oil

1 tablespoon minced fresh
　rosemary, plus 4 sprigs for
　garnish

Salt and freshly ground pepper to
　taste

6 ears fresh corn, kernels removed

2 pounds fresh green peas, shelled

1 small head leaf lettuce, leaves
　separated, rinsed, and dried

2 medium red onions, sliced into
　thin rings

1 green bell pepper, cored, seeded,
　and sliced into thin rings

Three 4-ounce cans boneless,
　skinless sardines, drained

4 medium ripe tomatoes,
　quartered

3 large hard-boiled eggs, quartered

½ cup small, cured black olives
　(preferably *niçoise*)

2 tablespoons capers

In a small bowl, whisk together the vinegar, mustard, and garlic till well blended. Add the olive oil and minced rosemary, and whisk till the dressing has emulsified. Season with salt and pepper.

In a large bowl, combine the corn kernels, peas, and about half the dressing and toss well.

Line the edges of a large oval platter with the lettuce leaves. Arrange overlapping circles of onions and bell peppers on the lower half of the leaves around the platter. Arrange the sardines in a tight row lengthwise across the center of the platter. Spoon the corn and peas evenly around the sardines and reserve the marinade. Alternate tomato and egg quarters at attractive intervals and scatter capers over the sardines. Arrange the rosemary sprigs around the edges and pour reserved marinade and remaining dressing over all the ingredients.

Serve the salad at room temperature or slightly chilled.

Salade Niçoise with Smoked Salmon, Cucumbers, and Chives

SERVES 4

¼ cup white vinegar

¾ cup extra-virgin French or Italian olive oil

1 tablespoon minced fresh dill weed, plus 4 sprigs for garnish

Salt and freshly ground pepper to taste

2 medium cucumbers, peeled and diced

½ pound fresh mushrooms, quartered

1 small head red-tipped lettuce or 2 medium heads radicchio

½ cup coarsely grated fresh horseradish

¾ pound smoked salmon, thinly sliced

1 pint cherry tomatoes, rinsed

3 large hard-boiled eggs, quartered

½ cup small cured black olives

2 tablespoons minced fresh chives

2 tablespoons capers

In a small bowl, whisk together the vinegar, oil, and minced dill till the dressing has emulsified. Season with salt and pepper.

Place the cucumbers in a large bowl. Add ¼ cup of the dressing, toss, cover with plastic wrap, and let marinate 1 hour. Place the mushrooms in another bowl, add ¼ cup of the dressing, toss, cover with plastic wrap, and let marinate 1 hour.

Line the edges of a large oval platter with the lettuce leaves and sprinkle the horseradish over the center of the platter. Trim the salmon slices, and form them into 2-inch-long rolls, and arrange the rolls attractively in a single row down the center of the platter. Using a slotted spoon, make mounds of cucumbers and mushrooms along both sides of the salmon, separating each with either a cherry tomato or an egg quarter. Arrange the remaining tomatoes and the olives artistically around the platter. Sprinkle on the chives and scatter the capers over the top. Decorate with the dill sprigs and pour on the remaining dressing.

Chill the salad about 30 minutes before serving.

SAVORY PIES

O F ALL THE IMPORTANT DISHES THAT LINK US MOST CLOSELY
with our rich culinary heritage, none has fallen victim more to the
modern appetite for fatuous novelty than the munificent, lusty savory pies
that once glorified (and should be restored to) the American table. This reality first struck home when I ventured to Plimoth Plantation in Plymouth,
Massachusetts, to find out firsthand what sort of food the original Pilgrims
cooked. Take my word, at that "first Thanksgiving" observed in 1621 there
was no stuffed turkey, no cranberry sauce, no creamed onions, no potatoes
in any form, and no pumpkin pie as we know it. What the early housewives
did pride themselves on preparing on a daily basis and for special occasions
were dramatic savory pies bursting with everything from chicken to venison
to cod to parsnips and dried fruits, pies that not only recalled those that had
been baked for centuries back in England but also were easily adapted to
virtually any ingredients found in the New World.

Historically, of course, almost every country in the civilized world has
been able to boast at least one savory pie (the Moroccan *bastilla*, the *pastit-
sio* of Greece and *pasticcio* of Italy, Canada's *tourtière*, Spain's *empanada*,
France's *pounti* and puffy *tourte*). There can be no doubt, however, that the
art of baking pies in simple and elaborate pastries attained its full glory only
in England, and that the tradition has maintained its reputation from the
Middle Ages down to the present day. Originally, this pie was most likely a
sweet and savory concoction perceived as a convenient and stylish way to
eat meat in gravy before the fork became a standard utensil. During
Chaucer's times, there would rarely have been a royal feast that did not
include a multilayered "grete pye" composed of cocks' combs, sweetbreads,

oxtails, oysters, prawns, pine kernels, pickled onions, dried fruits, rosewater, numerous herbs and spices, and heaven knows what else.

By the early seventeenth century—when the Pilgrims embarked—the "raised" savory pie (that is, one prepared using an intricate technique whereby the bottom and sides of the pastry "coffin" were raised free-form by hand) had evolved into a truly ceremonial dish, prompting Elizabeth Ayrton, in her authoritative *The Cookery of England,* to establish that "it was inconceivable [in 1615] that the table at any feast, or any grand occasion, should be without its pies and pastries." Little wonder, then, that meat and seafood pies (both hot and cold) were a major feature in the colonial kitchen and would evolve throughout the next two centuries as a staple in every American household.

In America today, just about the only vestiges of the long and illustrious savory pie custom are the occasional chicken and beef potpies, as well as hearty lobster and clam pies still prepared in certain areas of New England. Travel, however, through the mother country, as I have, and the surprises can be as delectable as they were two hundred years ago. Any pub-restaurant worth its supply of lard, for instance, prides itself on a classic steak and kidney pie, pork and apple pie, and ham and veal pie.

While staying with friends in private homes, the principal treat I've been served for lunch or dinner has been a spicy fish pie, a crusted beef cobbler, or a fidget pie of gammon, onions, and apples. On one special occasion, I enjoyed a Melton Mowbray pork pie flavored with anchovies. At a country inn in Yorkshire, there was a memorable pigeon pie with back bacon, mushrooms, and boiled eggs enveloped in rough puff pastry; at a manor house hotel in Cornwall, a pheasant and chibbles pie in a featherlight suet crust; in Shropshire, an herby rabbit pie studded with diced artichoke bottoms; and at the famous Horn of Plenty restaurant in Devon, without doubt the most elegant salmon pie I've consumed anywhere. Devizes pie, pork crumble, veal flory, stargazey, chicken caudle, rook pie—the intriguing savory pies in Britain are enough to fill a whole cookbook.

Some visitors to London, falsely but forever convinced that English cuisine begins and ends with breakfast, roast beef with Yorkshire pudding, or the Frenchified modern creations of Marco Pierre White and Gordon Ramsey, don't even know to stop by the legendary food halls of Harrod's or Fortnum & Mason to admire the vast displays of savory pies, must less to book a table at any one of the restaurants that feature this great British speciality. They might easily start at, of all improbable places, the Tate Britain Gallery, where each day at least one recreation hailing the pie's lofty role in culinary history is highlighted on the restaurant's acclaimed menu. There's always a nice selection of savory pies at both Maggie Jones and the more innovative Greenhouse, and a visit to Rule's is justified not only by the exemplary steak and kidney pie but by any one of the seasonal meat, game, and seafood pies that might appear on the all-English menu. Those who think that savory pies are not quite distinguished enough to be served in London's more fashionable establishments would do well to witness the periodic seafood beauties at the English House and English Garden, and any day I'd like to sink into a banquette at the Savoy Grill only to do full justice to the famous game pie, a golden pheasant-partridge-venison-oxtail wonder that's been satisfying gastronomes here since World War II.

One of the most appealing aspects of producing a savory pie is the overall simplicity of the undertaking. First you are at complete liberty to bake virtually any type of pie you think you and your guests might prefer, experimenting with all sorts of flavors and textures just as our Pilgrim forebears did. Second, there's scarcely a savory pie that cannot be baked well in advance, covered with foil, allowed to cool overnight or be kept chilled in the refrigerator, then, when ready to serve, finished off with the pastry lid or topping in place.

In the past, the cooked contents of most savory pies were entirely encased in a hand-raised pastry "coffin," and the experienced chefs I met at Plimoth Plantation would never dream of using a deep pie dish or casserole. Today, even in Britain, however, the complex affair of turning out raised pies is left generally to a handful of expert producers nationwide, so unless you're particularly adept at working with suet pastry, I discourage you from attempting to "raise the coffin." Also, given the present-day preference for pies with lighter, thinner, and crisper crusts than those in more expansive times, I recommend that you do not line the vessel with pastry but settle for a flaky top crust adorned with all types of attractive pastry decorations and designs.

Since savory pies are still not on the agenda of most American chefs and food writers out to reinterpret dishes from the past and incorporate them into our new styles of cooking, don't bother to search for exciting recipes in even the most ambitious cookbooks. Eventually, I'm sure, savory pies will reemerge to assume their rightful place in both restaurants and home kitchens. But till then, I suggest you start with one of the pies that were inspired by what the folks at Plimoth Plantation taught me, then proceed to create you own sumptuous shrimp and oyster pie, or chicken and sausage pie with a biscuit crust, or a festive turkey and chestnut cobbler, or a spicy lamb and eggplant pie with a glazed mashed potato topping. The possibilities are endless, and with the staggering array of wonderful meats, seafoods, vegetables, wild mushrooms, and fresh herbs now available all over the country, there's really no reason why "grete pyes" shouldn't play an updated role on the American table that would make our colonial ancestors proud and even envious.

Chicken, Leek, and Oyster Mushroom Potpie

SERVES 8

THE SHORT-CRUST PASTRY
2½ cups all-purpose flour
½ teaspoon salt
⅔ cup chilled lard or vegetable
    shortening
¼ cup ice water

THE FILLING
Two 3½ pound chickens,
    disjointed
2 medium onions, peeled and
    studded with 2 cloves
3 celery ribs (leaves included),
    halved
2 carrots, scraped and quartered

Salt and freshly ground pepper to
    taste
2 quarts chicken stock or broth
5 medium leeks (including 1 inch
    of green leaves), washed
    thoroughly, split in half, and
    cut into 1-inch pieces
8 tablespoons (1 stick) butter
1 cup all-purpose flour
1 cup heavy cream
6 tiny white onions, peeled and
    blanched for 2 minutes
½ pound fresh oyster mushrooms,
    sliced
1 large egg, beaten

To make the pastry, combine the flour, salt, and lard in a chilled mixing bowl and quickly cut the mixture with a pastry cutter till mealy. Stirring with a wooden spoon, gradually add the ice water till a firm ball of dough forms, adding a little more water if necessary. Wrap in plastic and chill.

Place the chickens in a large, heavy pot. Add the onions, celery, carrots, and salt and pepper, then add the stock plus enough water to cover the ingredients. Bring to a boil, reduce the heat to low, cover, and simmer 30 to 40 minutes, or till the chickens are tender.

Transfer the chickens to a working surface, and, when cool enough to handle, remove and discard the skin, pull meat from the bones, and cut into 1½-inch chunks. Strain the stock into a bowl and reserve.

While the chickens are cooking, place the leeks in a large saucepan and add salted water to cover. Bring to a boil, reduce the heat to moderate, simmer partially covered about 15 minutes, or till tender, and drain.

In a large saucepan, melt the butter over moderate heat till just sizzling. Add the flour and stir with a whisk till smooth. Gradually whisk in 5 cups of the reserved stock, increase heat slightly, and cook till the sauce is thickened. Stir in the cream and cook till the sauce is smooth.

Preheat the oven to 400°F.

In a wide 3-quart casserole, combine the chicken, leeks, white onions, and mushrooms; add salt and pepper to taste. Pour on the sauce and stir till the ingredients are well blended. On a lightly floured surface, roll out the chilled dough till slightly wider than the casserole, lift it up on the rolling pin, drape over the casserole, and trim to fit. Crimp the edges to seal, brush dough with the beaten egg, and cut 2 small slashes on the top. Bake 35 to 40 minutes, or till the crust is puffy and golden brown. Serve hot.

Farmhouse Pork and Apple Pie

1 pound slab bacon, cut into 2-
  inch slices about ¼-inch thick
3 medium onions, chopped
3 pounds boneless pork (preferably
  shoulder), trimmed of excess fat
  and cut into small cubes
All-purpose flour, for dusting
3 tart cooking apples, peeled,
  cored, and roughly chopped
1 teaspoon dried sage, crumbled

½ teaspoon grated nutmeg
Salt and freshly ground pepper to
  taste
1 cup cider
4 medium potatoes, peeled and cut
  into chunks
3 tablespoons butter, softened
½ cup milk
2 tablespoons melted butter

In a 3-quart casserole, fry the bacon over moderate heat till cooked through but not fully crisp; drain on paper towels. Add the onions to the casserole, stir till just soft, about 3 minutes; transfer to a plate.

Preheat the oven to 325°F.

Dust the pork cubes lightly with flour. Increase the heat under the casserole, add the pork, and sear 7 to 8 minutes, till browned on all sides; drain fat from the casserole. Return the bacon and onions to the casserole and add the apples, sage, nutmeg, and salt and pepper. Pour in the cider plus enough water just to cover the ingredients. Cover the casserole and bake about 2 hours, or till the pork is very tender.

Meanwhile, boil the potatoes in a saucepan till tender, drain off the water, and toss over low heat till dry. Mash with an electric mixer, add salt and pepper to taste, and gradually beat in the softened butter and the milk till the potatoes are a thick puree.

When the pork is cooked, spread the pureed potatoes over the top thickly and evenly with a spatula and make an attractive design with the tines of a fork. Brush well with the melted butter and bake in upper third of the oven about 15 minutes, or till the potato topping is nicely browned.

Venison Pie with Cornmeal Crust

THE FILLING

3 pounds boneless shoulder of venison, trimmed of excess fat and cut into 1½-inch pieces

1 cup all-purpose flour

½ teaspoon salt

¼ teaspoon freshly ground black pepper

⅛ teaspoon cayenne

5 slices bacon, cut into 1-inch pieces

3 medium onions, chopped

3 celery ribs (leaves included), chopped

3 garlic cloves, minced

Herb bouquet: ½ teaspoon dried thyme, ½ teaspoon dried rosemary, 1 bay leaf, 3 cloves, and 2 sprigs parsley tied in cheesecloth

2 juniper berries, crushed

2½ cups strong beef stock or broth

1 cup Madeira

Salt and freshly ground pepper to taste

3 medium carrots, scraped and cut into 2-inch pieces

½ pound mushrooms, sliced

2 hard-boiled egg yolks, crumbled

8 small red potatoes, peeled and cut in half

THE BATTER

2 cups all-purpose flour

1 cup yellow cornmeal

1½ tablespoons baking powder

1 teaspoon salt

1 cup milk

¼ cup melted vegetable shortening

2 large eggs, beaten

To make the filling, combine the venison with a mix of the flour, salt, pepper, and cayenne in a large bowl and toss lightly with a fork. In a deep, heavy skillet, fry the bacon over moderate heat till almost crisp, about 5 minutes; drain on paper towels. Add the venison to the skillet in batches without crowding and brown on all sides, about 8 minutes. Add the onions, celery, and garlic and stir 3 minutes. Add the herb bouquet, juniper berries, stock, Madeira, and salt and pepper. Bring to a boil, reduce the heat to low, cover, and simmer 1½ hours, or till the meat is tender.

Preheat the oven to 400°F.

While the meat is cooking, make the batter by combining the flour, cornmeal, baking powder, and salt in a large bowl. Add the milk, shortening, and eggs and beat till the batter is thickened.

Transfer the contents of the skillet to a 3-quart casserole. Remove and discard the herb bouquet, add the carrots, mushrooms, egg yolks, and potatoes, and stir to mix. Spoon the batter evenly over the top and bake 25 to 30 minutes, or till the crust is puffy and golden brown.

ITALY'S SWEET "PICK-ME-UP"

JUST TWENTY YEARS AGO, ONLY THOSE AMERICANS WHO HAD traveled widely in northeast Italy had ever heard of, much less tasted, tiramisu. Today, it is as popular a classic dessert in this country as zabaglione or zuppa inglese, so much so that the very respectability of a northern Italian restaurant that doesn't have some version of the rich, elegant, sumptuous *dolce* on its menu might well be questioned. I'd even go so far as to say that, for many, this sinfully creamy confection of layered ladyfingers slathered with custardy mascarpone cheese and sprinkled with cocoa has become the benchmark by which any serious Italian kitchen is judged. And long after such trendy contemporary conceits as pineapple-moscato *semifreddo,* peach-polenta cake, and chocolate tortellini have vaporized in culinary oblivion, I can assure that tiramisu will still be hailed as one of the true and lasting glories of Italian cuisine.

There's only one problem, and that problem is that very few people in this country—including the Italians themselves—actually know what constitutes an authentic tiramisu. I do, and the reason is that, utterly disheartened by the increasing number of dubious permutations I had sampled in even some of our most respected Italian strongholds, I spent a couple of weeks tracking down the genuine confection to its most logical source in Italy and getting the original, correct, irrefutable recipe. Although I had always been under the impression that the dessert originated in Venice, a famous New York restaurateur (from Florence) told me that tiramisu was unquestionably created some thirty years ago in Tuscany. Then an outspoken San Francisco enthusiast (from Milan) said it stemmed from the countryside of Lombardy. And, finally, a reputed food authority (from Turin) insisted it was definitely Piedmontese.

Trying heaven knows how many versions of this airy dessert both here and abroad, I heard all the arguments about whether a correct tiramisu should be made with *savoiardi* (Italian ladyfingers) or *pan di Sapagna* (sponge cake) or even leftover *panettone* (yeast cake). Should the custard contain only the yolks of eggs? Should it contain whipped cream? And what about substituting ricotta cheese mixed with cream for the mascarpone? At one restaurant, the tiramisu was flavored with rum, at another with Madeira, at yet another with amaretto. I had tiramisu with nuts, with chocolate bits, with orange rind, with glazed cherries. A so-called "summer tiramisu," topped with a damp layer of kiwis, strawberries, and heaven knows what else and served at an outdoor café was, well . . . a corruption that was nothing less than bizarre. And, horror of horrors, I was once even subjected to a treasonous dietetic version that contained no cheese whatsoever.

Well, I determined, enough of that nonsense. The truth is that tiramisu, which in Venetian dialect literally means "pick-me-up," is a very old, basically simple dessert that was, indeed, first concocted in or around Venice toward the end of the eighteenth century. Since, in those enlightened days, Venice boasted its fair share of lively brothels, legend has it that the confection was formulated for Casanova and other young rakes craving the energy generated by its high content of caffeine and sugar. A titillating story, to be sure, though hardly sufficient to explain why tiramisu was invented or how it evolved as one of Italy's most beloved examples of that distinctive class of creamy desserts known as *semifreddo.*

A far more likely explanation is that, by the end of the eighteenth century, the coffee, sugar, and cocoa so highly valued by the Venetians had begun arriving in the port in greater quantities. Although these delectable commodities were still relatively expensive, they were at least sufficiently available to be used in cooking. Equally important was a creamy, fresh farm cheese called mascarpone, produced in the Veneto and neighboring Lombardy. A comestible indigenous to the region, it is one that, to this day, cannot be reproduced elsewhere with full success. Most likely, the first tiramisu was little more than mascarpone sprinkled with sugar and powdered cocoa and eaten with strong coffee. By the mid-nineteenth century, however, there were already recipes for a *dolce* in which small biscuits, dipped in coffee, were covered with a sweetened, egg-enriched mascarpone flavored with cocoa and Marsala.

For at least a century, tiramisu flourished as a favorite dessert through-out northeastern Italy, and to hear locals of the Friuli-Venezia Giulia district talk, so common was the dish that a housewife's regular supply of mascarpone was almost as ample as her supply of pasta. Enter Alfredo Beltrame, who, in 1962, opened an elaborate restaurant in Treviso called Ristorante da Alfredo with the express purpose of exposing the traveling public to as many authentic specialities of the Veneto as possible—tiramisu included. So successful was the place that a few years later Beltrame opened a second restaurant in Cortina d'Ampezzo named El Toulà (Cortina dialect for "the farm"), again featuring the cuisine of his native region and highlighting tiramisu as the quintessential example. Then a third El Toulà, and a fourth, till there were no less than fourteen such restaurants spreading the creamy gospel of tiramisu.

"The dish was not well known outside the Veneto until Alfredo popularized it," I was told by the manager of the Relais El Toulà. Of course, every region in Italy began to lay claim to the dessert as chefs altered its original concept and came up with every variation imaginable. Then its fame spread to other countries, and before long you would have thought that tiramisu was invented just thirty years ago in some Tuscan or Bolognese or Ligurian farmhouse."

Now, I'm not about to say that there's no such thing as a fine tiramisu outside the town of Treviso since, after all, the Italians no longer have a monopoly on this yummy confection. But there can be no question that the most sublime, unadulterated, subtle, utterly addictive tiramisu I ever sank a silver spoon into was the one I watched the pastry chef prepare at da Alfredo according to the age-old regional tradition. Thus, as far as I'm concerned, there is no need for further discussion or debate about what is and is not a genuine, perfect tiramisu. From now on, I can easily ignore those who have strange ideas about the dessert's lineage and preparation.

To learn the prized recipe, I literally stood with measuring spoons and cup in hand as the chef and her assistants went about their business, scrupulously watching lest someone try to fudge a few measurements or camouflage a cooking technique. You can't cheat by substituting ingredients, or reducing the quantity of egg yolks and sugar and mascarpone, or adding seemingly innocent personal touches—not, that is, if you want to taste a real tiramisu like the one in Treviso and like the one I now serve proudly. Today, you should have no trouble finding imported Italian *savoiardi* (which are much less absorbent than our flimsy commercial ladyfingers) and acceptable mascarpone in specialty shops and even upscale supermarkets. And should you have no Marsala in the house, buy a bottle.

It has been suggested that, because of its decadent quality, tiramisu is the only Italian dessert that competes successfully with the more sensuous French delicacies. That may be something of an exaggeration, but it's for sure that the hedonistic confection is here to stay in the international repertory, and that, so long as it is prepared properly, this aristocrat of humble origins will never fail in its sweet power to seduce.

Tiramisu da Alfredo

SERVES 8 TO 10

5 cups strong, cold espresso coffee
32 *savoiardi* (Italian ladyfingers)
10 large egg yolks
½ cup plus 2 tablespoons sugar
1 pound mascarpone cheese

2 tablespoons Marsala wine
2 cups heavy cream
3 tablespoons unsweetened cocoa
 powder

Pour the cold coffee into a large pie plate. Dip 16 of the ladyfingers very quickly into the coffee and line the bottom of a 12 x 9 x 2–inch oval dish with the ladyfingers.

In a large mixing bowl, whisk the eggs and sugar till frothy. Add the mascarpone and Marsala and whisk till well blended and smooth. In another bowl, whisk the cream till stiff and fold into the mascarpone mixture till well blended and smooth.

Using a large pastry bag, pipe about half of the mixture over the ladyfingers. Dip the remaining ladyfingers quickly into the coffee, arrange another layer of ladyfingers in an attractive design. Cover with plastic wrap and chill at least 6 hours. (The tiramisu can be frozen up to 2 months.)

When ready to serve, sprinkle the cocoa powder through a fine sieve over the entire surface of the tiramisu. Spoon portions onto individual dessert plates and serve with large spoons.

SEVICHE AND
OTHER COMPOSITIONS
FROM THE SEA

STEPPING OUT ON THE LARGE DECK OF MY HOME IN EAST
Hampton on Long Island, I could already tell at eight in the morning
that the day would be still another July scorcher, relieved only by the blessed
stirring of a distant ocean breeze. Guests were due at noon, and although I
was determined to serve as nice a lunch as possible outdoors, I certainly had
no intention of spending the entire morning over a hot stove producing two
or three complicated dishes that most people really wouldn't enjoy. Salad
seemed to be the most logical solution, but not just an ordinary salad. I was
in the mood, for better or worse, to experiment, but the last thing I wanted was to go shopping again.

Studying what was available in the overpacked refrigerator, I spotted the
two-pound plastic bag of fat shrimp I'd bought the previous afternoon at
Gosman's Dock in Montauk and was planning to freeze in water. There
were fresh peas two friends and I had shelled while having cocktails before
dinner, as well as some beautiful pork fat I'd cut from a loin and reserved to
make a pâté or possibly some good country sausage.

Within minutes, the shrimp, peas, and a few eggs were at the boil, the
pork fat was diced and on its way to being rendered into tasty cracklings,
and some chicory and ripe tomatoes from my own vines were washed and
dried. By ten the work was done, and a few hours later, my guests were
eagerly finishing off the shrimp and pea salad with cracklings, rugged
homemade bread, leftover cold peach cobbler with nectarine sherbet, and a

modest chilled white wine. It was a simple lunch appropriate to the summer occasion, but it was also a lunch that proved to me how truly wonderful a cold seafood salad can be when a little imagination is applied to fine, fresh ingredients.

For a nation reputed to be made up of the most passionate salad lovers in the world, America seems only now to be embracing the kinds of sophisticated composed seafood salads that have helped nourish people of other countries for centuries. Needless to say, there are few of us who over the years haven't thrown together plenty of canned tuna or salmon, shrimp, crabmeat, or lobster with a little chopped celery, pickle, and mayonnaise. And from all my snooping around while traveling, I have every reason to believe that most citizens of Florida have the same fondness for their famous conch and red onions marinated in lime juice as Californians have for that legendary combination of Dungeness crab meat mixed with mayonnaise, heavy cream, chili sauce, onion, and green pepper known as Crab Louis salad. But, generally, that just about summarizes our past involvement with cold seafood served with greens and other ingredients as a main-course salad.

Today, however, with the trend toward lighter meals, not to mention all the regional and global influences, I'm beginning to see all sorts of luscious seafood being utilized in restaurants to produce impressive cold salads that appeal both to the eye and the tastebuds: small fillets of poached tilapia or grouper served chilled with tangy herb sauces atop beds of fancy greens and vegetables; shrimp and tender rings of marinated squid and octopus in a classic Italian *insalata di mare,* as well as any number of cold rice and other grain dishes bursting with clams, snails, and mussels; elegant lobster and crayfish salads enriched with small amounts of foie gras and truffles; and various South American seviches made with every form of marinated seafood from scallops to tile fish to Peruvian bass.

Although cold seafood salads lend themselves to almost limitless experimentation, we might do well, while developing this dimension of our ever-changing gastronomy, to consider first a few foreign examples that today might be termed classic. In Greece, for instance, you find not only myriad salads based on marinated seafood but also such superlatives as molded whitefish roe, cream cheese, and garlic (*taramosalata*); fresh tuna and chickpea salad; tabbouleh with tiny smelts; cold pilaf with octopus; and a lemony lobster salad chock-full of feta cheese, tiny cured black olives, capers, and shredded lettuce. For centuries in Italy, one of the most popular second courses to a festive hot-weather meal has been a pasta or rice salad containing bits of scampi, squid, or clams, and a great regional speciality of Tuscany is a salad made with fresh marinated tuna, creamy white beans, slivers of bell pepper, and rings of crunchy red onion. Herring salad made with curried macaroni is a curious favorite in Denmark, while the inhabitants of Norway love nothing more than leftover halibut or cod mixed with dandelion greens, chopped dill, tomatoes, and a creamy horseradish dressing.

If it's true that in Cuba, Mexico, and many South American countries both seviche (marinated raw fish) and whitefish *escabeche* (marinated cooked fish) salads are veritable staples in the national diet, it's equally true that no traveler to Brazil should have much trouble locating a good rice salad made with crab or salt cod and coconut milk. Salads composed of pickled herring and orange; soused shrimp, cucumber, and peas; and kippers, beets, and apples have been relished in the British Isles since the Middle Ages. Even in France, where the very concept of salad never implied much more than a few greens moistened with vinaigrette or a *salade niçoise* till the practitioners of the nouvelle cuisine introduced all sorts of *salades folles,* there's hardly a modern restaurant that doesn't turn out at least one delicate seafood example featuring smoked salmon, spiny lobster, mussels, sea urchins, and heaven knows what other creatures of the deep.

Culinary inspiration from other countries is no doubt producing some interesting results, but given the rich bounty of fresh seafood, fruits, and vegetables with which we're now blessed, I like to create composed seafood salads that have a distinctive American character. Possibilities might include potato salads that have been given new overtones by the addition of marinated shrimp, salt cod, or some variety of smoked fish; canned tuna salad perked up with fresh fennel, apples, or olives; ordinary coleslaw enriched with smoked salmon, herring, or crabmeat and served as a main course; eggs stuffed with deviled fish salad; half cantaloupes, mangoes, or papayas overflowing with Crabmeat Imperial or Crab Louis; big, ripe heirloom tomatoes stuffed with dilled herring or curried sea bass hash; an interesting combination of lobster and chicken vinaigrette atop sliced avocados and radicchio leaves; and any number of molds made with flecked fish, chopped mollusks, and small whole shellfish. Consideration should also be given to seafood salads based on basmati or wild rice, lentils, and buckwheat groats (kasha), as well as ones that involve arugula, chicory, celeriac, sprouted seeds, sorrel leaves, and dandelion greens.

Although half the pleasure in dealing with these salads is the freedom to experiment with all kinds of familiar and exotic new ingredients, don't get carried away to the point where inspiration begins to negate culinary logic. In the execution of any great salad, careful attention must always be paid to contrasting textures, delicate flavors, the discreet use of herbs, and the style of dressing. It hardly makes much sense, for example, to deemphasize the soft, pristine nature of bay scallops by mixing them with rugged greens, raw vegetables, or overwhelming herbs. On the other hand, nothing seems to complement the assertive flavor of fresh tuna more than zesty red onion and a good handful of mâche.

Combining lobster or shrimp with tangy orange or grapefruit creates marriages that somehow work, but dousing this sweet-sour melange with any other dressing than a plain crème fraîche or sour cream, or adding much more seasoning than a few gratings of fresh pepper or nutmeg, destroys the concept altogether. Salmon has the bold flavor and body to hold its own against such toothsome components as dill, bell pepper, radicchio, and a mustardy oil and lemon dressing; but to pit nuggets of elusive smoked sturgeon and delicate grains of caviar against anything more distracting than bibb lettuce or soft pasta and perhaps a touch of lemon zest would defeat the whole idea. Blending fresh crabmeat and corn at once brings out the sweetness of both ingredients and introduces a fascinating textural contrast, but stuffing pears with something like herring, raspberries, and nuts is a silly conceit that only courts disaster. As always, just use common sense, and before long, you'll grasp why more innovative cold seafood salads are almost destined to contribute considerable new scope to America's gastronomic revolution.

Shrimp and Pea Salad with Cracklings

2 cups diced fresh pork fat

2 pounds fresh medium shrimp

½ lemon

2½ cups cooked fresh or frozen green peas

2 small dill pickles, diced

1 cup mayonnaise

3 tablespoons lemon juice

3 tablespoons heavy cream

1 teaspoon prepared white horseradish

Salt and freshly ground pepper to taste

Leaves of chicory (curly endive)

2 ripe medium tomatoes, quartered

3 large hard-boiled eggs, quartered

In a large, heavy skillet, render the pork fat over moderate heat about 45 minutes, or till crisp and golden brown, watching carefully and reducing the heat if the fat threatens to smoke. Drain the cracklings on paper towels and set aside.

Place the shrimp with the squeezed half-lemon in a pot of tepid salted water to cover, bring to a boil, remove from the heat, let stand 1 minute, then drain. When the shrimp have cooled, shell, devein, and place in a large bowl. Add the cooked peas and diced pickles, mix well, and chill 1 hour.

In a small bowl, whisk together the mayonnaise, lemon juice, heavy cream, horseradish, and salt and pepper. Add the dressing to the shrimp and pea mixture and toss well to coat. Line a large salad bowl with chicory, mound the seafood salad in the middle, sprinkle the cracklings over the top, and garnish the sides with the tomatoes and eggs.

Artichokes Stuffed with Curried Crab and Corn Salad

4 to 6 unblemished artichokes
½ lemon
2 tablespoons olive oil
1 teaspoon lemon juice
1 teaspoon salt
2 cups fresh lump crabmeat
2 cups corn kernels (preferably
fresh), blanched and cooled
½ cup sour cream
1 teaspoon grated onion
½ teaspoon medium-hot curry
powder
Freshly ground pepper

Trim the artichokes: Slice off 1 inch from the tops of the artichokes. Cut the stems to make level bases. Snip tips of the leaves and rub all cut surfaces with lemon to prevent discoloring.

In a large pot, pour 2 inches of water, add the olive oil, lemon juice, and ½ teaspoon of the salt, and bring to a boil. Position the artichokes stem-side down in the liquid, reduce the heat to moderate, cover, and steam 35 to 40 minutes, or till the bases are easily pierced with a knife. Remove and drain the artichokes upside down. Spread the leaves, remove the fuzzy chokes with a spoon and discard, cover the artichokes, and chill thoroughly.

In a large bowl, combine the crabmeat and corn. In a small bowl, combine the sour cream, onion, curry powder, remaining salt, and pepper to taste. Stir till well blended, spoon the dressing over the crabmeat mixture, and toss gently. Fill the artichokes with the seafood salad and serve on colorful plates.

Herbed Tilapia and Rice Salad

1 pound fresh tilapia fillets
½ lemon, seeded
1 sprig fresh dill
3 cups cooked, dry, fluffy rice, cooled
2 tablespoons lemon juice
½ teaspoon Dijon mustard
Salt and freshly ground pepper to taste
¼ cup plus 2 tablespoons extra-virgin olive oil
2 tablespoons mixed finely chopped fresh dill, chervil, and parsley
3 tablespoons plain yogurt
¾ cup chopped green bell pepper
¾ cup chopped cucumber
3 tablespoons chopped scallions
4 to 6 large leaves of radicchio
Cherry tomatoes for garnish

In a large, heavy skillet, poach the tilapia fillets in salted water with the juice of the half lemon and the dill sprig for about 8 minutes, or till almost flaky. Drain, cool, remove any skin, and flake into 1-inch pieces.

Place the rice in a large mixing bowl. In a small bowl, combine the lemon juice, mustard, and salt and pepper; stir till well blended. Add the olive oil in a thick stream, beating well, then stir in the mixed herbs. Pour the dressing over the rice, add the yogurt, and toss well. Add the flaked tilapia, bell pepper, cucumber, and scallions. Stir the mixture till well blended, cover, and chill.

Arrange the radicchio leaves on individual serving plates, place a mound of salad on top of each leaf, and garnish each plate with cherry tomatoes.

Mussel, Eggplant, and Walnut Salad

2 quarts mussels, washed and
  scrubbed thoroughly
1 pound eggplant, peeled and
  diced
½ cup olive oil
½ teaspoon dried thyme, crumbled
¼ teaspoon dried summer savory,
  crumbled
Salt and freshly ground pepper to
  taste

¼ cup lemon juice
1½ teaspoons anchovy paste
1 teaspoon minced garlic
1 medium red onion, minced
½ cup chopped walnuts
4 to 6 leaves bibb lettuce
Minced fresh parsley leaves, for
  garnish

In a large pot, steam the mussels just till the shells open; discard any that do not. Detach the mollusks from their shells, remove and discard the black rims, and chill the mussels in a covered bowl.

Preheat the oven to 400°F.

In a baking dish, combine the eggplant, olive oil, herbs, and salt and pepper; stir to mix. Bake 30 minutes and let cool.

In a large salad bowl, combine the lemon juice, anchovy paste, and garlic and stir till well blended. Add the mussels, eggplant, onion, and walnuts, and toss well. Cover and chill at least 4 hours.

Arrange lettuce leaves on a serving platter, spoon the salad into the middle, and sprinkle with minced parsley.

Lobster and Grapefruit Salad with Crème Fraîche and Nutmeg

1½ pounds cooked lobster meat, cut into bite-size pieces

2 grapefruits

1 cup finely chopped celery

2 scallions (white and 2 inches of the green), finely chopped

2 sprigs parsley leaves, chopped

½ cup crème fraîche or sour cream

Salt to taste

Leaves of Belgian endive

Freshly grated nutmeg

Place the lobster in a large mixing bowl. Peel the grapefruits, removing all the white pith, and cut in half. Cut out the sections with a serrated knife, avoiding as much membrane as possible. Add the grapefruit sections to the lobster along with the celery, scallions, and parsley; toss gently. Add the crème fraîche and salt and toss just enough to bind the ingredients.

Line a serving platter with endive leaves. Arrange the salad in the center and grate nutmeg discreetly over the top.

Seviche Salad with Avocado

1 pound fresh bay scallops

½ pound red snapper or striped bass fillets, cut in ½-inch strips

½ pound boiled fresh medium shrimp, shelled and deveined

¾ cup fresh lime juice

¼ cup sliced scallions

1 medium ripe tomato, cored, seeded, and chopped

2 serrano or other hot green peppers, seeded and cut in thin strips

1 garlic clove, minced

1 tablespoon chopped cilantro

⅓ cup extra-virgin olive oil

Salt and freshly ground pepper to taste

2 ripe avocados, peeled, cut in bite-size pieces, and chilled

Red-leaf lettuce leaves

Place the raw scallops, fish strips, and cooked shrimp in a shallow glass dish. Pour the lime juice over the seafood, cover, and refrigerate 6 hours.

Drain and transfer the seafood to a large glass bowl. Add the scallions, tomato, hot peppers, garlic, cilantro, olive oil, salt and pepper, and avacados. Toss lightly but thoroughly and chill well.

When ready to serve, place a leaf of lettuce in each of 4 to 6 large seashells and mound the seviche on top.

PART FIVE

POTABLE PURSUITS

STALKING THE
GREEN FAIRY

I'VE ALWAYS HAD A PERVERSE PASSION FOR ANY FOOD OR DRINK deemed illegal, dangerous, moderately addictive, or, by virtue of the utter secrecy with which it's produced, covertly mysterious. I've wolfed down in single bites more of those whole, tiny outlawed birds called ortolans in southwest France than I care to count. I've ingested potentially poisonous blowfish in Japan, hallucinatory kif (hashish) candy in Morocco, and enough genuine Peruvian *mate de coca* (coca-laced tea) in one evening to pickle a normal human brain. One reason I board the *QE2* so regularly is to overindulge in fresh beluga caviar cured with sweet borax, long prohibited in this country. Nothing gives me more delight than successfully smuggling past U.S. Customs ample personal supplies of French Époisse, German *Mondseer Sachachtelkäse,* Italian *caprella,* and other forbidden unpasteurized fresh European cheeses. And, yes, I still know where and how to obtain top-quality moonshine whiskey in the mountains of North Carolina.

My obsession with Spain's peerless, long-aged Jabugo ham made from only acorn-fed, black-hooved Iberian pigs is equaled only by my preoccupation with piquant, moldy Italian *pecorino di fosse* ("ditch cheese"), cured uncannily in sealed ruts. And no doubt one reason I so love and respect original Chartreuse elixir is because the rare, sublime French liqueur not only contains 130 sacred flavorings, but is distilled at a whopping 136 proof. If the quasi-secret formula for Coca-Cola (locked in a bank vault for more than a century) did not include a "decocainized flavor essence of the coca leaves," I'm sure I'd probably prefer Pepsi.

My fervor over such items is indeed profound, but of all the illicit, risky, or furtive substances that pass down my seasoned gullet, none excites me more than absinthe, the notorious, putatively treacherous drink distilled with wormwood (or, more precisely, with the plant's derivative essence, called alpha-thujone), considered to be a convulsant poison. That the production of absinthe was taboo in most nations of the Western world since the beginning of the twentieth century is a phenomenon that can only be deplored. That the drink has once again been legalized in every country of the European Union (though certainly not the pietist, ever-vigilant U.S. of A.) is cause for nothing less than exuberant celebration for hedonists everywhere.

Exactly why and how this happened I don't know or care. Of course, Spain has never stopped making genuine absinthe (which explains why, over the years, I've often managed to have a bottle of Absenta on hand). But today all any eager *bon viveur* has to do to witness the spirit's comeback in Europe is to perch in raffish Paris bistros or London clubs, frequent virtually any popular bar in Prague and Copenhagen, or simply step into the wine and liquor shops of Vienna and Lisbon. (Although produced clandestinely by an estimated 130 bootleggers and readily available at the right places, absinthe is still technically banned in Switzerland—home, ironically, of its birth.)

Granted, it's not likely that waiters and bartenders in conservative bluechip European restaurants and hotels are going to begin recommending absinthe over Champagne or cocktails tomorrow (some with whom I've spoken didn't even know that its sale is again legal). But if the drinking habits of roguish sophisticates and younger, adventurous trendsetters serve as a benchmark, I predict that what was once known worldwide as the Green Fairy will resurface to captivate drinkers as much as it did well over a century ago. As one distributor in London told me recently, "When authentic absinthe with wormwood was finally relegalized a few years ago in Europe, the beverage was merely a novelty. Now, the market is becoming explosive."

As for myself, I've been drinking absinthe with impunity for the past forty years. (In that same span of time, curiously enough, I've smoked marijuana only once and never come close to sniffing cocaine or indulging in other heavy drugs, nicotine being my preferred poison.) My first exposure to the light green, extremely potent spirit occurred one frigid evening in France when, while studying at the University of Grenoble, I was offered a glass by a fellow French student who had come upon a contraband bottle of La Bleue in Switzerland and decided to throw an absinthe party for a few friends.

Although I knew absolutely nothing about what we were drinking, the entire ritual intrigued me. First, Yves poured about half an inch of the peridotic liquid into my heavy, stemmed glass goblet, added a couple of ice cubes, then placed a perforated silver spoon holding a lump of sugar over the rim. Ever so slowly, I began to dribble cold water over the sugar into the glass to neutralize the wormwood's bitterness and watched as the absinthe was transformed almost magically into a cloudy, opalescent amalgam called *la louche*. The aroma of the drink was complex but more herbal than anything, and when I took a first sip, the immediate taste sensation was that of licorice, or mint, or a combination of the two. A few more sips of the gentle, bittersweet, refreshing liquid, and I felt a strange warmth throughout my entire body. By the time I finished the glass and began to prepare a second, I was distinctly aware of a mellow exaltation and the urge to carry on serious but quiet conversation. Never once that evening did I feel drugged, or numb, or disoriented, or sluggish as I often had with gin and bourbon and even wine. I had come under the spell of the Green Fairy, and it was a trance that would stay with me for all the years to follow.

Perhaps my most important exposure to absinthe happened about a decade later, when, while visiting the expatriot American food and wine writer Richard Olney at his humble dwelling in Provence north of Toulon, I tasted for the first and last time a genuine Pernod absinthe produced before its abolition in 1915. As it happened, Richard was showing me his wine *cave*, which had literally been excavated from a massive rock formation and contained some of the most impressive French aristocrats I'd ever seen. Surveying the formidable collection of vintage clarets and burgundies, my eyes suddenly caught sight of a single, greenish, half-filled bottle of Pernod Fils with labels that read "Extrait d'Absinthe" and "60°" and featured a signature red-and-white cross. After explaining that the bottle had been discovered in a consignment of sundry old wines and liqueurs he'd bought at auction, Richard suggested we toast our recent slightly outrageous crossing from New York to Cannes with Hermione Gingold aboard the *Michelangelo* by indulging in a little of the illicit absinthe before dinner in her honor. For maybe an hour at sunset, we sat around his exquisite herb garden gazing at olive trees in the distance, smoking Gauloises, and discussing Hermione and food and music and art. But what I remember most—and what haunts me to this day—was that the clean, stimulating, almost mystical absinthe was like none I'd ever tasted—indeed, like *nothing* I'd ever tasted. The drink was unique, I've never had it again, and there hasn't been a time when I've sipped other absinthes or even various pastis that the memory of that blissful Pernod has not been evoked.

While absinthe's essential ingredient, wormwood (*Artemisia absinthium*), was used for over a thousand years as a medicinal tonic, antiseptic, aphrodisiac, vermifuge agent, digestive, and fortifying cure-all for every physical and psychological disorder imaginable, it was not till the late eighteenth century that a certain French doctor called Pierre Ordinaire, fleeing the Revolution, crossed into the Val-de-Travers region of Switzerland and perfected a formula for the high-proof, anise-and-wormwood-flavored elixir that would have such dynamic impact on drinking habits in the nineteenth century. When Dr. Ordinaire died shortly thereafter, the intricate recipe eventually passed into the hands of a Swiss named Henri-Louis Pernod who, to avoid high import taxes at the French border, opened in 1805 the first absinthe distillery in France in the small town of Pontarlier.

Absinthe first gained favor in the 1840s as a fever and dysentery preventative with French troops fighting in Algeria. When thousands of these men returned home with an acquired taste for the sapid, heady, potentially addictive drink, it was only a matter of time before other distilleries opened, both the quality and price of absinthe rose, and a new middle-class social pastime was established throughout France. When, however, phylloxera devastated most of the French vineyards in the 1880s and caused a drastic shortage of wine, the consumption of absinthe skyrocketed as producers began catering more and more to a working-class market and the drink became as popular in bohemian dives and seedy dance halls as in fashionable cafés that lined the grand boulevards of large cities.

Gradually, the French custom spread to New York, Chicago, San Francisco, and other major American cities, but nowhere in the United States was absinthe more popular than in New Orleans, tagged at one point "the absinthe capital of North America." Featuring such local brands as Milky Way, Green Opal, and Legendre (the predecessor of today's wormwood-free Herbsaint), the Absinthe Room in the French Quarter became the epicenter of absinthe culture in the late nineteenth century, boasting elaborate marble fountains on the bar that dripped cold water onto lumps of sugar suspended on perforated spoons over the glasses of absinthe and attracting distinguished visitors like Mark Twain, Theodore Roosevelt, O. Henry, Walt Whitman, and Oscar Wilde. Eventually, the name of the bar was changed to the Absinthe House, and it was here than such famous cocktails as Absinthe Frappé, Absinthe Suissesse, and, most notably, the Sazerac were created. (Today, the Old Absinthe House still exists on the corner of Bourbon and Bienville Streets, the bar adorned with an original green marble absinthe fountain topped with a statue of Napoleon.)

With an alcohol content as high as 72 percent (necessary to keep the various flavoring oils in solution), absinthe not only enjoyed a phenomenal vogue around the world by the late nineteenth century, but, during the Belle Epoque in Paris, gradually became associated primarily with the dissolute, rebellious lives of many great artists and writers who were addicted (sometimes fatally) to the seductive drink. Manet, Van Gogh, Degas, Toulouse-Lautrec, and virtually all the Impressionist painters, Verlaine, Rimbaud, and Oscar Wilde, even Picasso—all succumbed in some degree to the alluring sorcery of the Green Fairy. No matter that for millions who sipped it in moderation during what was called *l'heure verte,* absinthe was little more than a safe, pleasant drink, for by the turn of the century, nothing symbolized decadence, anarchy, and evil more than a glass of green absinthe shimmering on a café table, the drink was increasingly stamped "the French poison," and temperance zealots in both Europe and the United States were voicing their outrage loud and clear.

The truth is that, even at the height of its popularity, when no less than some thirty-six million liters were produced each year, absinthe never made up more than 3 percent of the alcohol drunk in France (wine accounted for about 72 percent). Yet every medical, social, political, civic, economic, and military problem imaginable was attributed to the scourge of this single beverage: alcoholism, suicides, street crime, family murders, insanity, syphilis, sexual sterility, unemployment, strikes, national defense, even anti-Semitism. (Certain obvious comparisons can be made with events leading to Prohibition in America later on, and in our own time, to the rampant crusade to eradicate tobacco products from the face of the earth.)

"Absinthe makes one crazy and criminal, provokes epilepsy and tuberculosis, and has killed thousands of French people," stated one petition drawn up in France by a temperance league in 1907. "It makes a ferocious beast of man, a martyr of women, and a degenerate of the infant. It disorganizes and ruins the family and menaces the future of the country." What's more incredible—if not utterly ludicrous—is that, at the time, the French authorities did not consider the consumption of wine to be a factor in alcoholism, and when it was once again in good supply, even recommended it as a healthy alternative to absinthe and other spirits.

In any case, with the threat of war looming in 1914, exacerbated by the fictive prospect of thousands of debauched, unhealthy, alcohol-addicted troops going into battle, the production, circulation, and sale of absinthe—the perfect sacrificial scapegoat—were finally banned officially in France in early 1915. Already, the drink had been outlawed in Switzerland, Belgium, Holland, and most other European countries, and when it was banished in America, a member of the United States Pure Food Board declared absinthe to be "one of the worst enemies of man, and if we can keep the people of the United States from becoming slaves to this demon, we will do it."

Only in Spain did production continue as usual (Pernod Fils opened an absinthe plant in Tarragona not long after the spirit was banned, and, like other producers, eventually resorted in France to making the innocuous pastis we know today). No doubt the only reason the sale of absinthe was never formally decreed illegal in Britain was because the beverage didn't really catch on socially till a few decades later, when it came to denote nostalgic French decadence and enjoyed a certain wanton popularity with the upper class.

What's most confounding about the history of absinthe is how what was originally perceived to be a clear-cut problem of alcohol abuse quickly shifted emphasis to the wormwood factor—the reason most often indicated now to justify the drink's danger and hence its abolition. It's absolutely true that thujone, the powerful oil derived from wormwood and used to flavor absinthe, is, like so many plant extracts, a psychoactive poison that could be toxic if consumed in inordinate quantities (though there are some modern scientists who disagree strongly with that theory). But, as Barnaby Conrad augers in his definitive book *Absinthe: History in a Bottle,* it's also probable that since a typical quart of genuine absinthe never contained more than about thirty drops of thujone (or absinthol), the culprit that could cause stupefaction, seizures, and even death was hardly this bitter, supposedly deleterious herb but the alcohol itself. "What most people object to in absinthe is mostly the name 'wormwood,' which makes them think that little maggots are eating their brains. . . . But the most harmful ingredient in absinthe is not wormwood or thujone but ethanol, which is drinking alcohol."

Further, nobody in the United States seems to care in the least that wormwood is a flavoring agent in such other popular (and legal) distillates as Bénédictine, Chartreuse, and virtually all vermouths (the word actually derives etymologically from the German *Wermut,* meaning wormwood). Or that, like tincture of cocaine, it is used in numerous salves, ointments, and creams we rub into our bodies every day. Or that it is a major component of sage, tansy, tarragon, and other herbs that flavor the foods we eat. Or that certain species of wormwood and its extracts are readily available in health-food stores and the more urbane head shops.

So what gives here? Before BATF (Bureau of Alcohol, Tobacco, and Firearms Control) approves any liquor formula in the United States, it must be 100 percent wormwood-free. Yet if my detective work is accurate, the suspicious agent is tolerated virtually everywhere—except in the infamous, evil absinthe, which has somehow not wiped out a segment of the European population that has sipped it illegally for the past ninety years, that is once again as lawful as water in most of Europe (and on other continents), and that American connoisseurs would relish sampling and judging for themselves. What national calamity would unfold, one wonders, if it were discovered that the closely guarded formula for Coca-Cola included a trace of perilous, felonious wormwood?

But no matter, for not only are travelers to Europe free again to indulge in this bewitching preprandial tipple, but American consumers curious about the legendary drink can now learn all about ordering bottles ("for personal consumption only," of course) on the Internet by logging onto www.absinthebuyersguide.com, www.absintheonline.com, or www.lafeev-erte.de—at least till the health gestapo in this country decides to clamp down. Officially, the EU authorities specify not only that all French absinthe must carry the declaration "Spiriteaux aux Plantes d'Absinthe" on the label of every bottle, but that no absinthe (French or otherwise) can contain more than ten milligrams per kilogram of thujone. Such safeguards are meant to impress, until, that is, you learn the startling fact that original, pre-ban absinthe—the drink that was allegedly poisoning the brains of millions—rarely contained more than six or seven milligrams of thujone.

It doesn't take a beverage scholar to figure out that scientific facts about absinthe and wormwood have obviously been manipulated and exaggerated over the years for whatever moral or political reasons. Nor do you have to be a wizard to realize that the absinthe being sold today in Paris and London or shipped to consumers in the United States is no more harmful than other spirits with high alcohol content. In truth, the only warning that merits any attention at all is that no genuine absinthe is inexpensive, and that premium brands like Emile Pernot, François Guy, and Absenta Segarra can cost up to one hundred dollars a quart.

Meanwhile, a brand like Versinthe is flying off the shelves of one upscale shop on the rue St.-Honoré in Paris so fast that it's hard to keep the item in stock, while in London, I was told by a representative of the distributor La Bohème UK Ltd. that sales to the United States of Sebor, Hill, Pilsner-Lor, and other absinthes distilled in the Czech Republic have been brisk and are increasing steadily. In the United States, a few curious drinkers are already investigating Logan Fils, Deva Absenta, and Emile Pernot. A group of enthusiasts in Houston have conducted a formal tasting of four authentic absinthes: French Pernod, Oxygénée, Spanish Absenta Serpia, and Absinthe N.S. And rumor even has it that efforts in the spirits industry to have the U.S. ban rescinded or at least modified are gaining momentum every day.

Although champions of absinthe can be found virtually all over America, none is quite as knowledgeable and downright fanatical about the drink as a maverick in (predictably) New Orleans by the name of Ted Breaux. A Harvard graduate and practicing microbiologist, Breaux, at the ripe age of thirty-seven, is not only one of the world's foremost experts on absinthe but an outspoken man on a serious mission. It all began a few years ago when, through an estate sale, he came upon an antique bottle of pre-ban Pernod Fils and, through a process of organoleptic analysis, succeeded in deciphering the spirit's basic composition. Next, he studied another classic absinthe, then others he managed to locate by one means or another.

"The whole project was an incredible revelation," he exclaims with real passion. "I'd tasted any number of cheap modern styles made in the Czech Republic, Spain, and even France, and there simply was no comparison between most of these vulgar adaptations using macerated herbs, added sugars, and artificial colorings and the complex, subtle, wonderful originals."

As to the wormwood factor, Breaux doesn't mince words. "It's insignificant, utterly inconsequential, since there's not and never has been enough thujone in the drink to hurt anyone. That's all one, big, exaggerated, deplorable myth. Contrary to the notion trumpeted for decades, thujone is not absinthe's only—or even primary—active flavoring ingredient. And besides, there are lots of nebulous compounds in absinthium—not to mention in the spirit's other herbal ingredients—that nobody's ever bothered to analyze and that help to explain the conjoined elated-sedative effect that most drinkers experience. In a word, absinthe has gotten a bum rap when it comes to this wormwood nonsense."

So how did Breaux confront the problem? Simple. With typical American entrepreneurship, he made contact with another chemist and absinthe aficionado, a New Orleans native living in Thailand, and the two partners established a foreign company, Jade Liquors Co., Ltd., designed to produce, publicize, and distribute at least six of Breaux's authentic recreations based scrupulously on the pre-ban originals. Breaux won't reveal all the details of the venture, but so far there's already a working facility in Thailand and plans for at least one in France. What he does make crystal clear is his objective.

"Others today seem to want to target youngsters interested only in getting drunk on something exotic. Our market is connoisseurs, serious consumers eager to learn what truly premium absinthe was all about a century ago. We have total control over the harvesting and processing of the herbs we grow, no compromises are made in distillation, and every Jade absinthe is refined, distinctive, and, considering how strong they are, remarkably benign when consumed in moderation."

The first Jade labels to look for in Europe and Asia and on the Internet in the future are Absinthe Pontarlier, Absinthe Edouard, Absinthe Nouvelle-Orleans, and Absinthe Gorgan, each of which will cost about one hundred dollars a bottle. Of course, Americans always run the risk of having a shipment from overseas confiscated by U.S. Customs, but, at least so far, that possibility seems minimal.

The question that is on the mind of anybody who's never indulged in absinthe is what the drink really tastes like and what its effects are. First, if you don't like French Pernod or Ricard, Greek ouzo, and other styles of wormwood-free pastis flavored with star anise and possibly gentian, you may not take to absinthe till after some exposure. If you are a devotee of pastis (as I certainly am when absinthe is out of the question), it's still possible that you'll find the more complex, powerful drink too bitter or alcoholic or slightly antiseptic even when diluted and sweetened with sugar. For some, absinthe is an acquired taste, but one well worth cultivating. Unfortunately, I've by no means had occasion yet to sample that many different absinthes on today's European market or by ordering on the

Internet—but indeed enough to know that the styles can differ radically in color, alcoholic strength, flavor, and overall quality.

Spanish Absenta, for instance, seems to have been dyed an orangish hue and has a mild bitterness and alcohol compared with one of the greenish, more aggressive, and often crude Czech distillates that can reach 140 proof. In Paris, I've sampled the new, vividly green Versinthe against a more traditional emerald-yellow Oxygénée and found the former's highly herbal flavor to be a pale imitation of the bittersweet, elusive, more classic formula redolent of what I assume is mainly wormwood. Most recently, in Vienna, I found a colorful bottle of Austrian Mata Hari that seemed to have just the right pale green hue, but when I tasted the absinthe, I found it curiously much too sweet. Ditto the sickeningly sweet Hill from the Czech Republic.

While I don't object to modern Pernod as vehemently as Ted Breaux, it certainly doesn't have the same sublime mellowness as the absinthe I sipped at Richard Olney's over thirty years ago and seems outclassed today by both François Guy (made, ironically, in Pontarlier) and Emile Pernot. Of course, I still go out of my way to snag an illicit bottle of the same herby, delightfully acerbic, milky-smooth Swiss La Bleue that initiated my mild addiction forty years ago, drinking it preferably on a cold winter evening with reckless friends in a louche French café or bistro with strains of Piaf or Poulenc in the background. As for Absenthe (the spelling is cutely correct), a new domestic "absinthe refined" that is flavored with something supposedly "safe" tagged "southern wormwood" and now available on the American market, all I can say after sipping a glass at a hip, ultra-chic bar in Manhattan that also uses the fake to make a Blue Hemingway, a Flaming Margarita, and any number of other exotic cocktails, is that it is obviously intended for sissy drinkers and can't be taken seriously.

The effects of real absinthe vary from person to person and depend both on the herb concentrations and, as with any high-proof alcoholic drink, on the amount consumed (my limit is usually two glasses containing about half an inch of watered-down absinthe each). Some enthusiasts imagine tropical isles, or calm waters, or the fragrance of summer grass; others report that their eyes are more sensitive to light after a couple of glasses; and still others are convinced that they feel *more* sober the longer they indulge. Personally, I've never experienced any of these particular "secondary-effect" sensations, only a blissfully heightened but lucid mood, the impulse to engage in keen conversation, and a ravenous appetite for good food. One thing is for sure: the psychic and gustatory impact of absinthe is like that of no other alcoholic beverage. Abuse the substance, and the consequences could be virulent; but sip the drink in moderation like a civilized adult, and the rewards are unique and inimitable.

Poets, painters, and composers of the past tried repeatedly to capture the mystery of the Green Fairy, but perhaps none was more baffled by its cryptic spell than the otherwise unflappable Oscar Wilde. "It has no message for me," he first told one famous art expert. "I never could quite accustom myself to absinthe, but it suits my style so well," he then said to another friend, only to profess on a later occasion that "Absinthe has a wonderful color, green. A glass of absinthe is as poetical as anything in the world. What difference is there between a glass of absinthe and a sunset?"

Sazerac Cocktail

I contend that a properly made New Orleans Sazerac—testimony to the nostalgic allure of absinthe and ideally sipped on a shady patio in the city's dignified Garden District—is the most sublime cocktail on earth. Created most likely at the Absinthe Room during the nineteenth century, and originally made with French Sazerac-du-Forge Cognac, absinthe, local Peychaud's bitters, and sugar, the Sazerac is believed by many to be the first American cocktail. At some point in the drink's mysterious history, the brandy was displaced by rye whiskey, then bourbon, and when absinthe was banned, either New Orleans Herbsaint or Pernod was used as a substitute.

While the Sazeracs I've made at home with genuine absinthe are no doubt haunting, I've become so accustomed to the imitation flavorings in New Orleans (first at the Absinthe House and the old Hotel Roosevelt, and later at my beloved Commander's Palace) that I can hardly tell much difference. Here is the one and only way to make a classic Sazerac:

2 ounces premium bourbon
1½ teaspoons superfine sugar
4 dashes Peychaud's bitters
2 dashes Angostura bitters

1 tablespoon absinthe, Pernod, or
 Herbsaint (available in fine
 liquor stores)
1 lemon twist

Fill a cocktail shaker half-full of cracked ice, add the bourbon, sugar, and bitters, and shake well but quickly. Spoon the absinthe into an Old Fashioned glass, spin the glass to coat the sides, then discard the remaining spirit. Strain the shaker contents into the glass, rub the rim with the lemon twist, and drop the twist into the drink.

DEAR LITTLE WATER

THE INITIAL SENSATION IS MYSTERIOUS, SYNESTHETIC, EVEN DELIciously foreboding. Out of the freezer comes a frigid bottle so speckled with crystals that you can hardly read the label, followed by an equally frosted tiny glass that, when touched, sticks momentarily to your fingertips. You pour a neat shot of the viscous, somewhat syrupy spirit, wait a few seconds for the icy haze on the pony to disappear and reveal the liquid's pristine clarity, and gradually begin to detect an aroma that is familiar and complex. You toss back half the glass and wait. Unlike a martini or a manhattan, which quickly inundates the mouth with recognizable tastes before delivering its ultimate jolt, this deceptive drink makes a direct path to the midsection, releasing a warmth that, like a sunrise, extends slowly in all directions. A second swallow and other flavors are released. You take a bite of fresh caviar or smoked salmon or tuna tartare, then pour another glass, and eat, and wonder why it all tastes so good and at what point you should stop. You are indulging, in other words, in one of the most sensuous and gratifying gustatory pastimes of all: the premium vodka experience.

Perhaps I should first confess that, until a few years ago, I always loathed vodka for the simple reason that my lifelong exposure to only the sharp, odorless, tasteless domestic stuff was so offputting that I was never moved to so much as try one of the imports coming on the market. Then, while on a trip to Finland with my dear, eccentric cohort, the food writer Paula Wolfert, to finally eat fresh reindeer tongue and whale meat, roast ptarmigan, buckthorn berries, Janssen's Temptation, Karelian hotpot, baked anchovies and eggs, and a few dozen other exotic items that had been piquing our insatiable curiosity, the epiphanal moment occurred when a waiter in a pretty snazzy restaurant automatically placed a small bottle of

Finlandia vodka encased in ice and two tiny frosted glasses on our table after we ordered different styles of Baltic herring.

"Is this on the house?" Paula whispered to me suspiciously.

"I have no idea, but I hate vodka."

"Me too. Why didn't he offer us the wine list?"

Craving something alcoholic, I eyed the blue-and-white bottle, then noticed that those around us were sipping the same vodka and also drinking beer.

"What the hell," I muttered, reaching for the bottle just before the waiter brought the herring. "Let's try a shot."

Suffice it that after the first few slugs of the icy, thick, aromatic spirit, we were both transformed on the spot, and when we continued to drink the luscious vodka with the herring, then with crayfish, then reindeer chops, then cloudberry crêpes, we were both ecstatic for more reasons than one. The bottle, indeed, was not on the house, but we didn't care. I don't believe we drank a single glass of wine the entire week, only different brands of Scandinavian and Russian vodka and plenty of rich, yeasty Finnish beer—at restaurants, at elaborate lakeside smorgasbords, in saunas, in private homes, everywhere. We were converted forever by what the Finns and Russians lovingly call "dear little water," and today our addiction to premium imported vodkas with certain foods is as passionate as ever.

It's certainly no news that vodka long ago surpassed bourbon, scotch, and gin as the most popular spirit in the United States, but what continues to utterly baffle me are the thousands who still prefer the insipid domestic product (which, by law, can have no "distinctive character, aroma, or taste") to such robust, ethereal imports as Russian Stolichnaya, Swedish Absolut, and Finlandia. To be brutally frank, drinking what is virtually generic vodka distilled in the United States is not unlike drinking most mass-produced American beer (once likened by a particularly candid and horrified friend as "a brew extracted from the wrong end of a donkey").

No doubt a lot has to do with some people's puritanical perception that odorless, tasteless vodka, whether mixed with soda or tonic, used to make Bloody Marys, or combined with dry vermouth for an historically questionable martini, is cleaner, more healthful, and "safer" than the more assertive spirits. Another possible explanation is that much of the vodka-drinking public actually believes that there are radical differences between domestic brands (there aren't, which is why anybody who drinks domestic vodka is a fool to buy anything but the cheapest labels). Maybe the relatively low prices of American vodkas compared with the high tags of imports (thirty to thirty-five dollars a fifth) are a major factor. My guess is that those who've not become captivated by the nuances of Iceland's Elduris and ICY, the illusive flavorings in Polish Wyborowa and Luksusowa, the silky finish of Stolichnaya's noble Cristall, and the way Dutch Oliphant or Vox can enhance any number of foods have simply never been readily exposed to many of the foreign aristocrats.

One thing for certain, however, is that truly serious tipplers are as familiar with and excited by Norwegian Vikin Fjord, Austrian Baczewski, and Danish Frïs as oenophiles are au courant with the latest vintages of cabernet coming out of Napa Valley in California. It's also true that the foreign producers, out to capture an even larger and more sophisticated segment of the drinking public, are not only promoting their better-known upscale brands like never before but introducing any number of new-wave plain and flavored vodkas (Polish Chopin and Belvedere, Swedish Thor's Hammer and Absolut Mandrin, Italian Mezzaluna, French Grey Goose L'Orange, pepper-flavored Stoli Pertsovka) aimed at young and old aficionados alike. It is assumed, I judge, that if the uninitiated have stubbornly resisted just the superior tastes and elegant textures of premium vodkas, perhaps all the romance and innovation implicit in the sleek, colorful new labels will provide the necessary stimulus to nudge consumers to a loftier realm of drinking pleasure. (I had great hopes when I learned that a small distillery in California, Charbay, is now producing fruit-flavored vodkas; but when I sampled two made with trendy blood oranges and Meyer lemons, the citrus was so intense that I thought I was drinking a fortified fruit juice.)

Since the Russians and Poles are forever at odds over who actually invented vodka somewhere between the eighth and fourteenth centuries, it's futile to attempt to trace the spirit's early technological, cultural, or medical history. Nor is it worthwhile trying to verify or negate various (and often absurd) claims: that genuine vodka was originally distilled from potatoes, or rye, or wheat; that vodka is the legitimate national drink of Russia, Poland, or Finland; that the spirit "leaves you breathless"; and that it doesn't give you a hangover.

For centuries, vodka has played a very important role in the social life of almost all Slavic and Scandinavian countries, each of which has developed and perfected its own unique style of spirit and incorporated it into rich gastronomic traditions. Today, Russia and Poland distill not only some of the world's finest clear vodkas, but also delectable ones that are either aged or flavored with everything from honey to wild herbs to rowanberries to buffalo grass. Whereas the tendency in the United States is to blend vodka with any convenient beverage, in northern and eastern European countries the icy spirit is almost never mixed, but consumed neat, often in one gulp, and complemented by some form of food (the copious Russian appetizers known as *zakuski* are considered ideal, as is the fare included on an elaborate Scandinavian smorgasbord).

Until the 1930s, when Vladimir Smirnoff sold to another Russian emigré the rights to reproduce in America his family's age-old formula, vodka had remained virtually unknown in this country. For over a decade, no more than six thousand cases of Smirnoff vodka were sold a year, but once an enterprising tavern keeper in Los Angeles created the Moscow Mule in 1946 by blending vodka with English ginger beer, the day of the Bloody Mary, screwdriver, vodka Collins, and a host of other vodka-based cocktails was not far away. Soon other American companies began to produce their own brands of vodka, often fabricating regal names reminiscent of Mother Russia; federal law spelled out the strict distillation procedure that would guarantee a neutral spirit "without distinctive character, aroma, or taste"—a regulation that exists to this day—and by the mid-seventies, vodka had not only surpassed scotch in sales but was on its way to overtaking bourbon as "the light generation's" favorite spirit. That the premium imports would eventually pose a serious challenge to the domestic industry should have been a foregone conclusion, but only in the last few years has the threat become a vital reality. And today, the vodka wars, as it were, are only intensifying.

Opinions concerning the taste and texture of any spirit (or wine or food) are always highly subjective, and never more so than in the case of imported vodka. Relatively speaking, there are still not that many foreign brands available in the United States. (Russia alone produces more than seventy varieties of plain and flavored vodka, but only a few are imported here), but every year the number of labels multiplies—and from many places besides Russia, Poland, and Scandinavia. So, how are these vodkas different from one another when each is technically no more than a distilled neutral grain spirit, and what determines why one might be considered superior to the next? There is no easy answer. At the Finlandia distillery outside Helsinki that I've visited, for example, you are told that the greatness of its product is due partly to the spring water from a vast underground lake in Rajamaki. At the Stolichnaya plant in Moscow, there's talk about the use of pure, soft glacial water from Russia's Lake Ladoga, and how the vodka is filtered not only through special charcoal to remove impurities but also through native quartz. And at the Absolut distilleries near Ahus, Sweden, a good deal is made of the superiority of the grain found in the south of Sweden.

No doubt such natural geographical phenomena do contribute to the overall quality of the finest imports, but why pursue causes when so much of the pleasure of these pedigreed vodkas lies in the mystery of their body and flavor? I find a world of difference between most imports and the domestics, and often wonder whether, as in the case of genuine French Champagne and Scotch malt whisky, it is simply outside the domain of American producers (or because of ridiculous government regulations) to duplicate those elusive variables that can make the premium spirit so special: the finesse of Absolut Citron, the almost unctuous texture of Finlandia, the earthy taste of Wyborowa, the satiny finish of Denaka and ICY, not to mention all the subtle flavorings that go into the various styles of Stolichnaya.

One is certainly free to guess at the faint taste of honey, caraway, and, possibly, heather in classic, plain Stoli; or the intimations of pine in the English Borzoi; or the flowery nose of Wyborowa; or the high alcohol of one-hundred-proof Absolut and J.A. Baczewski. But what matters most in the long run is quality and enjoyment, and the only way to develop a sense of one brand's appeal over another is to sample as many vodkas as possible, first by themselves then, in traditional fashion, with various foods. (Unfortunately, the one great vodka you can no longer purchase in this country is the legendary Polish Zubrovka flavored with buffalo grass, condemned some time ago by the ever-vigilant and zealous FDA for containing an excess of coumarin, an anticoagulant.)

The only way to drink a premium import is ice-cold from the freezer and poured neat into a small, frosted shot glass. (Vodka does not actually freeze but assumes a beautifully viscous quality when kept in the freezer.) There is no comparison in taste and texture between neat "frozen" vodka and that served at room temperature, on the rocks, or just chilled, and I've been known to call restaurants (and the kitchen aboard *QE2*) in advance and politely demand that a bottle be tucked away for my arrival. An exceptionally smooth, flavorful vodka may tempt you to drink quickly and pour another, but even I have learned that not pacing myself can only result in postprandial havoc. Straight vodka sipped in moderation as a cocktail is harmless, but when it is served at intervals throughout a meal—as I often love to do—it's best to follow the Scandinavian practice of also drinking fine beer or ale.

Along with sauternes and foie gras, Chablis and oysters, and port and Stilton, superlative iced vodka and fresh caviar or smoked salmon are marriages made in heaven. As for other foods enhanced by vodka, almost any of the items found on a traditional smorgasbord—and often served separately as canapés or first courses—would qualify: fish tartares, pickled shrimp or mushrooms, herring in a dozen forms, small cocktail sausages or meatballs, fowl or meats in aspic, liver pâtés, various types of hard-boiled eggs, steak tartare, and assertive cheeses. In Scandinavia and Finland, I've drunk vodka blissfully with everything from grilled perch to *vorshmack* (baked mutton, herring, beef, and onions) to juniper-flavored reindeer to bear steaks with buckthorn berries, and while it's not usually practical here to throw a typical Finnish feast at which mounds of dilled crayfish are washed down with vodka and beer, I've duplicated the ritual successfully by substituting giant shrimp boiled and served in the shell. Also, shots of flavored vodka make an ideal accompaniment to spicy Indian and Asian food. As for Paula Wolfert, I think she'd now drink premium vodka with bouillabaisse and couscous.

I'm certainly not about to suggest that vodka could—or should—replace wine as the ideal companion to most foods, but I am convinced that the imported spirit has the dynamic character to add a whole new dimension to our dining sophistication. Bartenders and restaurateurs across the country assure me that more and more customers are specifying Grey Goose, Absolut, or iced Stoli when vodka cocktails are in order, proof enough that the premiums are here to stay and only gaining in popularity with fastidious boozers. Now, when I begin to notice folks serving frosted shot glasses of Polish Shakespeare with shrimp or crabmeat cocktails at home, and ordering an icy bottle of Finlandia or Wyborowa in restaurants to wash down salmon and tuna tartares and—why not?—sushi, I'll know that the mysterious "dear little water" is finally playing its proper role and deserves a resounding *Za vashe zdorovye!*—"To Your Health!"

BUBBLY I:
PINK EXTRAVAGANCE

MY PRODIGAL TASTES SEEM TO RISE AND DIMINISH QUITE NAT-urally with the aging process, with my level of jadedness and boredom, and, of course, with the status of my bank account. Once was the time when I decked myself out only in English bespoke suits, sported about in a spiffy BMW convertible, and boarded the *QE2* just to devour unlimited mounds of fresh beluga caviar for five straight days and nights. At the moment, howev-er, these lavish habitudes have been toned down considerably in favor of more restrained refinements, the one salient exception being my newly acquired, wanton, and utterly decadent passion for *Champagne rosé*.

Now, before anyone raises a skeptical eyebrow, be assured that I'm not referring to that domestic product known simply as pink champagne, a ghastly plonk that has poisoned the gut of more than one unwary young reveller, and one that should have been banned from the marketplace decades ago. No, indeed. What has captured my most recent attention, and what I predict will eventually be poured at more and more savvy gatherings and truly serious restaurants, is the ultimate and most costly Champagne of France, a frivolous but indescribably sublime pink bubbly that, while still rare, could become the passion of every high-lifer in America.

Already, *Champagne rosé* has taken many of the finest European restau-rants, hotels, and resorts by storm, and, as usual, it's only a matter of time before America catches up on the trend. On the French Riviera, for exam-ple, I've observed sybarites at the luxurious Hôtel du Cap in Antibes gazing over the Mediterranean while sipping Laurent Perrier Brut Rosé instead of the more familiar golden fizz. In Paris, it's no longer unusual for guests at

Taillevent, Guy Savoy, and Lasserre to wash down sinful desserts and cheeses with a few flutes of vintage Moët et Chandon Brut Impérial Rosé or Veuve Clicquot Ponsardin Rosé. At the Ritz in London, the hotel's private De Lahay Rosé Reserve is in such demand in the restaurant and at receptions that management has decided to sell it at the hotel to the public. And at a snazzy dinner I attended in Barcelona, the worldly host thought nothing of serving a robust Heidsiech Monopole Rosé throughout the entire meal. My eyes have been popping, but without doubt the most impressive collection of *Champagnes rosés* (no less than eighteen different labels) I've come across lately is to be found not in France but at the magnificent Nassauer Hof in Wiesbaden, Germany, a hotel where guests can imbibe such snappy pink Champagne cocktails as a Casino Royal, Piroschka, and Admiral's Cup.

Rosé Champagne is by no means a new wine, having been around in Europe since at least the late eighteenth century (the firm of Veuve Clicquot claims it was created by the widow herself) and possibly as far back as the reign of Louis XIV. But it is a style of Champagne that seems always, for whatever reason, to have had its ups and downs in popularity. Long esteemed as a wine of romance and gaiety, it appealed particularly to naughty late Victorians and Edwardians who, to distinguish the pink tipple from its golden cousin, often referred to it as *oeil de perdrix* ("eye of the partridge") and who poured it to toast their courtesans and celebrate their amorous occasions. Since then, the Champagne has moved mysteriously in and out of fashion about every twenty years or so, and although many still associate it with wild and dissolute lifestyles, present-day connoisseurs are, perhaps for the first time, truly beginning to respect it as the very rare, special, and noble wine it is.

And well they should. Genuine French *Champagne rosé* is, and always has been, one of the most difficult and risky wines to make, one that many producers actually shy away from. The Champagne is made from only the finest vintage wines, by one of two legal methods. With the first, classic procedure, the pressed, dark pinot noir grape skins are allowed to remain in contact with the white fermenting juice just long enough to impart a desired color and add a certain depth to the cuvée. With the second, more modern process, a given (and always secret) quantity of superior still red wine from the Champagne district (the red of Bouzy is usually preferred) is poured directly into the champagne bottle before the second fermentation.

Each method is extremely complex and unpredictable, requiring consummate skill on the part of the wine maker.

If the white must remains in contact with purple skins too long, there can emerge, in the words of wine historian Patrick Forbes, "a Champagne that is blue or green or yellow or brown or orange." Add too much or too little still red wine to the cuvée and not only might the color turn out disastrous, but the Champagne might be undrinkable because of unwanted deposits that can form in the bottles. Little wonder that it takes a good deal of commercial courage to make even limited quantities of pink bubbly (*Champagne rosé* accounts for no more than 2 percent of all Champagne production). And since a firm can lose its entire rosé cuvée if color or taste is incorrect, little wonder, too, that this fizz is considerably rarer and more brutally expensive than regular Champagne.

Even with such odds, however, virtually no major French Champagne producer today is about to miss out on a segment of this increasingly lucrative market. (A couple of top California sparkling wine producers have tried making a superior rosé, but I've yet to sample one that can begin to compete with the French aristocrats.) Currently, the French and English still consume the most rosé Champagne, but statistics prove that nowhere does the pink bubble boom show more potential than in the United States, which is the second-largest export market of Champagne in the world. In 1987, only twenty-five thousand cases of rosé were imported into this country; by 2000, the figure had at least doubled. *Champagne rosé* is hardly about to become America's everyday beverage—not when rosé production is still miniscule relative to golden Champagne, and not when a bottle of pretty and racy Dom Pérignon Rosé can command—are you ready?—a cool $350. But the fact is that producers are intensively monitoring our consumption, and that when knowing Americans want to sip something truly special or entertain with real style, they are thinking pink.

At present, there are at least thirty-five different French rosé Champagnes available in our finer wine shops and restaurants, as well as a few acceptable (and less expensive) California rosé sparkling wines, like Schramsberg's vintage Cuvée de Pinot, Domaine Chandon's nonvintage Blanc de Noirs, and Scharffenberger's Brut Rosé. With few exceptions, the pink French cuvées are all basically quite dry (Brut). Color ranges from pale copper (such as '96 Bollinger) to coral ('93 Pol Roger) and brilliant amber ('90 Perrier-Jouët Fleur de Champagne). And the flavor varies, depending on how the bubbly is made, from simple and lean (Gosset Rosé Brut Champagne IV nonvintage) to slightly fruity (Billecart-Salmon Brut nonvintage), rich and toasty ('90 G.H. Mumm Gordon Rosé), or highly intense and complex ('85 Veuve Clicquot Ponsardin).

Prices also vary enormously—repeat, *enormously*—depending on whether the Champagne is vintage (some experts feel that the better, more expensive rosés age beautifully, while others insist that all pink fizz should be drunk while it is young and fresh), and also on availability, consumer demand, and dealer markup. You can find a casual but well-made nonvintage Bouvet Rosé Brut for under $40, but you can also shell out $300 for a vintage Krug and considerably more at a blue-chip New York restaurant for a bottle of '90 Roederer Cristal. I can't emphasize enough (especially after having auctioned some of my own *Champagnes rosés*) that never is the advice of shopping around more wise than when dealing with *Champagne rosé*. In general, though, you should expect to pay at least $40 retail for a bottle of nonvintage Laurent-Perrier, Moët et Chandon, or Taittinger Prestige Rosé; $75–100 for vintage Mumm Cordon Rosé, Bollinger, or Dom Ruinart (the best recent vintage years for rosé Champagne, to my mind, are '90, '93, '96, and '97); and $200–350 for such prestige vintage labels as Taittinger Comtes de Champagne, Krug, Dom Pérignon, Roederer Cristal, or, in magnums, Veuve Clicquot Ponsardin. Be aware, especially, of the hefty markups in restaurants of such status labels as Dom Pérignon and Roederer Cristal, either of which can be tagged at a staggering $425 to $475.

If you decide to take the plunge into the dazzling world of *Champagne rosé*, I do have a few tips on how to deal best with this exquisite wine. I suggest, for instance, that the ideal way to show off the delicate, floral qualities of nonvintage Ayala, Pol Roger, and Billecart-Salmon is by offering any one of them as an apéritif when no appetizers are being passed. If foie gras or smoked salmon is being served, I recommend a crisp but medium-bodied vintage Deutz. If you decide to splurge with an iced tin of fresh caviar, you might as well go all out with flutes of Taittinger Comtes de Champagne or Dom Pérignon. To my mind, almost any Piper-Heidsieck, Simonnet, or Dom Ruinart is perfect for lazy holiday brunches and light midnight suppers. And when it comes to pairing *Champagne rosé* with foods, give me a meaty, round nonvintage Laurent Perrier or plummy '97 Bollinger Grande Année with duck; a toasty Mumm Cordon Rosé or Lanson Brut Rosé (both '96 vintage) with roast turkey, veal, or rabbit; a calm but grapy nonvintage

Perrier-Jouët Blason de France with fish and goat cheese; an intense nonvintage Krug with rich, elegant desserts; and a beautifully clean '93 or '96 Moët et Chandon Brut Impérial with anything.

Whether America will eventually prove to be the largest market yet for a bubbly that continues to evoke wanton lifestyles and hedonistic celebrations remains to be seen. But already the indications are strong. Importers, retailers, and restaurateurs from New York to St. Paul to San Francisco report that percentage growth in rosé Champagne sales has been mounting steadily since the late 1900s. In New York, pink fizz now figures prominently on the wine lists of such boldface bastions as Daniel, the Four Seasons, and Le Cirque 2000; the most recent talk of the town in both upscale wine shops and trendy Eurotrash clubs and lounges is Nicolas Feuillatte's Cuvée Palmes d'Or Rosé '96, tottering at around $170 the bottle (the brand's regular rosé, however, can be priced retail as low as $26); and at a recent small private dinner party attended by the country's three most famous chefs, Daniel Boulud, Rick Moonen, and Thomas Keller, nothing would do to celebrate the august occasion but for the hostess to pop the cork of a splendid Taittinger Rosé. Well-heeled guests at the exclusive Bel Air in Los Angeles have been introduced to the hotel's "Bel Air Rose," concocted from rosé Champagne, Irish liquor, and a peach slice, and I've noticed in Chicago that when certain gents want to impress their kittens at fashionable hotel and wine bars, they often now do it with flutes of vintage Krug, Roëderer Cristal, or Bollinger—all pink.

Someone I know has suggested the perfect scenario for drinking *Champagne rosé:* a pink sunset, a dining table set with a pink table cloth, pink flowers and pink candles, and a menu with an emphasis on lobster, beets, and strawberries. An enticingly decadent idea, I must say, and one that certainly reinforces this bubbly's mischievous and sexy reputation. But, you ask, is it really worth shelling out a hundred or more bucks for any bottle of Champagne (not to mention $35 for a single flute)? To which I respond by asking if the outrageous prices charged for fresh beluga caviar, white truffles, genuine Dover sole, and Château d'Yquem are justified. Today, some people think nothing of plumping down $200 for an Hermès necktie that will probably be spotted in a month, $60,000 for a new SUV that will devalue ten percent the second it's driven off the lot, and $75,000 for a summer rental house in the Hamptons. Reckless spending is only relative to the consummate pleasure we derive from rare exposure to commodities that are truly distinctive and unique, and *Champagne rosé* is near the top of the list. Periodic hedonism is our natural birthright, a privilege that not only contributes to our sophistication but can often be the catalyst that makes life bearable at all.

And this is exactly the way I was thinking when, after learning not long ago that a much-anticipated eating foray in France had to be cancelled, I marched into the Four Seasons restaurant in New York one evening with a beloved date to lick my wounds and, with no hesitation or qualms whatsoever, ordered a $475 bottle of Dom Pérignon Rosé '90. With the tiniest of beads, a texture of velvet on the tongue, and a subtle, fruity savor that was literally indescribable, the wine was liquid perfection. Later, I crassly calculated that every single consoling sip of that lustrous fizz had cost about $10. Please don't ask me if it was worth it.

BUBBLY II:
GRAND SHAM-PAGNES

ALTHOUGH I DO HAVE A TENDENCY TO VACILLATE BETWEEN the sublime and ridiculous in my bibulous habits, when it comes to champagne, my convictions couldn't be stronger or more steadfast. Succinctly, I am resolutely convinced that genuine French Champagne (and not just the rosé-style but all French Champagne) is a wine that can *never* be duplicated outside the blessed area where nature has always played as important a role in its production as the craftsmen who have spent over three hundred years developing the complex, laborious method by which it is made. Nor do I believe that the popularity of French bubbly will ever diminish for those who demand and are willing to pay for the ultimate in drinking.

That said, the time has arrived to address seriously a phenomenon to which I would not have paid the least attention just a couple of decades ago, namely the rise in quality and popularity of other sparkling wines both here and abroad. To be sure, nothing will ever equal a special, costly bottle of Dom Pérignon, Taittinger Comtes de Champagnes, or Bollinger. But it's also true that the scene is rapidly changing as I and other American tipplers become more and more aware of the excellent, reasonably priced sparklers now being produced not only in France outside the official region of Champagne but also in Italy, Spain, Germany, even Argentina, and certainly in the United States. Brut Royale and Boyer Blanc de Blancs from France's Jura and Haute-Savoie departments respectively; Ca' del Bosco from Lombardy and prosecco from the Veneto in Italy; Codorníu, Segura Viudas, and Montserrat from Spain's Penedés region; Kupferberg Riesling Brut from Germany's Rhine Valley; Chandon Argentina; Iron Horse Brut; Roëderer

Estate and Piper Sonoma Blanc de Noir from California—the number of premium sparkling wines now on the market is nothing less than staggering.

I well remember when these exciting, affordable wines either were not available in this country or simply didn't exist, but visit today's wine shops or check out the wine lists in many of our finest restaurants and it becomes pretty obvious that the world of sparklers has already changed forever and will no doubt only intensify as production increases and consumers become more familiar with the labels. Often selling for as little as $10 to $12 a bottle (compared to $40 or $50 for the renowned French Champagne bottles), these alternatives are positioning themselves not only to influence the nation's overall approach to sparkling wines but also to give the producers of French Champagne a good run for their money. And if I and many of my hedonistic cohorts are now drinking and serving the delectable wines on a fairly regular basis, I see no reason why thousands of others shouldn't follow suit.

Exactly how, when, and where this action began is still a question that confounds nearly everyone. As early as 1952, Beaulieu Vineyard in California was making a small amount of sparkling wine in the French manner, and by the early 1970s large-scale efforts were underway by other winemakers on the West Coast to produce premium wines that might one day compete favorably with French Champagne. "You just wait, someday the sparkling wines in this country will be truly great," I recall Jack Davies telling me back in 1972 as we sipped his Schramsberg Blanc de Blancs, one of the first American sparklers made with classic pinot noir and chardonnay grapes and in strict accordance with *la méthode champenoise*—the traditional process of producing Champagne in France by which the wine is subjected to two lengthy, complicated fermentations in the bottle. Then, no sooner had President Nixon elevated the world reputation of California wines by choosing to take Schramsberg rather than French Champagne on his historic trip to China than we all learned that the French house of Moët et Chandon had purchased 1,200 acres in California's Napa Valley with the ultimate intention of producing 200,000 cases of sparkling wine under the Domaine Chandon name. "Since we decided not to put the word 'champagne' on the label, some people thought we were crazy," recalls today's general director of Domaine Chandon. "But every sign pointed to the fact that consumers were starting to think of champagne as a white wine rather than a symbol of celebration, and we're now competing with some of the most prestigious houses in France."

Inspired by Chandon's resounding success, the French firm of Piper-Heidsieck was the first to follow suit in the 1980s by negotiating with wine-master Rodney D. Strong at Sonoma Vineyards and launching Piper-Sonoma. In just two years, the winery was marketing 100,000 cases of lean, austere, beautifully balanced bubbly, and the experts raved. Next, the noble French houses of Roëderer, Deutz, and Lanson began to capitalize on the proven potential of northern California as a prime region, and when I stalked the vineyards once again back in the 1990s, even I was utterly amazed at the progress that has been made in just twenty years.

While the well-known French houses were sinking roots in the California wine country, other producers of sparkling wines wasted little time exploiting what promised to become an explosive market in America, and today sparkling wines register one of the largest percentage gains in growth of any wine category. Thumb through any magazine, wine-store catalog, or serious restaurant wine list and you'll be impressed by such Spanish *cava* wines (made in the traditional French manner) as Freixenet Carta Nevada and Cristalino Brut; Italy's Bolla Brut and elegant proseccos; Germany's Fürst von Metternich Brut and Kupferberg Riesling Brut; and France's Aimé Boucher and Veuve Amiot, from the Loire Valley. Back home in California (where no fewer than thirty wineries now produce *méthode champenoise* sparkling wine), such established makers as Korbel, Domaine Carneros, and Wente are expanding production and upgrading their entire lines at a record-breaking pace, while such smaller still-wine houses as Chateau St. Jean, Iron Horse, Jordon, and Scharffenberger are adding thousands of bottles of French-style bubbly to their inventories.

With no intention of being left behind, Chateau Frank in New York's Finger Lakes district is now producing a very respectable sparkling blanc de blancs; Texas has entered the scene with Cap Rock's crispy vintage brut; and even Virginia's nonvintage Oasis Brut, made according to the classic French method, is edging its way into the highly competitive market. Of the recent foreign imports, Australia's French-style Green Point and Salinger, and New Zealand's Deutz (licensed by the famous French house) are starting to make their mark, and while I doubt that many of the fruity sparklers coming out of Argentina's Río Negro area will put any French or California producers out of business, a wine like Chandon Argentina is definitely one to keep an eye on.

The intricate details involved in the production of sparkling wine (yeast varieties used in fermentation, residual sugar, acid levels) are much too complex to discuss in depth; but suffice it that the quality and character of any bubbly springs largely from the climate and soil conditions of the location where it is made, the grape varieties, the blending skills of the winemaker, and the method itself whereby still wine is magically transformed into a miracle of elegant effervescence. In Europe, the Common Market dictates that only sparkling wines produced in the French district of Champagne can carry the term *Champagne* on the bottle, a ruling that explains why Spanish, Italian, and German sparklers are referred to by such respective appellations as *espumoso, spumante,* and *sekt,* why even French bubbling wines made outside the classified district must be called *vin mousseux,* and why American winemakers should not be using the word *Champagne* on their bottles. The one key expression, however, that any producer can affix to his label is *méthode champenoise* (in Spain, it's usually *cava;* in Italy, *metodo classico*), advertising the fact that, as in Champagne, the wine has undergone a secondary fermentation in the bottle with sugar and yeast to develop fine bubbles, has aged a specified length of time to enhance flavor, has been riddled (or rotated) on a regular basis to accumulate sediment in the neck of the bottle, has been disgorged of sediment, and then finally recorked. The finest sparkling wines are made according to this time-consuming, costly *méthode,* whereas the less distinguished (often wretched) ones are produced in large quantities by either filtering out the sediment from the second fermentation in large tanks (the transfer method)—thus bypassing riddling and disgorging of the original bottles—or simply pouring the primary fermentation in tanks with sugar and yeast, filtering, then bottling (the bulk method).

Processing a given wine in the classic French manner does not guarantee the same quality you expect from genuine Champagne, since so many other important factors are involved. But, generally, there can be no doubt that most of the best sparkling wines employ the *méthode,* and that more and more Americans are demanding wines made in this manner. Such giant domestic producers as E. & J. Gallo (who, under the André label, distribute more low-priced, bulk-method sparkling plonk than all the American *méthode* producers combined), Tott's, and Cook's still account for the vast majority of sparkling wines available in this country, but it's also true that sales are increasing steadily among such high-quality *méthode* wines as Korbel, Domaine Chandon, Schramsberg, Piper-Sonoma, and, indeed, France's Brut Royale and Spain's Codorníu (the largest producer of French-style bubbly in the *world*).

Trends and statistics are intriguing, but in the final analysis the most important question is how these sparklers compare in taste and cost with the aristocratic French bubbly that is so complex and harmonious, so well balanced between acid and sugar, so yeasty clean and refreshing, so subtly elegant—and generally so expensive. American sparkling wines have always tended to be lighter, fruitier, and much less yeasty than the French, while those made in Spain, Italy, and, in some cases, Germany and Austria often have a mild sweetness that can offend purists. Since most vineyard climates in the United States are warmer than that of Champagne (where cool weather almost assures that the grapes never ripen completely), our wines are also usually sweeter and less acidic.

The most serious winemakers, however, are now using classic chardonnay and pinot noir grapes exclusively, following the *méthode champenoise* to the letter, leaving the bottles longer on the yeast, learning how to reduce residual sugar, and, in short, producing some beautiful wines. As quality continues to increase, so do the prices, alas, to such an extent that after record vintages in Champagne, and with the French producers determined to combat the competition, it's often possible to pay more for a bottle of premium California bubbly than for certain discounted labels of genuine Champagne. (Annually, France produces about twenty million cases of *méthode* Champagne, compared with about two million cases in California.)

Where the real value comes today, therefore, is with the growing number of well-made, clean-tasting, comparatively inexpensive sparkling wines being shipped from other areas of France and from Spain, Italy, and other foreign countries. But where does the consumer start? That, of course, depends largely on individual taste, but there are a few generalities I can offer as a result of sampling heaven knows how many brands. Most French *vins mousseux* shipped here, for instance, are produced according to the *méthode,* are lighter and more fruity than Champagne, and can make for delightful casual drinking. They've been turning out fine sparklers made with the chenin blanc grape in the Saumur and Vouvray districts of the Loire Valley for centuries, and for under $20 you can't go wrong with Veuve Amiot, Bouvet Brut, or Aimé Boucher. Brut Royale, made from 100 percent chardonnay grapes in the Jura district, comes as close to genuine Champagne in body and taste as any wine you'll find, and so convincing is the Boyer Brut Blanc de Blancs from Haute-Savoie, selling for about $12 a bottle, that I'd go on record as saying that the bubbly is one of the best sparkling wines of France. Also now available is Alain Longchamps from Alsace and Finette Brut Blanc de Blancs from the Jura, both strikingly reasonable in price and completely acceptable for those occasions (leisure lunches, picnics, and certain large parties) that call for an honest sparkling wine that can be served in quantity without costing a small fortune.

Spain produces enormous amounts of sparkling wine in the Penedés region south of Barcelona, and since the 1990s, the market growth of these delightful wines (most of which are made by the French *méthode*) in the United States has been meteoric. The major reason for their popularity is, of course, the low price made possible by cheap labor in Spain, but by no means does the $10 a bottle necessarily indicate a third-rate product. A warm climate and entirely different grape varieties do give the wines an intensely fruity, almost musty character, but when left on the yeast a long time during the second fermentation (a producer like Montserrat goes so far as to import its strain of yeast from Champagne), the best sparklers attain excellent flavor balance. While not even the most naïve palate is going to mistake a Spanish sparkling wine for the highly refined, delicate French counterpart, only a hardened snob can fail to admit that vintage Castellblanch, Freixenet Carta Nevada, and Cristalino Brut represent some of today's most attractive values in the world of sparkling wines.

More care and precaution should be taken when approaching the sparkling wines of Italy, a country where the business is still in the midst of complex experimentation as more and more producers move closer to the *méthode* and expand their inventories. Of course the Italians have loved their highly perfumed, fruity, well-known Asti spumanti made from the muscat grape as long as the French have sipped their Champagne, and no doubt when you find a clean, dry, zesty Asti like Vibosa or Fontanafredda costing no more than about $12, the rewards are memorable. Unfortunately, there's also plenty of poorly made, cloyingly sweet, cheap Asti on the market, so be careful. The very best spumanti are the French-style bruts of northern Italy, where the preferred chardonnay, pinot noir, and pinot grigio grapes thrive beautifully in a relatively cool climate and chalky soil and yield wines that can be almost as complex as Champagne. For obvious reasons, the brut spumanti cost considerably more to produce than the Asti spumanti made by the transfer method in and about the town of Asti; but $15–20 is hardly an excessive amount to spend for the most distinguished labels. As in America, producers in Italy are determined to make sparkling wines that can compete with French Champagne at considerably lower cost. But until that day arrives, consumers unwilling to pay the price for premium brut spumanti (Ca' del Bosco, possibly the finest of the Italian sparklers, is at least $30 a bottle) would be wise to begin sampling the readily available, inexpensive Asti spumanti of such large producers as Antinori, Bersane, Cinzano, and Gancia.

As the American fascination with sparkling wines intensifies, it seems there's hardly any wine-producing nation that is not out to stake its ground in the international competition. *Sekt,* the generic name for German sparkling wine, is still scarcely known in the United States due to the small amount exported and the absence of publicity, but producers in Germany are also in the process of upgrading their lines and initiating promotional campaigns in hopes of breaking into the lucrative American market. The famous Rheingau estate of Schloss Johannisberg is supremely proud of its premium Fürst von Metternich, made in the French style, and I have noticed more of the house's low-cost *Sekt* obviously positioned to compete with the sensibly priced Spanish and Italian sparklers. The house of Kupferberg in Mainz has garnered a number of gold and silver medals in leading wine competitions with its Riesling Brut and is already distributing in the United States both this prestigious bubbly made with 100 percent riesling grapes and a popular-priced blend called Kupferberg Gold. Also interesting is Prémiat Méthode Champenoise Brut from Transylvania in central Romania. As for the few sparkling wines from Israel, Portugal, and Hungary now available at some locations in the United States, who knows if they will survive alongside the huge quantities of other wines being so heavily promoted, or if one day they too may prove to display the quality of our best sparklers.

In one issue of the authoritative *Wine Spectator* devoted entirely to the ascendancy of sparkling wines on the American market, it was made perfectly clear that sales of genuine Champagne have more than kept pace with those of the aggressive competitors. Great, I say, for who can deny that there's still quite nothing that makes a more definitive, albeit expensive, statement about one's sophistication and esteem for others than a beautiful bottle of real French bubbly? On the other hand, intelligent connoisseurs can't help but heed the writing on the wall: now, for the first time in our history, the shelves are full of excellent sparkling wines that almost everyone can afford to drink on a fairly regular basis, and consumption in upscale bars and restaurants seems to mount every month. (Just recently, a new wine bar called Proseccheria specializing in Italian prosecco opened in Manhattan to great acclaim.) Considering all the energetic efforts within the international industry, it seems pretty obvious that the feisty sparklers can only get better and better, and that the more these wines improve, the more discerning and demanding Americans will become. All we need now to put ample fizz in our lives without wrecking solvency is plenty of curiosity and perhaps a bit less snobbism.

A Selective Guide to the Best Sparkling Wine Producers

USA

California
Domaine Chandon
Roëderer Estate
Domaine Carneros
Iron Horse
Korbel
Gloria Ferrer
Jordan
Mumm Napa Valley
Schramsberg
Pacific Echo
Cordoníu Napa

New York
Chateau Frank
Benmarl

Washington State
Domaine Ste. Michelle

Texas
Cap Rock

Virginia
Oasis

FRANCE
Bouvet
Boyer
Gratien et Meyer
Langlois-Château
Kriter
Aimé Boucher
Veuve Amiot
Brut Royale
Alain Longchamps
Finette

SPAIN
Grand Codorníu
Freixenet Carta Nevada
Cristalino
Segura Viudas
Castellblanch
Montserrat

ITALY
Ca' del Bosco
Vibosa Asti Spumante
Fontanafredda Asti Spumante
Antinori

ITALY (*continued*)
Bolla
Santa Margherita Prosecco
Mionetto Prosecco

GERMANY
Deinhard
Kurt Darting
Schlossgut
Hubert Gänz
Schloss Johannisberg
Kupferberg

AUSTRALIA
Green Point
Salinger

NEW ZEALAND
Deutz

AUSTRIA
Schlumberger

ARGENTINA
Chandon Argentina

LIQUID GOLD

THE COLOR OF THE WINE CAN BE GOLDEN, OR AMBER, OR LIGHT caramel, or translucent mahogany, depending on the years, the decades, or indeed the centuries it has aged. Poured slowly into a small tulip glass, it releases a bouquet suggestive of orange blossoms, or honey, or peaches, or maybe almonds. You sip. The texture is soft on the tongue, creamy, voluptuous, like nectar. The first taste sensation is an electric sweetness that explodes within the mouth, but what emerges after swallowing is a mellifluous, lingering flavor so rich and complex, so incredibly luscious, that every nerve in the body is literally stunned. The overall synesthetic experience of drinking Château d'Yquem is not unlike stroking a pelt of Russian sable or hearing Flagstad sing Isolde. After a singly sensuous quaff, even those who disparage any sweet wine begin to get some idea of why Yquem is the rarest, most mysterious, and costliest white wine on earth.

Produced by the same aristocratic Lur-Saluces family for more than two hundred years in France's Sauternes district south of Bordeaux, Château d'Yquem has been sought by kings, emperors, and potentates; poured at coronations, royal weddings, and state banquets; and immortalized in literature by Proust, Colette, Turgenev, and Mauriac. By 1787, Thomas Jefferson, who was then the U.S. ambassador to the court of Versailles, was ordering Yquem directly from Comte Louis-Amédée de Lur-Saluces, not only for himself, but for President Washington back in the States. Yquem's cellar books record consignments to Napoleon Bonaparte, to the czars of Russia, and to King Alfonso XIII of Spain.

In more recent times, not only has the liquid gold been poured at various state occasions in the White House; it's also the perennial favorite of Prince Charles when he entertains in the royal manner. Serious wine collectors the world over (yours truly included) think nothing of paying up to $300 a bottle for the most recent releases of Yquem. It's not unusual for a prestigious restaurant like the Four Seasons in New York to charge $350 for *half* a bottle of the renowned '88 vintage, and not long ago at Morrell & Co. in New York, one gold-plated aficionado placed an order for three cases of the '83 vintage of Yquem and six cases of the '86, and thereupon scribbled out a check for $24,300. It's always crude and unsavory to measure quality in terms of cost, but if ever a commodity justified its high price by virtue of its rarity and true value, that commodity is Château d'Yquem.

Unlike the arid Médoc region to the north of Bordeaux, known for its legendary dry clarets, Sauternes is a relatively verdant grape-growing region blessed with some of the most beautiful topography in all of France. It also boasts gracious old châteaux and tiny villages, a bucolic pace of life, and, most important of all, the ideal microclimate needed to make the area's distinctive sweet white wines. Scattered about the vine-covered territory are such respected wine-producing estates as Château Suduiraut, Château Filhot, Château Rieussec, and Château Coutet. On Sauternes' highest point, dominating the landscape, is the majestic Château d'Yquem, a seigneurial castle with imposing Renaissance towers, crenellated walls, and unobstructed views over the undulating panorama of vines on all sides.

Inherited in 1968 by Comte Alexandre de Lur-Saluces from his uncle, Marquis Bertrand de Lur-Saluces, the château, like the regal wine it produces, evokes another epoch—or, in the words of Richard Olney in his definitive book *Yquem,* "a vague sense of timelessness, of touching something that is eternal." Although Château d'Yquem has been technically owned by a French luxury goods conglomerate since 1999, the estate is still run exclusively by Count Alexandre. Here he and the countess entertain visitors of every nationality in their baronial dining room, and here, every autumn, unfolds a drama that has fascinated oenophiles for centuries: one of the most remarkable collaborations between nature and man ever devised.

By September of each year, when the grapes of most other wine-producing areas are already fermenting in vats, there begins to appear on the golden-leaved Sémillon and Sauvignon Blanc vines of Sauternes a strange parasitic mold that generally flourishes in the region's climate, with its misty, moist mornings and sunny afternoons. Known officially as *Botrytis cinerea* but referred to locally as *la pourriture noble* (noble rot), this benevolent fungus (which would destroy any crop grown for the purpose of making dry wine) penetrates the skins of the ripe grapes and causes water in the fruit to evaporate, thus gradually increasing the concentration of natural sugar. Eventually, the mottled grapes turn dark and shrivel as the fungus feeds ravenously on the various acids, initiating a chemical transformation that in the end yields a viscous, sweet liquid with a taste like no other.

Not every grape, not even every cluster, is attacked by botrytis, but only those that are can be used to make sauternes. Day after day, week after week, female pickers (who are used because they've proven to be much faster than men) return to the vines with their small wooden baskets and special scissors, searching for new, pulpy victims of the mold, snipping ripe berry after ripe berry, and rushing their harvests to a sharp-eyed foreman to be assessed and then pressed. It's primitive, back-breaking work. What makes this labor seem almost absurd is that, while one grapevine in the Médoc might yield half a bottle or more of dry wine, a single vine in the best vineyards of Sauternes rarely produces more than a small glass of concentrated nectar. And the risks involved in obtaining even that are high. Some years, when the weather is not right, botrytis may not develop, or if it does, it may not spread properly in the vineyards. Let there be too much rain while the fruit is ripening, or not enough sunlight to reflect warmth from the gravelly soil to the grapes, or a crop infested with invisible worms, and disaster is certain. Grapes may appear to be perfectly ripe to the most experienced pickers, but once the fruit is analyzed, a cellar master may find that it has an insufficient sugar concentration to produce a perfectly balanced wine.

The labor, costs, and whims of nature involved in producing such regular First-Growth sauternes as Suduiraut and Climens are daunting enough. But the painstaking effort required to maintain the standards of perfection for Château d'Yquem—the only classified First Great Growth in all of Bordeaux—is nothing less than appalling. Many of the smaller châteaux simply cannot afford to wait past the season for the grapes to attain their ultimate ripeness, to send dozens of pickers into the vineyards time and time again, to create the ideal sugar concentration and alcohol content in the juice balance, and then to age their wines a full three-and-a-half years before bottling. But no concessions to practicality are ever made at Yquem.

To realize their profit, other winemakers may be forced to use grapes not fully botrytized, blend questionable vintages, chaptalize (add sugar), or store their wines in something other than new oak barrels. At Yquem, such cost-cutting procedures are unheard of. Adherence to such rigorous standards can prove financially devastating in bad years, when the cellar master determines that 80, 90, or even 100 percent of the natural juice must be rejected because of poor sugar concentration and therefore sold to *négociants* as generic sauternes. The loss can amount to millions of dollars on the U.S. market alone.

"We do work here that bears quite a resemblance to Russian roulette," Comte de Lur-Saluces moans. Even in the best of years, Château d'Yquem averages only seven thousand cases (compared with four times that for the greatest clarets), a figure that translates into about seventy-five gallons per acre, or the equivalent of a single four-ounce glass of wine per vine. Little wonder that today Yquem is released at double the price of the First Growths and phenomenally more than that of lesser sauternes.

What, then, does this mean to the average consumer wishing to serve a bottle of Yquem at a special occasion or simply eager to drink the wine for the first time? It means, quite frankly, that you splurge, the only justification being that by investing in so costly a wine you are not only indulging in one of life's unique pleasures but perhaps sharing that supreme pleasure with those you care for the most. It also means that you should shop around, since the prices of Yquem (depending on availability, demand, and, of course, vintage) can vary enormously from region to region and from shop to shop. Most reputable retail stores stock at least a few precious bottles or cases of Yquem for discerning customers. While it is virtually impossible today to lay hands on such sought-after vintages as '66, '67, '70, '71, '75, and '76 (most of which were swept up by eager investors during the buying frenzy of the 1980s and have since moved into the domain of the prestigious auction houses), there still seems to be a fair supply of the great '81s, '83s, '89s, and '90s. The years 1996 and '97 were also excellent for Yquem, but since these wines were released just recently and really should be allowed to age in the bottle at least another two or three years, they are being acquired mainly for future consumption.

I have seen bottles of '95 Yquem selling for as little as $145 in New York, but I've also seen that same vintage for $179 at one shop in Houston and $215 at another. By the same measure, I was recently told by a Chicago merchant that he had a single bottle of the prized '86 vintage tagged at $750—a rare find, I agreed sheepishly, until shortly thereafter I was stunned to notice on the wine card at a famous New York restaurant a regal '28

Yquem for a mere hundred dollars more. My conclusion about the pricing of Yquem is that practices are as flexible as those governing the purchase of fine jewels and furs; allowances must be made for how quickly a given source wants to move its inventory, for clever bargaining, and for sheer luck. James Beard once told me about spotting a dusty half-case of '45 Yquem in the back of a small Midwestern wine shop. The clerk told him that it was "just some old sweet wine that nobody ever buys," and he walked away with the valuable bottles for $5 apiece! (Today, a single bottle of that extraordinary vintage might well bring $1,500 at auction.) Such things do happen, I suppose, but generally the consumer must assume that professionals know exactly the worth of Château d'Yquem on the world market and that no bottle comes cheap.

And what, you might ask, is the risk that a $200 or $300 bottle of Yquem might turn out to be bad? Suffice it to say that a few years back Michael Broadbent, the celebrated wine authority and auctioneer at Christie's in London, was privileged to participate in the uncorking and tasting of a bottle of the fabled mahogany-hued 1784 "Jefferson" Yquem. The wine was "perfect in every sense," he reported ecstatically. I personally have been fortunate enough to drink a number of old Yquems (including an '04, '29, and '55), and can truthfully say that none was even faintly oxidized or overly acidic—never anything less than well balanced, vibrant, and utterly sublime.

Allowing for the fact that Château d'Yquem has always refused to produce any (or very much) wine in difficult years, one of the most distinctive qualities of this wine is its mysterious, almost miraculous ability to remain sound and mellow no matter what its age or appearance. In fact, it only gains in richness and complexity over the years. Like a fine violin that becomes more and more radiant with age, Yquem seems to defy the destructive onslaught of time by maintaining its integrity generation after generation—one of life's true wonders.

Connoisseurs argue heatedly over just when, in the course of a festive meal, Château d'Yquem should be poured. Indeed, the wine's role at the table has been reinterpreted dozens of times over the ages. In the nineteenth century, the custom was to serve sauternes with fresh oysters, turbot or sole, crayfish, and many types of fowl. It was not unusual, on the frightfully expansive formal menus of that era, to find Yquem paired with foie gras, composed salads, and all sorts of cold terrines, pâtés, and mousses, served *after* the main course and the red wines. Never, before World War I, was sauternes considered to be a dessert wine (Champagne always held that place of honor), and even when its position shifted from the depths to the end of the menu, there were still plenty of epicures who found the idea of drinking Yquem with sweet instead of savory dishes an outrage.

For some years now, the general practice in more elevated circles has been to serve Château d'Yquem either with foie gras at the start of a special meal or with a fairly bland dessert—or both. Yet, as if the cycle seemed destined to repeat itself, some enthusiasts are once again touting the wine as an ideal accompaniment to such main courses as poached lobster or red snapper, duck *à l'orange,* apricot chicken, and, appropriately enough during the holidays, roast turkey.

Some years back, California chef Jeremiah Tower went so far as to serve (to great acclaim) a '55 Yquem with an entrecôte of beef, while more recently, at the celebrated Taillevent in Paris, an experimental dinner featured a number of old Yquems with such dishes as braised turbot, sweet-and-sour duckling, and a ragout of sweetbreads, truffles, foie gras, and cockscombs. Richard Olney used to heartily recommend trying Yquem with figs and prosciutto, sautéed squid, roast pork stuffed with apricots, and almost any simple fowl preparation. And there's one avid collector in Texas whose idea of gastronomic bliss is fresh fettucine with shaved white truffles washed down with his favorite sauternes.

As for myself, I must confess that I remain a semipurist when it comes to Château d'Yquem, especially when I include it at an elaborate dinner involving many contrasting (and often assertive) flavors. Unlike a few respected fanatics I know, who will sip the nectar only by itself after a fine meal, I love nothing on earth more than to begin a joyous repast with a small slab of *terrine de foie gras* accompanied by a small glass of slightly chilled Yquem (one of life's greatest gustatory marriages) and to end the event with no more, perhaps, than a few mild cookies, bread and butter pudding, crème brûlée, or poached pears with more of that same noble wine. Yquem (like a great port) also holds its own with such aristocratic blue-veined cheeses as Roquefort and Stilton, and it can absolutely blossom in the presence of a light cheese soufflé or any simple dessert prepared with almonds, dried fruits, fresh peaches, or honey.

Contrary to what others believe, I find that Yquem is usually paralyzed by acidic fruit tarts or ice creams, and never would I dream of serving this nervous wine with something so potentially shattering as chocolate. Test what you will, but remember that the true glory of Château d'Yquem manifests itself only when the wine comes in contact with flavors considerably less sweet and aggressive than itself.

Every year for more than a decade, I've managed to overcome one of the most painful temptations in my life: to uncork that rare, slightly amber bottle of '67 Yquem resting peacefully in my cellar in celebration of my birthday. Last year I settled on a golden '90 to highlight a dinner for close friends, and this year—unless my willpower fails at the last minute—I'll probably pour a young but seductive '96. I treasure my '67 since it was given to me by Alexandre de Lur-Saluces himself, but I almost resent the gift because of a maddening condition to which I virtually agreed when I accepted the bottle.

"And Monsieur le Comte," I asked innocently, standing in the courtyard of the château and cradling my prize with both hands, "when do you suggest I drink this?"

Blinking his eyes rapidly, the count stared at me with a polite but stunned expression. "Ah, Monsieur," he decreed, "this bottle is not for you to open. This bottle is for your children—or your grandchildren."

SUPER SUDS

J UST THE NAMES INTRIGUE: DILLON'S SIX SHOOTER, BRIDGEPORT Old Knucklehead, Rogue Shakespeare, Golden Monkey, Coopersmith's Horsetooth, Dixie Blackened Voodoo, Rattlesnake Premium, Moonlight Twist of Fate. Some are described as clean, toasty, fluffy, or honeyed; others as musky, cheesy, or skunky. The best manifest volatile odorants, a subtle delicacy or suave aggression, and impeccable character, while the worst look flaccid, or have no alluring personality, or fail to challenge the senses. All crave and demand compatible fellowship, and a few are so amenable, so irresistible, and so virile that they inspire immediate adoration and loyalty.

Welcome to the world of premium American microbrews, a relatively recent phenomenon that is already adding a whole new dynamic dimension to the way we eat and drink. Call it the high-browing of beer, if you will, or the wine challenge, or the return to our earliest bibulous roots. Not, mind you, that beer is likely to totally eclipse wine as the choice beverage with great food—not after the decades it's taken for wine to finally assume its proper place at the American table. But today you really have to be almost blind not to notice both the ever-increasing variety of regional speciality brews filling the market shelves and the number of sophisticated consumers who are buying or ordering in restaurants bottles of smoky Sierra Nevada Pale Ale from California, New York's fruity New Amsterdam lager, malty Allegheny Penn Pilsener from Pittsburgh, Red Oaks Ale made in Greensboro, North Carolina, and a staggering aggregation of other princely domestic microbrews that can compete with and often surpass the best of the imports.

Of course, unenlightened snobs will be the first to raise eyebrows and snicker at the very idea of elevating any style of beer to the same level as fine wines, and, given the embarrassing, disgraceful quantities of light, low-alcohol, mass-produced swill on which most Americans have been weaned and which is the staple of college fraternities, smoky bars, and rowdy ballparks, I'm not at all surprised by such protest. Nor does it really amaze me that when even many food professionals occasionally opt for a beer to accompany their Asian, Mexican, or highly spiced American dishes, they automatically ask for a familiar, respectable, but not necessarily challenging Dutch Heineken, German Beck's, English Bass, or Canadian Molson. Once was the time when I, too, had little alternative but to drink a zesty, full-bodied, well-balanced foreign lager, stout ale, or porter, but today, for the first time in nearly a century, the quality of beer being produced by relatively small, artisanal microbreweries all over the country is generally so high that I literally go out of my way to find shops and restaurants that stock San Francisco Anchor Steam Ale, Brooklyn Lager, Alaskan Amber Alt, or San Antonio Jax Pilsener.

In case you believe that the beer drinking world in the United States has always revolved around Bud, Schlitz, Miller, and Coors, perhaps it's time to learn that, till the advent of that insanity known as Prohibition in the 1920s and early 1930s, some of the best beers in the world had been brewed by small American regional operations ever since Colonial days. Virtually every founding father, including Jefferson, Adams, and Madison, had enormous love and respect for the hoppy lagers, bitter stouts, and highly malted porters made in Massachusetts, Pennsylvania, and Virginia, and so enamored of beer was George Washington that he even maintained his own brew house at Mount Vernon. With the arrival of German immigrants in the early nineteenth century, elaborate beer halls and beer gardens began to flourish in every major city, brewing innovations and techniques became more and more elaborate as different types of beer evolved, and by the end of the century, there were well over four thousand customized breweries turning out barrel after barrel of every delectable style imaginable.

The infamous Volstead Act of 1920, which instituted Prohibition, spelled utter disaster for the beer industry, and after Repeal in 1933, competition and price-cutting among the larger companies to open eventually drove most of the small, local breweries out of business and made way for the real giants to take complete control and begin producing prodigious amounts of the almost generic, lifeless suds that would eventually flood the market. By the late 1970s, there were no more than a few dozen local and regional breweries left in the entire country, and just fifteen years ago, it was still next to impossible to find much domestic beer produced by anyone except the half-dozen or so national megabreweries churning out millions of barrels a year.

Exactly what inspired the return of regional microbeer activity in the 1990s is not easy to pinpoint, but my guess is that it was not only a reaction to the low quality of mass-produced beer but also still another reflection of the vibrant national fervor over all specialized native foods and beverages sweeping the nation: cottage-industry cheeses and olive oils; exotic new vegetables, fruits, and varieties of seafood; unusual regional rices, flours, syrups, and cured meats; and, indeed, first-rate, highly personalized varietal wines that could compete with the best France had to offer. Whatever the reason, it's for sure that in almost no time, microbreweries were once again making their mark in almost every state of the union—to such an extent that today enthusiasts can choose from over five hundred local, regional, and national brands that stretch across the landscape from Chico, California, to Fort Mitchell, Kentucky, to Norwalk, Connecticut.

By definition, these are relatively small enterprises with a brewing capacity of thirty to forty thousand barrels annually (compared with a megabrewery like Anheuser-Busch that turns out five to six million barrels a year at one plant alone). And while the microbeers so far represent no more than about 2 percent of U.S. beer production and are often distributed only in their respective regions (in bottles or on draft), such is the growing demand for these well-crafted, complex beers that I have no doubt that their market ranking can only soar and their availability widen as people learn more about them.

Since it's much too complicated to go into the technicalities of microbrewing (malt extracts, hops, yeasts, special flavorings, kraeusening, top versus bottom fermentations, etc.), suffice it that most of the smaller operations produce anywhere from three to a dozen different styles of beer. All the average drinker needs to know is that lagers (which include pilsener, bock, and malt liquor) are generally lighter, crisper, more carbonated, and less hoppy and aromatic than other beers. (In its watery, tasteless disguise, this is the major style of beer made by the megabreweries.) Ales, by contrast, are light amber to almost brown in color, higher in alcohol and more malty, either subtly bitter or delightfully flowery, and soft-textured. Most varied of all are the stouts and porters, both of which are dark in color from their principle component of roasted barley, but each of which can be dryly alcoholic or malty sweet, bitter or fruity, heady or tame. Steam ale, a style created originally in California, is beautifully amber, well-hopped, and very yeasty, while beers flavored with everything from herbs and spices to fruits to woody smoke comprise a vast, exciting category unto itself. It takes only one visit to a brewery like Brooklyn in Utica, New York, or Dillon's in Chatsworth, California, to realize that the production of premium American microbeers is as much (if not more) a fine art as the making of distinguished wines. There are now even beer competitions around the country that have all the seriousness of the most solemn wine tastings.

So exactly which beers complement which foods, and when does it make lots more sense to opt for an exceptional, reasonably priced micro over a costly cabernet or chardonnay? (And yes, price does indeed matter these days when greedy restaurants are charging almost as much for a single glass of dubious bar wine as they do for a main course.) Needless to say, it all depends on personal taste, the style of food, and even the locale and mood of the moment. For years, I couldn't imagine drinking anything but wine with French or Italian cuisine, for instance; but when I was once forced for medical reasons to lay off the grape for a month, I learned in a matter of days how compatible a local, malty Manhattan Stout on draft was with rich coq au vin and the amazing ways both Anchor Steam Ale and Cold Springs Lager from Minnesota integrated with various pasta dishes. (I also recalled watching many Parisians drinking Kronenbourg pale lager with their *choucroûtes* and *boudins*. And once, in Venice, a table of Italians sipping Messina Pilsener with an elaborate seafood risotto.) I'll choose a hoppy micro pilsener over white wine any day with virtually all simply grilled or broiled seafood; I much prefer a toasty, chewy, full-bodied stout or nutty pale ale with steak, hamburgers, meat loaf, ribs, and other such traditional American fare; and, quite frankly, I can't imagine drinking anything but prickly, robust, well-tempered beer with Indian, Asian, Mexican, and most Scandinavian dishes, as well as with spicy American ones.

Unlike wine, which, contrary to many popular and naive perceptions, does—or should—have limitations in terms of food compatibility, beer is so versatile and conducive to such a broad spectrum of cuisines that it's almost foolish not to become better acquainted with the first-class microbrews, sample as many regional ones as possible while traveling about the country, and ask what's available in every restaurant. If friends or waiters give you a snooty look, just pity and ignore them.

Drinking fine beers, like great wines, is an art with certain rules that should always be respected. First, I resolutely refuse any canned beer because of the metallic taste the container tends to impart, and I'm very wary of clear bottles, which may have exposed the sensitive brew to sunlight and changed its structure. Distinctive beers, like good wines, demand their own style of glass to manifest textures and aromas to best advantage, be it thick glass mugs for lagers meant to be kept slightly chilled; tulip-shaped glasses or large tumblers for ales, stouts, and porters to capture volatile odorants (aromas) and maintain sufficient head foam; or tall, conical glasses for pilseners that need to be pressured upwards to keep the bubbles intact. All of these glass vessels are relatively inexpensive, and I've noticed that more and more savvy restaurants are beginning to stock the different styles to suit the appropriate beers. (The only thing more uncouth and grotesque, by the way, than drinking beer directly from the bottle or can is having it served in an appalling plastic glass as if it were Pepsi.)

A cardinal sin committed all too often in homes and restaurants is over-chilling premium beer, which can not only make it cloudy but suppress the head and kill much of the flavor. For these same reasons, I also disapprove of serving beer in highly frosted glasses and mugs, a strictly American custom that provokes horror in British, German, Scandinavian, Japanese, and other European and Asian zealots who've been drinking quality beer with food for centuries. An even worse offense is serving beer in glasses washed with soap and water and dried with a soiled towel, procedures almost guaranteed to leave trace residues that can totally destroy any frothy head and produce off-tastes. (The best method is to wash in a solution of salt or baking soda and water and air-dry the glasses.) Finally, to protect its aroma, effervescence, and head as long as possible, never pour beer till the food arrives; and, unless you want a glassful of worthless foam, pour it very slowly down the angled inside of the glass till a gentle head gradually forms almost an inch from the rim. Pouring premium beer correctly is not unlike pouring fine Champagne, so that the essence is manifested initially on top while the flavorful fizz continues to rise in the glass.

I doubt seriously that even the most noble domestic beers will ever dominate American drinking habits the way the premiums do in Ireland and Scotland, Asia, Scandinavia, and, to a large extent, England and Germany, though I'm sure there will always be as many tipplers chugging indiscriminate quantities of Bud and Miller as those who find nothing objectionable about guzzling glass after glass of inferior generic wines—at both table and cocktail parties. There can be no doubt, however, that the micros are not only gaining popularity with more sophisticated palates but also inspiring such financial arbiters as the *New York Times* to now recommend Boston Beer, Redhook, and other highly successful companies as sound investments.

Perhaps even more relevant is that potential younger gastronomes are quickly learning the many advantages of choosing a spritzy lager, mellow ale, or bold stout to wash down both certain classic foods and countless New Wave dishes with complexities that almost demand the most versatile of beverages. One trendy restaurant in New York, for example, reports doing an astounding business in pricy Michelob Ultra, a premium beer specifically targeted to vernal diners on a low-carb diet. (I've tasted Michelob Ultra, and while it's certainly not in the same league as Red Feather Pale Ale from Pennsylvania or California's Rhino Chasers Lager, it's at least a start for some.)

I don't know of any popular grill-restaurant in San Francisco that doesn't serve in bottles or on draft such local favorites as North Coast Scrimshaw, Anchor Steam, and Santa Cruz Lighthouse. In all the major cities of Texas I've visited, Jax Pilsener is the beverage of choice at high-end Mexican and Tex-Mex locales. Most young drinkers in the Windy City already recognize the distinct differences between Chicago's Legacy Lager, Legacy Red Ale, and Big Shoulders Porter. As for Philadelphia, which I'm ready to tag the microbeer capital of America, virtually every hip downtown restaurant now carries labels like Love Stout, HopDevil, and Dogfish Head, all handcrafted at dozens of small breweries in and about the city. (Monk's Café and Beer Emporium even boasts a "Beer Bible" for truly dedicated aficionados.) I haven't had the chance recently to check out the activity in Atlanta, but apparently it's lively enough for the city's *Journal-Constitution* to appoint a "beer columnist" (who, appropriately, has become quite an expert at home-brewing his own red ale).

Whether consumed on a national or strictly regional basis, microbeer is without question a reemerging phenomenon that not only pays proud testimony to our heritage but promises to intensify as the number of brews multiply across the nation and Americans take them more and more seriously. As for myself, what I'm waiting for at the moment is for someone to arrive at my house and, instead of the same old predictable cab or third-growth claret, present me with a dozen rare bottles of dark, satiny-smooth Coopersmith Horsetooth Stout from Fort Collins, Colorado.

A Selective Regional Guide to Premium Micro Beers

While, generally, a microbrewery is a relatively small operation producing about forty thousand barrels or less of premium beer annually, some better known ones such as Anchor in San Francisco, Samuel Adams of Boston, Sierra Nevada in Chico, California, and Seattle's Rainier have either expanded operations considerably to reach a wider national market or contracted with other breweries (often out-of-state) to increase production under tight quality control. Many of the beers are still available only in the region of production, and consumption of a few (Schlafly, Old Columbia, and Coopersmith) is thus far limited by state law to the actual locale where the beer is brewed. Regulations, production, and distribution change constantly from state to state, so consumers should remain on the alert. The beers listed below are some of the finest in the nation.

Alaska
Alaskan Amber Alt

California
Anchor Steam and Porter
Anderson Valley Oatmeal Stout
Dillon's Six Shooter Red Ale
Mendocino Black Hawk Stout
Old Columbia Black's Beach Porter
Rhino Chasers Lager
Sierra Nevada Pale Ale
North Coast Scrimshaw

Colorado
Coopersmith's Horsetooth Stout
Odell's 90 Shilling Ale
Connecticut: New England
    Holiday Ale

Hawaii
Maui Lager

Idaho
Sun Valley Holiday Ale

Illinois
Chicago's Big Shoulders Porter

Iowa
Millstream Lager

Kentucky
Oldenberg Weisse

Louisiana
Abita Dark Ale
Dixie Lager

Michigan
Old Detroit Amber Ale

Minnesota
Cold Springs Lager

Missouri
Schlafly Oatmeal Stout

New York
Brooklyn Brown Ale and Lager
Manhattan Stout
New Amsterdam Lager

North Carolina
Red Oaks Ale

Oregon
Bridgeport Old Knucklehead
Rogue Maierbock Ale
Rogue Red Ale
Rogue Shakespeare Stout

Pennsylvania
Allegheny Penn Pilsener
Yuengling Porter
Prior Double Dark Bock
Red Feather Pale Ale
Love Stout
HopDevil
Stoudt's

Texas
Celis White Hefe-Weizen and Pale
    Bock
Jax Pilsener

Washington
Grant's Imperial Stout and Special
    Ale
Rainier Ale
Red Hook Blackhook Porter

Wisconsin
Angsburger Pilsener
Capital Gartenbrau Lager

BYOB REVISITED

NOT LONG AGO, AFTER RECEIVING A PRINTED INVITATION TO still another early-evening "cocktail" reception in Manhattan, I decided at last to take the bull by the horns and invest in a handsome, thin, pewter pocket flask that I subsequently filled with Jack Daniel's sour mash whiskey. Arriving at the party, I declined the predictable glasses of white or red wine and mineral water proffered on a tray by a roving waitress, located the area where a so-called bartender was pouring nothing but the same, and politely asked for a glass of water with a few ice cubes from a wine bucket. I then boldly withdrew the flask from the inside pocket of my jacket, poured a good measure of booze into the water as those around me gawked sheepishly, swirled the ice with a finger, and proceeded blithely around the room to socialize with the other guests.

No doubt there are many in these vapid times who would consider my gesture unmannerly if not downright uncouth, but the truth is that I'm fed up to the gills with shindigs falsely blazed as cocktail affairs where the only alcoholic libations to be had are Niagaras of still or sparkling wine. (I won't even deign to comment on all the mineral water, seltzer, fruit juice, cola, and other inane beverages that are usually also available.) Such a phenomenon might be regarded as savvy and chic in today's jejune social world, but I'll have no part of the nonsense. Even if they're pouring '90 Lafitte Rothschild and Taittinger Comtes de Champagne, I resolutely do not drink wine at cocktail parties. Wine, after all, is not—repeat *not*—a cocktail, and when some gig is pegged as a cocktail party, is it really asking too much to have a simple gin and tonic or bourbon and branch? To deny guests this option is, to my mind, not only egregiously pretentious but disingenuous and rude.

Don't get me wrong, for there's not a creature on earth who loves and respects wine as much as I do—except at cocktail parties. I attend wine tastings, mull over wine lists in restaurants, read extensively and write about wines, and even auction some of my own rare labels, and just the idea of savoring any noteworthy meal without at least one bottle of fine wine on the table is ludicrous. This does not preclude the fact, however, that I also relish and esteem an honest highball and expect to be offered one when an invitation calls for "cocktails." That my conviction has been shared by James Beard, Craig Claiborne, Julia Child, Paula Wolfert, Jeremiah Tower, Marcella Hazan, and a host of other past and present culinary swells only serves to heighten my outrage and courage when I'm denied my pleasure.

I have no idea when or why or how the distinctive, proud, all-American tradition of sipping legitimate alcoholic mixed drinks at social functions succumbed to the jaunty practice of swilling wine (any wine, any style, any label). Utopians would probably say it is due to our gradual exposure to better and better wines and a change in taste patterns; others to the facility of pouring wine over mixing cocktails; and cynical I to the puritanical and erroneous perception that wine is much more tolerable, safer, and healthier than liquor. Whatever, I often wonder if most tipplers have actually forgotten how subtle and delicious distilled spirits can be when consumed fastidiously and in moderation, or if our society is simply doomed forever by the tyranny of Prohibition and alcohol abuse.

I know that some drinkers really do prefer wine at parties, and, although I do find it intensely depressing watching the mobs (some of whom will not hesitate to drive a car afterwards) typically guzzle glass after glass of cheap domestic sauvignon blanc, South African chablis, Chilean merlot, and other such plonk while I nurse my single, sublime tumbler of mellow sour mash, I acknowledge their right. On the other hand, it truly is appalling that I'm now forced to pocket my own hooch like some sleazy reprobate.

The irony of all this mess, of course, is that many more people at cocktail parties than you might imagine would actually prefer the real McCoy to still another routine, ordinary, boring glass of wine—especially in view of all the new, wildly popular cocktails (e.g., the cosmopolitan) being created in bars and served in restaurants all over the country. At a recent upscale charity event I attended at a small museum, for example, lined up on the bar next to a couple of respectable red wines and a bucket of chilled chardonnay and Champagne were bottles of premium gin, vodka, bourbon, and scotch, plus various mixers and garnishes. Some guests opted for bubbly, but by far the majority (young and old) chose a highball—and quite a few simply single malt or Stoli on the rocks. I notice in restaurants that more and more of my friends and colleagues, freed momentarily from the fashionable wine-as-cocktail syndrome, order everything from exotic martinis to whiskey sours to margaritas to concoctions I've never heard of, and when guests in my own home catch sight of the inspiring array of liquor labels on the bar, I bet I don't pour two glasses of wine. Perhaps most revealing of all are the lustful glares aimed at my Jack Daniel's manhattan each and every time I prepare or order in a restaurant my favorite cocktail, a proceeding that never fails to inspire at least one person to ask for a taste, then mumble in ecstasy, "Oh, I think I'll have one of those, too."

I'm not an unreasonable man. I bend to anybody's putative licence to serve what they please at their own get-togethers; I'd never be so audacious these days as to expect anything really civilized like a manhattan, vodka gibson, or Negroni; and, in fact, I'm perfectly willing just to stay away from parties and not cause any commotion when I know that wine is being fraudulently and tackily passed off as a cocktail. Like any dedicated boozer, all I ask, indeed beg, is to be given advance warning should the dubious decision be made not to tender so much as a jigger of the hard stuff. If not, I simply have no alternative but to continue exercising my BYOB right. After all, even my dear 88-year-old mother wouldn't be caught dead at a suspicious "cocktail" party without a small, silver, trusty flask filled with fine bourbon stashed in her handbag, so why should I or anybody else have qualms about indulging in a little old-fashioned, stylish bootleg delight when times are tough?

DISPATCH FROM THE RESTAURANT ARENA

DINING IN
THE PLAYPEN

IS IT JUST ME, OR HAS ANYONE ELSE NOTICED THAT DINING OUT in certain restaurants during these testy first years of the twenty-first century is becoming about as brainless as a Jim Carrey potboiler? No, I'm not referring to such theme places as Olive Garden or the Hard Rock Café, which are at least honest and good-humored about their blatant silliness and can actually turn out some pretty tasty food. I'm talking about the increasing number of putatively serious restaurants in America that thrive on childish pretense, artifice, and gimmickry to such a degree that I could easily fall prey to acute anorexia. I'm certainly not prepared to predict that their ubiquitousness is leading us to the fall of Western civilization, not when—thanks be to God—there are still enough estimable locales to keep us afloat. But as one who views respectable dining—adult dining, if you will—as a treasured part of a hedonistic life, I'm understandably alarmed by the prospect of the hypertrendy and downright dippy infiltrating the very soul of fine dining.

I mean, there are certain basics I feel I have the right to expect of any grown-up restaurant: an attentive reception, a civilized ambiance, a well-groomed staff and clientele, polished service, and a halfway intelligent menu and wine list. Fine dining, like great art, music, and literature, ought to be keen-minded, luminous, and uplifting; and restaurants that adhere proudly, even boldly to this notion—such as the Four Seasons in New York, Valentino in Los Angeles, and Le Bec-Fin in Philadelphia—cater to adult behavior and tastes. But when an otherwise sensible New York establishment sees fit to offer so absurd a menu entry as "Grilled Swordchop" (cutely numbered, no less, so you know how many have been served before), or a fashionable San Francisco haunt touts "noncholesterol soufflés," I have to wonder if some of today's culinary playpens aren't wielding a bit too much influence over their more worldly brethren.

And what do I mean by a playpen? Well, it's a venue that takes shape when someone with little or no professional experience decides to open a snazzy, usually overpriced restaurant, comes up with a name that might be better suited to a TV sitcom, and then hires a high-profile decorator to create something out of a fantasy (and probably best kept there). The postpubescent chef, preferably a pedigreed culinary school graduate, is generally lured from another similar-style restaurant to fashion his or her eclectic version of "New American," "Mediterranean," or global "fusion" cuisine, hopefully free of salt, cream, butter, flour, and all those other poisons. Everything is decidedly casual and laid back—the exposed kitchen optional—and there must be sufficient noise for utmost relaxation and psychological security. Tables are placed painfully close together to foster social interplay and eavesdropping, not to mention big profits. If anybody orders a cocktail, it is a jazzed-up sweetened, spiced, or herbed concoction with a name like Cristo Cooler, Forbidden Fig, or Cranberry Surprise; and mineral water (at outrageous prices), generic wines by the glass, and diet colas flow in Niagaras. Unseasoned waiters and waitresses (sorry, "waitpersons") hastily recite a litany of specials so contrived that they're usually forced to repeat or—worse yet— try to explain them, and there's no need for a professional wine steward.

The laboratory food itself has no real national identity, but the copycat menu is sure to include some form of foie gras (domestic) and fresh tuna (raw or undercooked), about a dozen salads and pastas (the old stuff till a dietetic substitute comes along), a roast organic baby chicken and boneless meat (sauce on the side), plenty of flavored mashed (oops! I mean pureed) potatoes (preferably Yukon gold), surely a few intriguing items made with lemon grass or truffle oil, and indeed, an updated rendition of yolkless crème brûlée and some molten chocolate dessert. Most important of all is presentation (i.e. "plating"), so no matter how the food might taste, the chef sees that every dish includes clever squiggles, drizzles, and stacks. The atmosphere encourages indiscriminate grazing and nibbling from one another's plates, and at the smoke-free tables, there's lots of talk about calories, fats, organic this-and-that, and gyms. (French, Italian, or Japanese diners in the room are, of course, dumfounded.)

This is hardly to suggest that every contemporary entry on the nation's restaurant scene has gone the way of what I consider child's play, not when such redoubtable places as Locke-Ober's in Boston, Wildwood in Portland, Highlands Bar & Grill in Birmingham, and Daniel in New York truly strive to enrich America's gastronomic tradition. But you wouldn't believe (or maybe you would) the nonsense I've witnessed about the country over the past couple of years: a restaurant in San Francisco where the noise is so piercing that the chefs providing entertainment in the open kitchen must wear headsets to communicate with each other; a hot Italian spot in Atlanta where waiters introduce themselves by writing their names with crayons on paper tablecloths; a wildly fashionable boîte in Manhattan that encourages foodies to assemble their own do-it-yourself meal like children arranging colorful blocks; and—no joke—a glamorous place in Miami's Coconut Grove that caters to calorie-conscious nibblers and provides tall stacks of tiny plates on each table amid paint pots, easels, brushes, and other clever trappings of an artist's atelier.

To be sure, playpen dining is nothing novel in Chicago, not after the stupefying success of the pioneering Lettuce Entertain You company and such fun houses as Café Ba-Ba-Reeba! and Scoozi! If not for seasoned havens like L'Orangerie and Rex Il Ristorante, dining out in Los Angeles would make a visit to Disneyland seem like a long night at the opera, and while it's been some years since Wolfgang Puck sported his first baseball cap in the display kitchen at Spago and wooed Hollywood's most saturnalian honchos with his fussy boutique pizzas and orchidaceous pastas, today even the antics of this adulated wunderchef are being upstaged by menu histrionics ("Okra Winfrey Creole Gumbo," "Ty Cobb Salad," that sort of thing) that give a whole new dimension to funville.

Since the emergence of the restaurant as theme park seems to be a natural by-product of our juvenile times, I suppose it's only inevitable that the shrinking of the nation's collective attention span has spilled over into the dining experience. Consequently, more and more establishments, as if catering to antsy children, feel the need to keep customers constantly entertained—even if that means serving food in unrecognizable formations and stacked as high as the Washington Monument. And as running a restaurant increasingly becomes just one more hobby—like taking up hang gliding—the restaurateur's calling, that French notion of *devoir*, seems about as quaint as a rotary telephone. Even my hometown of Charlotte, North

Carolina, hasn't escaped the playpen phenomenon, a fact that became all too clear when one upscale favorite with the locals recently came up with a roasted fresh Dover sole with sweetpea vanilla sauce and a "potato lollipop." Likewise, I suppose regulars at one restaurant in Rye, New York, are still raving as much about the "Screaming Oysters from Hell" with lemon grass, cilantro, and ginger as they were when I had my first and last meal there a couple years ago.

Although nothing in Manhattan can quite top a restaurant on Long Island where professional physical therapists massaged guests' upper extremities between courses, never doubt that my own adopted Big Apple has evolved into an even more unruly culinary sandbox than Los Angeles. One illustrious restaurant after another (the Coach House, La Réserve, Sign of the Dove, La Côte Basque, Arcadia) has closed, so what's replaced them? Let's ignore the mobs swarming to the fun dives along West Fifty-seventh Street and take a peek—without cruelly calling names that most blessedly won't be around for long—at other playgrounds dazzling the public and a number of trend-seeking restaurant critics alike. One current Latin American cave serves up such fanciful conceits as a chocolate "Puro" cigar with marzipan cigarette butts and a sugar matchbook, only to be challenged by a pseudo-American newcomer featuring chocolate vodka cocktails topped with Hershey's Kisses. At the city's hottest Japanese restaurant, patrons perch on chopstick stools at the sushi bar, the service bar is located in a bank vault, and such surprises extend even to the restrooms, where repose is shattered by rain-and-thunder sound effects.

For the moment, crowds rush to a new West Village bistro that boasts a dessert of "Nori'O's," consisting of chocolate fondant between squares of caramelized nori seaweed. At a swank so-called Scandinavian temple uptown, there's a lobster roll not only made with pear, caviar, and "potato foam," but also enhanced by a ginger ale granité. And, incredibly, none other than a lionized French chef has opened a venture with little pots of peanut butter and grape jelly on each table. At least we're now spared one curio that finally died a deserved death: Twins, owned by a set of them, bartended by identical brothers or sisters, and serviced by squads of look-alike siblings. But never fear, however, for what trendites are now flocking to instead is Bed—yes, Bed—a restaurant where customers dine shoeless on actual beds. (It was reported that designer Karl Lagerfeld left in a huff when told that he'd have to remove his shoes.)

Does this silliness have its place? Of course it does. I just don't happen to believe that a restaurant is one of them—or at least not one that expects to be taken seriously. Thankfully, those of us who wish to dine like adults can always exercise our option to steer clear of the playpens and simply hope that their creeping talons don't grow any longer. Otherwise, the day isn't far off when somebody's sure to open . . . Cafe Toyland. Now, let's see. The walls of the crowded dining room are finger-painted with updated versions of nursery rhymes. Rock music and *Sesame Street* ditties alternately drown out all conversation. Tables are decorated with toy soldiers and blocks, and waiters and waitresses dress as clowns and Raggedy Anns, respectively. Customers, who sit in sturdy high chairs and don house-label bibs over their jogging garb, can be spoon-fed for a small additional fee. The food, served in compartmentalized plates, is fatless, saltless, and eggless low-cal purees. Dessert? Exotic fruit-flavored sorbets only. Alcohol? None served here. The check is written in crayon and delivered by kiddie car. And . . . well, it could never come to that, could it?

THE FRUGAL GOURMAND

"I'LL HAVE THE CREOLE PRAWNS, THE BRAISED LAMB SHANK, ROAST-ed Yukons, and Parmesan asparagus," I tell our waiter while nursing my bourbon manhattan and nibbling on a sesame stick. "And could we please see the wine list?"

My table companions, sipping mineral water or house wine and mumbling nervously about calories, continue to survey the tempting menu. Two finally succumb to their carnivorous instincts, but only by agreeing to share the giant porterhouse and a side of cottage fries. The third opts for grilled triple lamb chops, and before it's all over, orders are also recklessly given for Caesar salad, portobellas filled with crabmeat, frizzle onion rings, chive potato pancakes, cauliflower au gratin, and . . . for dessert, blueberry cheesecake, hot apple crisp with vanilla ice cream, and molten chocolate pie.

A feeding frenzy, to be sure, but while my otherwise cautious friends clean their plates as if food rationing were the law, complain about feeling stuffed, and suffer the guilt of the damned, I'm quite satisfied with exactly two prawns, about half of my shank, a few tiny creamy potatoes and asparagus spears, maybe a taste of the cauliflower, and a morsel of each dessert.

"Well, I can tell that this place won't get a rave from you," muses the sated lady on my left, eyeballing the remaining lamb on my plate.

"On the contrary, my dear," I counter to everyone's astonishment. "Except for the undercooked asparagus, it's one of the best meals I've had in months."

Who says restaurant lovers can't and shouldn't dine out intelligently? For years, people have been amazed at how a professional gastronome like myself manages to shamelessly indulge his passions yet somehow remain reasonably fit and trim—without resorting to torturous diets, silly fitness programs and gyms, or periodic sojourns at health spas. The immodest but truthful answer is that, like other of my colleagues devoted to eating, cooking, and writing about food and drink, I've learned to dine out sensibly without relinquishing so much as a trace of the hedonistic joys associated with *la bonne table*. To eliminate the need for gorging at any one meal, for instance, I religiously consume three wholesome meals a day, the first two being relatively moderate affairs compared to the almost ritualistic dinners out that I usually plan with fanatical precision and share with friends and associates. While I never give much thought to such things as cholesterol and fat and sodium when I'm dining out, I remain generally healthy, energetic, and in control of my weight, and quite frankly, I just don't understand those for whom eating is an exercise in either gluttony or self-denial, like social nibblers more concerned with lipids and avoirdupois than the sensible orchestration of a fine meal.

Of course, there was a time when such trenchermen journalists as A.J. Liebling, Lucius Beebe, and James Beard could and would polish off, in a single sitting, three dozen oysters with Champagne, soup, a hot sausage *en croûte*, a seven-rib rack of lamb with ratatouille and souffléed potatoes, wedges of ripe Stilton with port, and a full bottle of vintage burgundy. That was not only considered a culinary adventure but a veritable badge of courage. Well, such displays of virtuosity—never mind the stamina—are rarely seen today. Naturally, there are salient exceptions, but to observe such eminent compatriots as Julia Child, Jeremiah Tower, Paula Wolfert, and Ruth Reichl in restaurants is to enjoy the company of people who, like myself, savor their "work" precisely because they know how to eat wisely.

Of all the practical rules that govern my gustatory way of life, none is so inviolate as limiting myself to one major restaurant meal a day—even when I'm reporting on many places in a given city or country. If I'm planning an important dinner out in New York or London, no amount of coaxing can get me to eat an elaborate three-course lunch the same day. Instead, I'll opt for something like a good soup and sandwich at home or maybe in a nice pub or café. It's not only foolish but amateurish for travelers in, say, Paris or Rome to feast on a huge lunch in one celebrated restaurant, only to face (or, more to the point, face down) a full dinner at another. The French and Italians certainly love food and wine as much as—or more than—anybody else, but it's rare that after a traditionally copious lunch, they wouldn't settle in the evening for something like a simple composed salad or a bowl of pasta, a little bread, and a few glasses of wine.

Almost as important as the one-restaurant-a-day principle is my determination to order exactly what I want and nothing more. That's not as easy as it sounds. At certain high-profile restaurants, for example, it's no longer uncommon for a table captain to strongly suggest that the chef be allowed to prepare a "tasting menu" for the entire table. When I hear this I cringe, for not only is it a costly proposal that presumes all present enjoy the same dishes; it virtually guarantees a staggering three-hour eating marathon involving God knows how many courses. ("The meal loses its cadence," as one seasoned colleague so aptly puts it.) When confronted with this trendy nonsense, I do all in my power to politely steer my tablemates away from the risky option, ask to see a menu, and point out that we might just as easily sample one another's à la carte dishes—much as I basically loathe this rather fatuous practice. If the persistent waiter then tries to push perhaps "a salad and selection of potatoes and vegetables," I decline, pretty sure that at least a couple of the main courses are sure to be sufficiently garnished.

Few things befuddle serious reviewers more than those diners who order with little discernment, devour an entire dish or slug a glass of wine, and then proclaim either or both to have been unpalatable. ("For some people, there's this urgency to gobble, like they'll never have another meal," Ruth Reichl observes.) Nobody should have to eat or drink anything that's unacceptable, and I'm by no means adverse to sending back poorly prepared dishes, choosing alternatives from the menu, or asking the manager to taste a questionable wine. But night after night on the starched-tablecloth circuit teaches you to order with care—and that can take time. "The big problem with a lot of people in restaurants is that they simply don't stop to apply the senses to what they eat and drink," contends William Rice, food and wine columnist for the *Chicago Tribune*.

To dine out these days is to hear some variation of the cry: "Oooh, this dish looks wonderful, but Lord, there's so much," the implication being that capital punishment should be meted out to those who don't polish off everything in sight. Yes, today some bistros, steak and seafood houses, and indeed, blue-chip havens, pride themselves on large portions, no doubt a reaction to the more anemic nouvelle offerings that once dominated the restaurant scene. Never, however, am I intimidated by even the most glorious overabundance, not when the doggy bag has become as socially accept-able as ordering fine wines by the glass. "When I'm shelling out thirty-seven bucks for a veal chop, I'll be damned if I let half of it go down the chute," huffs another colleague who shares my sentiments on such matters.

Surely the most welcome feature of dining out in these increasingly lib-erated times is the willingness of many serious restaurants to accommodate virtually any reasonable customer request. As a result, I think nothing any-more of making an entire meal of two, three, or even four appetizers I'm eager to taste. Often I'll order a substantial soup or mound of prosciutto, followed by a half-portion of pasta as the main course, and I never hesitate to request that two portions be split for four people if my tablemates and I can agree upon the selection. Nor is it unusual for a frequent dinner com-panion and me to order four different desserts and take just a single bite of each. You might consider that a blatant insult to the pastry chef and the quintessential act of waste, but those of us whose jobs require a consistent-ly piqued palate just don't see it that way. What matters as much to us as memorable food, drink, and good company is an admittedly crazy notion behind our sybaritic impulses: *Always* stay hungry!

RESPECT
MOTHER NATURE

WHILE THE STAGGERING DIVERSITY OF FOODS AND BEVERAGES now available in American shops and served in restaurants is enough to make even the most picky gastronome swoon, I must insist that much of what is imported, shipped across regional borders, and duplicated pales in comparison with the real thing. I have no qualms with the integrity of such well-traveled specialities as English marmalade and Stilton cheese, numerous dried chilies used in authentic Mexican dishes, French mustard and Champagne, Idaho potatoes and Vidalia onions, German lagers, and finally Italian prosciutto. And I readily admit that transplants and imitations such as fresh domestic goat cheese, chorizo sausages, dried pasta, and exotic rices can taste almost as good on home turf as in alien climes.

But there are times when I absolutely draw the line at what I'll order in restaurants (or purchase in shops), fully convinced that the only way to satisfy certain gustatory passions is to go where sacred boundaries cannot be breached. I'm certainly not as radical as one old friend who resolutely refuses to touch a morsel of French cuisine anywhere but in France and won't eat Dungeness crab except on the coast of Washington State. But when I dine out, I have developed serious prejudices that manifest themselves each and every time my eyes slowly and carefully peruse a menu or wine list. French bread, *boudin noir,* and crème fraîche, fresh Italian scampi and white truffles, German pork sausages, and Alsatian wines are indeed among the provender I consider topographically sui generis, but I find that the compromising of even these delectables is modest compared with the liberties taken with Mother Nature's very finest.

Russian and Iranian Caviar

I suspect the reason most Americans don't wax blissful over the sublime flavor and texture of Russian and Iranian caviar is because either they're exposed only to the strong, fishy, processed sludge found in bottles on market shelves or that most of the fresh stuff they're served in the United States—due both to absurd government regulations and, most recently, to false labeling on an appalling black market—is far too salty. Petrossian's fresh beluga *malossol* ("little salt"), sevruga, and ossetra are the only imports I'll touch—to the tune of a small fortune in blue-chip restaurants. But even these respectable products disappoint alongside the delicate, celestial caviar made with eggs lifted from giant (and possibly endangered) sturgeon in the Caspian Sea, lightly cured with both sea salt and sweet borax, then shipped to reliable outlets like Harrods in London, Fauchon in Paris, and my beloved *QE2*. No European, to my knowledge, has yet perished from eating caviar preserved with borax, but until the United States eases its restriction on the cleaning agent, you'll simply have to leave American soil to taste this delicacy in all its glory—either that or wait till the Sterling *transmontanus* caviar from farmed white Pacific sturgeon currently being tested in California under Petrossian supervision proves its worth.

Foie Gras

I think of the ultimate foie gras as goose liver (prepared as a chilled truffled-and-jellied terrine, *en brioche,* or in mousse form) and wouldn't buy or order it anywhere but in France. Yes, it's true that D'Artagnan in New Jersey produces a respectable duck foie gras now used (or overused) in fine U.S. restaurants (and when *will* our chefs finally stop the nonsense of sautéing delicate foie gras?). But—well, *par Dieu*—it's worth catching the next plane to Paris just to nestle at Lous Landès over a sumptuous slab of force-fed goose foie gras (illegal in the United States, naturally) consumed ever so slowly with a wee glass of chilled sauternes. I also rave about the fresh foie gras at L'Ami Louis in Paris, not to mention the luscious examples found throughout Alsace and Gascony. Domestic duck foie gras is certainly better than no foie gras at all, but once you're addicted to fresh goose foie gras in France, poached and seasoned ever so expertly and lovingly, you have no doubts about heaven.

Sushi

The express purpose of my last trip to Tokyo was to frequent as many *sushi-ya* (sushi bars) as possible, partial explanation of why today, to the consternation and utter shock of many friends and colleagues, I virtually refuse to eat the questionable stuff that has become such a trendy rage in Japanese restaurants across America. Another main reason is that, compared with the bonhomie and almost intimate rapport between knowledgeable, well-dressed, relaxed customers and veteran sushi chefs in Japan, I find the scene of mostly unschooled, slipshod people crammed together anonymously at sushi counters before rookie chefs, or wolfing down bland tuna rolls, listless salmon tartares and carpaccios, silly sashimi salads, and watery tea at tables, downright depressing. Despite being so damnably chic, Masa Takayama's authentic, exotic, and beautiful dishes at Ginza Sushiko in Beverly Hills are reminiscent of what I relished in Tokyo, but for that inimitable aroma of rice vinegar, well-fermented miso, and freshly grated wasabi; for unblended sushi rice, crisp dark purple nori, mysterious hot sake, and *maccha*-enriched green tea; and for such indigenous, glorious, glistening-fresh fish as *hamachi, saba,* and *chu toro,* there's really no alternative to the modest but great *sushi-ya* in Ginza and other districts of Japan's capital.

Bouillabaisse

I contend that no soup on the planet has been more bastardized than this aromatic, gutsy, unique potage native to Marseille and the French Riviera. Sure, the version served in your favorite bistro might be a fine preparation in itself, but without the special fish indigenous to this strip of the Mediterranean, such as *rascasse, rouget,* and *Saint-Pierre*—not to mention plenty of garlicky rouille paste and the bread called *marette* over which the intoxicating concoction is ladled—it is simply not authentic bouillabaise. To savor one that can bring tears to your eyes (for more reasons than one), book a table at Restaurant Bacon the next time you're anywhere near Cap d'Antibes, or even better, slip into virtually any of the lively seafood restaurants around the Old Port in Marseille.

Louisiana Redfish

This aristocrat of the Gulf is what was originally "blackened" before the trendy (and opprobrious) Cajun cooking craze was applied to everything from snapper to salmon. Even if Louisiana law made it painless for the relatively scarce, sweet redfish to be shipped out of state (generally only frozen is available), I'd continue to make periodic trips to the Big Easy just to savor the fish simply broiled with pecan butter or classically baked in court-bouillon, stuffed with vegetables, and served with a Creole meunière sauce. Tip: next time you're in New Orleans, call Brigtsen's, Commander's Palace, or Broussard's and ask if they have any redfish. If they don't, my bet is they will by the time you arrive. People are like that in the great restaurants of this food-obsessed city, and they're proud of nothing more than their redfish.

Cassoulet

Contrary to what you read, hear, or think, true southwestern French cassoulet is not just about sausage, preserved duck, pork, and white beans. It's about very special local garlic sausages, homemade confit, many unusual cuts of pork, ham hocks, perhaps mutton or partridge, fresh goose fat, and above all, indigenous bean varieties such as Tarbes, Coco, and Lingot, which must be simmered slowly to toothy perfection. Although respectable versions can be found stateside in a few unpretentious French restaurants and bistros, to really see what you've been missing you must travel down to the Domaine d'Auriac in Carcassonne, Le Colombier in Toulouse, or numerous other restaurants throughout Gascony where I've stalked this greatest of French stews.

Couscous

How sad that this indigenous Moroccan dish now found in myriad forms at trendy American restaurants never comes close to the fresh, featherlight grains prepared by women *dadas* (cooks) at such traditional Marrakesh strongholds as El Bahia near the luxurious Mamounia hotel and the unforgettable Yacout. The problem is not so much that American chefs all use dried, commercial couscous but that, as our expert on the subject, Paula Wolfert, contends, "They insist on fixing it instantly—and wrongly—according to package directions." Making absolutely fresh couscous (unlike making fresh pasta) is a highly specialized, difficult task, so . . . anybody for the Marrakesh Express?

Dover Sole and Loup de Mer

Let's get one thing straight once and for all: Dover sole is not lemon sole or gray sole, and *loup de mer* is not striped sea bass or grouper. And since neither exists in American waters, I turn green around the gills when I see these noble, meaty, succulent fish tagged as "fresh" in even our best shops and on the most serious restaurant menus. The real Dover sole thrives only in the

English Channel, the "wolf fish" only in the Mediterranean. To test this orthodoxy, order what passes for Dover sole or *loup de mer* in any upscale U.S. restaurant, then sample the originals, respectively, at Wilton's in London (simply grilled) and La Belle Otéro in Cannes (cooked over fennel twigs). The difference is astounding and will make you cringe when you realize what you've been paying outrageous prices for back home. Since our fresh flounder and striped bass are two similar aristocrats of the sea, it's simply beyond me why some restaurants insist on serving the ill-traveled imports. As usual, I suppose, it's a question of snobbism.

Corned Beef and Pastrami Sandwiches

You don't have to be kosher to know that corned beef and pastrami sandwiches found *anywhere* but in that garish, brusque, wonderful New York institution known as the Jewish delicatessen never come close to, ahem, cutting the mustard. Maybe it's partly a state of mind, but I've eaten imitations in Chicago, Miami, Los Angeles, and even London, and I don't hesitate a second to say that most are pretty ridiculous. The genuine article is made with moist, tough-crusted local rye bread, often carelessly stained with briny kosher-pickle juice; brownish, mellow, sweet-sour, German-style mustard; and, above all, meltingly soft, aromatic, spicy, amply fatty, house-cured or pickled meat—piled four inches high and dangling over the edges of the bread. In Manhattan, the Carnegie and the Second Avenue delis are exemplary, but for the quintessential sandwich (and deli) experience, nothing beats Katz's down on East Houston Street. If you're craving a great sandwich outside New York City, order a Club or a burger, but never a corned beef or pastrami.

Southern Barbecue

Restaurants everywhere outside the South have tried and tried to reproduce it: North Carolina chopped pig barbecue, Memphis dry barbecued ribs, Texas barbecued beef brisket, and Georgia pulled-pork barbecue (Kansas City barbecue is an oxymoron to Southerners). And they all fail—not dismally but significantly enough to send me racing home three or four times a year for the genuine stuff. Southern barbecue just doesn't travel (and that includes, alas, a pretty damn good North Carolina version I produce on Long Island). Maybe it's the breed of hogs or steers and what they feed on. Maybe it's the various smoking woods indigenous to the respective regions.

Maybe it's the obligatory open-pit methods of cooking deemed illegal in most urban areas. Or maybe it's all the secret basting sauces that have been handed down for generations. Frankly, I don't know exactly what the problem is, but I do know that only Southerners have the know-how and knack—plain and clear—and that if you crave real que, you simply must aim the car for Dixie.

Soft European Cheeses

It's wonderful that, finally, Americans are beginning to appreciate great cheeses as an integral part of the fine dining experience, and that restaurants specializing in cheese and cheese dishes are now popping up all over the country. What's not wonderful is that, because of draconian U.S. regulations that ban the importation of any raw-milk cheese less than sixty days old, you can forget about ever tasting the same unpasteurized, crusted, mold-innoculated, ideally aged soft cheeses you find in most European countries. An authentic, unadulterated Brie de Meaux, de Coulommiers, or de Melun, for example, as well as a genuine Norman Camembert from the Pays d'Auge, a pungent Italian Taleggio, or Spain's vivid Cabrales and Picón, are the results of century-old traditions, the respective area's natural assets, and man's ingenuity. Such cheeses at the peak of deliquescent perfection are reason enough for me to reject any import, no matter the pedigree of the shop or restaurant offering it.

Instead, I always opt for a well-aged English or American cheddar, Swiss Tête de Moine, French Roquefort or aged chèvres, or hard, perfumy, aged Dutch Gouda. Of course, part of the problem could be solved if some of our ambitious, talented artisanal cheese makers would devote a little less time to making one goat cheese after another and set about creating more delectable soft cheeses with distinct American identities.

Fraises des Bois

In recent years, efforts have been made in the United States (at White Flower Farm in Litchfield, Connecticut, for example) to transplant and cultivate these tiny, intensely sweet wild strawberries. *Fraises des bois,* at their best in the very beginning of summer, have been laboriously gathered for centuries in the French Alps and other mountainous European regions. Now appearing in more and more of our markets and restaurants, the costly facsimiles are rarely grown in the necessary cool, alkaline, gritty soil that lends so much to the savor of their foreign archetypes, and too often they're not allowed to fully ripen before shipping. Alas, the pretenders—even the great ones—seem to me a weak excuse for the nectarous berries found in France, Switzerland, and parts of Spain (ideally topped with a little genuine crème fraîche or doused in fresh orange juice—preferably extracted from blood oranges).

Fino Sherry

Not since I made my way through the bodegas of Jerez de la Frontera, Puerto de Santa María, and Sanlúcar in western Spain have I once tasted the delicate, clean-smelling, dry, slightly salty, and utterly exquisite fino sherry served in every tapas bar and restaurant. Most of the so-called "dry" sherry drunk as an apéritif or with tapas in the United States is a sacrilege compared with the sublime wine produced exclusively in this tiny area of Spain, the single reason being that genuine fino depends on air to keep its *flor* (a special local yeast) alive and thus begins to lose its distinctive freshness and finesse the second it's bottled for export. (In its natural locale, fino comes only from the cask, in small, unsealed glass containers in wicker, or in half bottles for quick consumption.) Think twice, therefore, when you see "Fino" on any sherry bottle, and by all means plan a westward excursion the next time you're in Madrid.

WINE SAVVY

SINCE, OVER THE YEARS, I'VE SIPPED AN EMBARRASSING AMOUNT of great wine in restaurants around the globe, you'd think by now I'd be completely at ease when it comes to dealing with wine lists. Think again. And, quite frankly, I know very few people, including many of those self-appointed, boring wine "experts," who are—especially when confronted with the bewildering array of new California and other domestic bottles now flooding the market. To make matters worse, rare is the time when the list is presented that my tablemates don't simply thrust it at me and intone, "*You* choose." Naturally, with something so chancy and subjective, there is never any guarantee of total satisfaction, but I have found, when faced with a lengthy, often mind-boggling selection of labels, diverse vintages, and even suspect prices, that there are strategies for ordering wine confidently and painlessly.

Setting the Scene
Given my preference for sipping a legitimate cocktail while carefully perusing a menu and wine list, the only wine I ever drink *without* food is fine Champagne. If, however, you like a red- or white-wine apéritif and don't care to be stuck with inferior generic swill, it's essential to ask the captain or waiter what is being poured and, if necessary, request a fairly exact description of that wine. I shiver when I hear someone order merely "a glass of red wine."

Trust the Expert
Although the truly professional sommelier is almost as rare today as a bottle of '61 Pétrus, there are numerous proprietors, table captains, and even

waiters who take great pride in their restaurant's wine collection and their ability to discuss it. To determine their competence, usually all I have to ask is, "What would you recommend with the dishes we've ordered?" If I'm convinced that they're really on the ball—and not out to gouge me—I'll gladly defer to their expertise. By placing yourself in these adroit hands, you'll be surprised how often you're exposed not only to some of the world's most interesting varietals (sturdy Italian reds from Apulia, dry German Spätlese, subtle French Rhône wines) but to such unexpected, delightful, and relatively inexpensive surprises as Australian Riesling, Oregonian pinot noir, South African chenin blanc, and minor-growth French and Italian wines seldom seen on standard lists.

Charting the Course

When it becomes obvious that I'm going to be the one delegated to make vinous decisions, I inform my company that I'm out of all conversation while I buckle down and study labels, vintages, and prices. For my part, I carry a folded vintage chart copied from one authoritative wine publication or another (particularly reliable is the one updated annually in Robert Parker's *The Wine Advocate*) and proceed to search for the most drinkable wines of the best vintages. This gesture can astound (or impress) others, but when I consider shelling out sixty bucks for a Puligny-Montrachet, I want to know for sure that the '96 vintage is superior (and ready to drink) to the '93 (probably already over the hill). A sharp owner or captain may be able to recite some of this very particular information, so if you're listless, don't hesitate to press him or her for the details you need to make a wise choice.

No Wine Before Its Time

I know arrogant wine buffs who think nothing of ordering bottles (never mind the price) without so much as considering what food is being served or what others at the table might opt to drink—the height, in my eyes, of shabby sophistication and rudeness. Some people enjoy only red or white wine, just as there are those who, no matter what dishes they may have ordered, much prefer a dry, flinty German Riesling to a more herbal California sauvignon blanc.

Once I've analyzed the list, I might suggest that a certain sturdy chardonnay would go nicely with everyone's chicken or sauced fish. If one person just doesn't care for white wine, I have no qualms about also proposing a simple red Italian Dolcetto, a light-bodied French burgundy from the Côte de Beaune, or even a fragrant Spanish rioja. Likewise, if three out of the four at the table (or a majority in a larger party) opt for red, I might search the list for half bottles of white (in those increasingly few restaurants that still stock half bottles) or suggest that the loner settle for a good house white by the glass. The point always is to match the food and wine as harmoniously as possible while respecting the tastes of everyone at the table.

Breaking the Rules

In the days when virtually all white wines were light and reds considerably heavier, most sophisticated diners adhered to the same dictum: white with fish and poultry, red with meat. Today, however, when many California chardonnays, white French burgundies, and even Rhône whites are more robust than most pinot noirs, *Chianti classico*, and, yes, some cabernets, gustatory couplings are governed by a much more liberal set of rules aimed not so much at color distinctions as at balancing the body and intensity of the wine with that of the food being served.

As a result, it is now perfectly acceptable to pair perhaps a rich salmon or tuna steak with a modestly astringent (tannic) Pomerol or medium-bodied merlot, just as it can be very gratifying to match an oaky chardonnay, an Italian Gavi, or a well-bred Pouilly-Fuissé with sautéed duck breast or a meaty pasta dish. I'm certainly not denying that fresh oysters with Sancerre, foie gras with sauternes, and braised lamb shanks with a luscious Brunello di Montalcino are marriages made in heaven, but there are dozens of other exciting options open to anyone willing to experiment.

Strange Bedfellows

Most of the fuss made about wine clashing with such things as artichokes, tomatoes, garlic, anchovies, hot chili peppers, and certain Asian ingredients is grossly exaggerated. Yes, some of these items do, by themselves, have chemical properties that tend to disrupt the integrity of complex wines, but I almost never encounter a dish that is so overwhelmed by one of these assertive ingredients that I'm forced to abandon all hope of drinking wine. Generally, I find that a crisp, fruity, slightly sweet or spicy red or white (beaujolais, Valpolicella; Gewürztraminer, chenin blanc) manages to counter even the most offensive culprits. So when I notice that a chef has been a little too indiscreet with the number of artichoke hearts, garlic cloves, etc., I do what any sensible diner does: pick them out—judiciously, of course— or opt for a good, sturdy beer or ale.

Some Like It Cold

Chilled beaujolais and zinfandel? Meursault at room temperature? Ice-cold Château d'Yquem and Alsatian Gewürztraminer? Grape aficionados will never agree on the best temperature for pouring certain wines. Today, it's becoming more and more trendy to sink even such mellow classified beaujolais as Juliénas and Saint-Amour, not to mention some of the lighter California and Oregon reds, into ice. I disapprove adamantly, convinced that the chill muzzles the wine's racy fruitiness. I also consider it nearly sacrilegious to lower the temperature of a noble white burgundy or great California chardonnay.

Yet when it comes to an Italian Orvieto, a French Chablis, or a German Riesling, I do, indeed, like a frosty edge. What to remember is that cold generally tends to mute flavor and mask sweetness (in both food and wine), and, in red wine, it emphasizes its astringency. Keep in mind, too, that both cold and spicy foods almost beg for the refreshing texture of a light, chilled wine such as muscadet, chenin blanc, or even red Valpolicella.

Sniffing Out Trouble

Though the public is becoming more sophisticated about wine than ever before, I think there's a bit too much nonsense these days about checking corks, decanting, swirling glasses, sniffing bouquets, and tasting. The truth is that the process of determining the soundness of any wine can be made quickly and without affectation. Since a cork that smells acrid or feels moldy or too dry usually forecasts big trouble, I don't so much as look at a glass of wine until the cork has been offered for inspection, given a whiff, and squeezed, but these are gestures that can be carried out almost in an instant.

I ask to have a wine decanted only if it's a distinguished, relatively old, expensive vintage red (like an '84 Château Figeac or '88 Barolo Montezemolo) that has obviously thrown sediment; and no sooner is it in the decanter than I insist it be poured into a glass to breathe further before being swirled briefly, sniffed, and ultimately tasted. I never swirl a white wine, but any red—no matter the pedigree—automatically gets a quick whirl around the glass to help release tannins and other flavors. (The trick to swirling without sloshing wine on the tablecloth? Simple. Never allowing the base of the glass to leave the table, grasp the bottom of the stem between the index and middle fingers, keep the wrist firmly in place, and swirl safely—but gently—away.)

When to Say No

Since you are always within your rights to question any standard wine (a modest French Chablis, Greek Demestica, or Swiss Chasselas) that either smells or tastes unsound or simply doesn't meet your expectations, most fine restaurants are usually more than willing to offer a second bottle or deliver a substitute that might be more acceptable—no questions asked. On the other hand, you're out of bounds in sending back a second bottle of an identical wine that is perfectly drinkable but happens not to suit your taste. And no captain or waiter should be expected to tolerate a rube who orders a distinctive Caymus chardonnay or Château Gruaud-Larose and, just to show off, sends it back without soliciting the opinion of others. If I have reason to splurge—say, on a regal claret such as the '83 Ducru-Beaucaillou or an exceptional cabernet like Heitz's '92 "Martha's Vineyard"—and certain doubts arise, before rejecting the bottle outright, I ask not only those at my table to taste the wine but also the person who served it. As for the grand gesture of having that rare, magnificent, irreplaceable bottle of La Tâche from Burgundy costing hundreds of dollars, one rule only applies: If you order it, you drink it.

The Final Word

Today, there are hundreds of publications covering every facet of the wine experience, some highly authoritative, others limited in scope but extremely helpful, and still others that are utter bunk. By far the most comprehensive and respected is Robert Parker's *The Wine Advocate,* a bimonthly guide primarily designed for and subscribed to by professionals and truly dedicated grape lovers. More commonly available is Parker's splendid sixth edition of *Parker's Wine Buyer's Guide* (Simon & Schuster), a highly readable compendium of the global wine regions, the greatest vintages, and numerous ways to purchase and serve wine. For the practical-minded amateur eager just to have a quick, concise, inexpensive guide to tote to restaurants, nothing can top the consistently revised, updated, and expanded *Hugh Johnson's Pocket Encyclopedia of Wine* (Fireside). As for myself, I'm quite satisfied with my little, ragged, badly stained chart that tucks very nicely into my wallet and can be consulted with minimum folderol.

Drink up!

THE RESERVATIONS WAR

I T'S ENOUGH TO MAKE YOU WANT TO PULL OUT YOUR HAIR, BUT the hard-core truth is that at many fashionable, wildly popular restaurants today, you simply never seem to be able to snag a reservation—unless, that is, you're willing to wait a month or your name happens to be Rockefeller or Zagat. Of course, it goes without saying that if you're an established regular (a "friend of the house") at such bastions as Nobu or Daniel in New York, Charlie Trotter's in Chicago, and Canlis in Seattle, booking a table on a moment's notice usually involves no more than a quick phone call. But just try your luck for eight o'clock on a Friday night at Joël in Atlanta, Campanile in Los Angeles, or the Inn at Little Washington outside Washington, D.C., and I can almost promise you'll be met with a very polite but definitive "Sorry, but we're fully booked." It's maddening, to be sure, the only consolation being that even professionals such as yours truly can also be tortured in reservation hell when we take an unassuming approach to booking a table. Just ask *New York* magazine's veteran restaurant critic Gael Greene, who once anonymously called the city's outrageously successful Gramercy Tavern and was finally awarded a table only after agreeing to dine midweek—at 10:30 P.M.

Actually, the inability to score at the stylish restaurant of your choice should never be construed as some disaster, not when there are so many attractive alternatives and when the trendy place in question might well be clamoring for *your* business nine months hence. No restaurant on earth is worth groveling over once it's perfectly obvious that nothing short of a papal writ can secure a hearty welcome. Still, even I can be as curious as the next gudgeon when tales of culinary wonder and social dazzle surround a place, at which point I don't hesitate a second to engage any number of well-crafted strategies intended to fracture, or at least relax, the reservations barrier.

Confronting the experienced, shrewd voice on the line at Le Bec-Fin in Philadelphia or the French Laundry in Napa Valley is not an exercise for the timid, the soft-spoken, or, for that matter, the morally correct. While you know as well as I do that, despite proclamations to the contrary, restaurants always have a "spare table" available at even the busiest times, seasoned reservationists, maître d's, and managers are not dummies, meaning they know—and know how to deal with—just about every obvious trick in the book: calling to confirm a reservation you never made; pretending you know so-and-so the restaurant critic, restaurateur, or famous chef; claiming to be in town for only one day or to have just flown in from London; having a "secretary" falsely identify you as a corporate hotshot or, for the more brazen, the duke or duchess of some questionable republic. Consequently, winning over one of these skilled professionals requires not only cunning, poise, a confident tone of voice, and indomitable clout but also a certain flair for human psychology.

I can't guarantee that the following tips will always net an otherwise impossible reservation, but I can assure you that each has at one time or another achieved a small miracle for me. Calling a sensible three days in advance, the main goal here is to land a table for two to four persons on a Friday evening. (Demanding a Saturday night on such short notice is unreasonable and only invites argument and frustration.)

Off-Hour Smarts

Never, ever call a restaurant to make a reservation during peak serving hours (12:30 to 2:30 P.M. and 7:30 to 9:30 P.M.), when the entire staff is frazzled, nobody has the time or the incentive to discuss possibilities, and serious mistakes can be made.

"If somebody rings at one o'clock and demands that I explain why it's impossible to be seated Friday evening at eight, I'm usually so busy handling lunch customers that all I want to do is get the person off the phone," admits Brian Jontow, longtime manager of Manhattan's forever crowded Ben Benson's Steak House.

I've determined that the most advantageous time to call for a difficult reservation is about thirty minutes after the lunch rush, or between 2:30 and 3:00 in the afternoon.

Love at First Sound

No matter who answers the phone—reservationist, manager, table captain—I like to create a personal bond by immediately saying, "Could I please ask who's speaking?" This puts the other person on the defensive, even as it appeals to his or her ego. (I must add that one of my more devious ruses has been to say, "Oh, I didn't recognize your voice" to someone I've never spoken with in my life.) Once your initial authority has been established, politeness is an absolute must. The victors in this war of wills know that something like "Good morning, this is Mr. (or Ms.) . . . and I'd like to make a reservation for four people on Friday evening" will always go farther than a blurted "Hi, I need a table" or an unthinking "How about a table?"

Linguistic Prowess

I've learned how to proffer a greeting in at least ten different languages, an affectation that might rub some people the wrong way but one that has helped get me over reservation hurdles at such restaurants as Jean-Georges in New York, Tony's in St. Louis, and even L.A.'s opulent Diaghilev (it's "Kak pozjivayetskya"). Of course, this can backfire if, after your "Bonjour, madame" at a French shrine, you must respond to *"C'est moi qui souhaite à monsieur le bonjour, et comment puis-je vous servir?"* On the other hand, if you're indeed capable of negotiating the reservation entirely in the applicable foreign tongue, let me assure you that half your battle is won.

Dinner at Eight

Even if your habit, like mine, has always been to dine at eight o'clock, try booking a difficult table for an hour later, because: 1) the most frantic rush at any fine East Coast restaurant is generally spurred by the eight o'clock arrivals (seven o'clock on the West Coast and in the Midwest); and 2) fairly or not, dining later is perceived by most places as more urbane—and the level of service might be affected by that perception. I resolutely refuse to dine anywhere at 6 or 10:30 P.M. and make it sound almost like an insult when some overinflated cretin on the line arrogantly dictates those times as the only options.

The Magic Number

Tables for two tend to be scarce in most restaurants—not to mention uncomfortable and often poorly located. To help ensure that my companion and I will be seated at a roomier table for four, I try reserving for no less than a party of three. When I call back with the revised number—and it would be unconscionable not to—at least I know that I'm "in the book" and that all sorts of juggling can be done. Restaurants are defenseless against this admittedly naughty ploy, but this is often the only way to get one of those spare tables they always hold back. (Warning: Do this at your own peril. When you change the number in your party, you might be asked to change nights as well, so be prepared.)

Secondhand Connections

Some of the closest and most productive friendships on earth are between administrative assistants and those who handle reservations at high-profile restaurants. The people who breeze into the finest establishments at the most sought-after hours have probably trained their assistants to establish a working relationship with numerous preferred restaurants, and if I've learned nothing else talking with those in control, I've learned that a sharp assistant *never* puts a reservationist on hold.

"I deal constantly with both local and out-of-town secretaries," says Benito Sevarin, manager of Le Cirque 2000 in New York, "and when one I know well calls, I go out of my way to please."

The same holds true for concierges at first-class hotels, the best connected of whom communicate continually with the reservation desks at many prestigious restaurants.

The Way to the Heart

One of the cleverest ways I know to disarm even the most steely restaurant arbiter—and maybe expose his or her vulnerability—is to demonstrate serious curiosity and suggest culinary expertise by requesting in-depth descriptions of the menu and wine list.

"I love potential customers who are eager to know what we're up to and who pose a challenge to reservation managers," says one overseer of reservations at Charlie Trotter's in Chicago (where a weekend table normally must be booked at least a month in advance). "If they're serious about food and wine—and believe me, I can tell instantly whether the players are real or phony—and almost desperate to dine on a certain evening, well, let's just say we can make it happen."

Storming the Top Brass

If my enthusiasm about the promise of superlative cuisine and wines fails to sway a stubborn Cerberus, the next move is to ask firmly to speak with the owner, the manager, or even the chef. I explain that I'd like to set up a very special dinner on Friday and was wondering if he or she would be able to propose a menu with wines and orchestrate the whole evening. (Needless to say, I'm always prepared to pay for such a custom-made meal.) Since nowhere are egos more inflated than in high-end restaurants, I know few proud professionals who can resist such a challenge.

Comic Relief

Not long ago, a gentleman who phoned the gold-plated Fleur de Lys in San Francisco on a Wednesday was told by co-owner Maurice Rouas that a table for dinner on Friday would be impossible. Unfazed, the man asked what President Bush would be told if he called with the same request, only to hear the obvious reply. "Well, sir, President Bush is not going to be using the table that evening, so why not let me have it?" Rouas laughed for a full minute, then granted the reservation. I've pulled similar stunts using other famous names, and you'd be surprised how often this approach has cracked the ice of rejection—and even made a couple of lasting friends.

In the reservations war—and often it is just that—determination is a strong instinct that can put not only one's authority but one's very character to the test. If you're adroit enough to overcome the odds, so much the better; but never forget, for heaven's sake, that you can always just forego all the aggravation and nonsense as I tend to do more and more, head for the nearest friendly bistro or *ristorante,* and tuck into the sort of coq au vin or risotto you'd be damn lucky to find in the snootier haunts. Now that, in my opinion, is a real test of character.

A SHAMELESS UPDATE
ON GREASING PALMS

AFTER MAKING A RESERVATION AT THE MICHELIN THREE-STARRED
Le Grand Vefour in Paris and requesting a right-hand-side banquette,
a friend and I are very ceremoniously ushered to a choice table by the maître
d' and told to let him know if he can be of further help. Throughout the meal,
he watches, hovers discreetly, and generally checks to make sure things are
going smoothly, and once we've paid the bill—with its automatic service—he
asks if lunch was enjoyable and bids us return. Are we expected to palm this
commandant a few extra euros and, if so, how many?

Two companions and I have booked a table at the wildly popular Babbo
in Manhattan for another fix of Mario Batali's seductive Italian cooking,
but on this particular night, we're asked to wait twenty minutes, only to be
led to "Siberia." There, our drink order is taken by a friendly but hassled
waiter, and eventually we're served lukewarm minced lamb ravioli and overcooked veal liver. Is it justifiable to show our disappointment by stiffing the
waiter?

Tipping. Over the centuries, few subjects have spurred more universal
debate, bewilderment, embarrassment, self-righteousness, and downright
contempt and loathing, so much so that it's reasonable to assert that the age-
old custom has now become as much a fact of life as death and taxes. One
apocryphal theory traces tipping's origins to Elizabethan England, where,
"To Insure Promptness" of service in taverns and roadhouses, guests tossed
coins into pots inscribed with the letters T.I.P. (Morbidly enough, wise
unfortunates about to lose their heads on the block also handed the execu-
tioner a few tuppence to guarantee a clean cut.) Wherever and whenever the

tradition started, the tips collected around the world by today's aggregation of waiters, chambermaids, taxi drivers, bellhops, croupiers, tour guides, and bullfight ushers amount to a veritable multizillion-dollar industry.

And nothing is more personal and complex than the practice of tipping in restaurants, a domain where, by profession, I face the eternal dilemma of distributing gratuities with prowess and where I must stay alert to even the slightest changes in the rules. Of course, I take for granted that anyone who dines out frequently is familiar with the standard formulas: 15–20 percent of the pretax bill for table service; two to three dollars per bottle of wine poured in restaurants with wine stewards; and so forth. But here I'd like to explore the finer points of tipping and offer a few highly subjective opinions that seem to be in tune with the dining styles of the early twenty-first century.

Proprietors

Time was when big spenders in first-class restaurants might, with impunity, slip the owner a crisp bill to guarantee special favors or impress their guests. Today, however, the gesture of trying to tip such gentlemen as Sirio Maccioni at Le Cirque 2000 in New York, Robin Gundry at Wiltons in London, or Jean-Claude Vrinat at Taillevent in Paris would be viewed as gauche and met with a polite refusal. Beware of any restaurant where the owner might accept a "bribe." Things could get just a bit complicated if the owner is also the maître d', a not-uncommon circumstance these days in the case of more sophisticated restaurants. (If I have any doubt, I never hesitate to discreetly ask a table captain or waiter.)

Maître D's

If you're greeted—particularly in Europe—by a formally dressed maître d' (who is *not* the owner) but goes out of his way to supervise the meal, making sure things click, a farewell tip of between ten and twenty dollars (or the equivalent) is not out of order. I would almost never grease a maître d's palm upon my arrival just to procure a premium table, except if I were, say, at a restaurant with spectacular views (Tavern on the Green in New York, La Tour d'Argent in Paris, the Mandarin in San Francisco) and discovered that placement meant as much to my guests as food and service.

Another time that might occasion a gratuity (of perhaps twenty dollars) would be when making advance reservations and asking a maître d' for a specific table or to arrange for particular dishes and wines to be served. I refuse, however, to be intimidated by a haughty maître d' who makes no special gestures yet appears to expect more than a cordial handshake at evening's end.

Table Captains

Although well-trained and dedicated table captains are virtually nonexistent in most of America's less formal restaurants today, the ones you still find at such redoubtable establishments as Commander's Palace in New Orleans and Locke-Ober's in Boston can literally make or break a meal. They show what they're made of in the way they discuss dishes, supervise waiters and busboys, and, now and then, even help prepare dishes. I realize tradition in this country dictates that captains (who, unlike waiters, often receive substantial salaries) should be tipped 5 percent of the pretax bill for good service. When I encounter a superlative captain, though, I'm quite capable of splitting the tip evenly on the credit-card slip—or palming the person an extra five- or ten-spot beyond the customary percentage. Having once served as an undercover captain in a fancy Chicago restaurant, I know, believe me, what this gesture means. On the other hand, a captain who simply takes my order then disappears forever is lucky to get 2 percent of the total.

Policies may vary from restaurant to restaurant, but remember that quite often all cash or credit-car tips left on the table in deluxe establishments are pooled among the entire serving staff, meaning that if you're determined to reward an especially solicitous captain, you'd best bestow the cash personally. Ditto in France and other European countries, where all service (normally no more than 15 to 18 percent) is included in the total bill.

Waiters

With millions of waiters and waitresses in the United States alone now making an estimated $3 billion in tips, it's little wonder that the IRS is more than mildly perturbed by the way many restaurants report the wages of these employees—and why the agency would probably be much happier with the European system of incorporating all service charges into the total bill. As it stands, waiters in the United States (and in many other countries) generally earn minimum wage, meaning that roughly two-thirds of their income is derived from tips.

I usually hold to the norm of tipping waiters 15 percent of the pretax bill for respectable, affable service—or in New York City, of simply doubling the sales tax, for a yield of about 16.5 percent. (For extraordinary service, I certainly up the ante to 20, even 25 percent, but on no account do I, unlike more intimidated and insecure diners, make it a policy to automatically tip waiters 20 percent for standard service—a practice, quite frankly, I find crude.) Good service is good service, whether rendered in a hallowed den of haute cuisine or a bistro, and I am just as apt to tip an efficient but unremarkable veteran 15 percent in an elegant restaurant as I am to leave 20 percent in a neighborhood pub for a waitress who knocks herself out to make the meal special.

Likewise, at today's casual spots where a single waiter seats you, discusses the menu, suggests wines, takes orders, and even helps clean the table, I might well overtip that conscientious pro as if he were maître d', captain, waiter, and wine steward rolled into one. To stiff a waiter who has performed with expertise and care is a crime. On those rare occasions, however, when I'm confronted with a rube who obviously dislikes me as much as the job, it doesn't faze me to leave a symbolic 5 percent and calmly tell both the waiter and the owner why. While penalizing a waiter for sloppiness, indifference, or rudeness is one thing, punishing him for kitchen or management that stumbles beyond his control is another—something that should always be carefully considered.

When I dine alone, or when a table for four has been given to a companion and me, I tend to compensate for the waiter's loss in numbers through my tip. Should extra dishes or wines be served compliments of the house for one reason or another, I take into account this increasingly popular gesture when figuring the waiter's tip.

I don't balk at bills that include an automatic 15 or 18 percent gratuity (both in the United States and abroad), even though some American diners find this either an inconvenience or insulting. On the other hand, this policy doesn't stop me one minute from taking out a pen and making adjustments when the service has been wretched. Should I be confronted by an indignant waiter, I ask to speak with the management. I have noticed in certain areas of this country that some restaurants have begun to ask for "cash tips only." It may be too early to say whether this minitrend will catch on elsewhere, but while some diners may not object to the tactic, I find it ungracious and have no problem, when paying by credit card, with disregarding it altogether.

Wine Stewards

Even though wine consumption in fine restaurants remains healthy and impressive, legitimate sommeliers are a dying breed in America, victims of increasingly relaxed dining styles and owners who are eager to maintain all-purpose staffs. In Europe, blessedly, the tradition continues to thrive, and at such distinguished restaurants as the Auberge de l'Ill in Alsace, London's Savoy Grill, and the splendid Il Sambuco in Milan, I consider it a privilege to palm the fervent experts, after a meal, the equivalent of about five dollars (in cash, of course) per bottle poured. Not that the "acting" wine steward should ever be overlooked: I'll tip a captain or waiter extra for wine service (perhaps five dollars) if he is exceptionally knowledgeable and helpful. Never, though, will I reward anyone—wine steward, captain, waiter—who does little more than hand me the wine list and later pour only the first round.

Busboys

From time to time, I find myself slipping a fiver to a particularly vigilant busboy who deftly clears dishes, repeatedly fills water glasses, replaces ashtrays, and so forth. Some might consider the gesture unnecessarily patronizing, but watching a face light up with appreciation can kindle a mutual respect that only enhances the overall dining experience. And, after all, these menial guys are not slaves but human beings trying to earn an honest living the best way they know how.

Coatroom Attendants

The posting of a sign informing patrons of a coatroom charge (a practice I personally loathe) is an almost certain guarantee that the attendants are adequately paid, in which case I'm less inclined to leave behind much more than a thank-you. Otherwise, my standard tip (both in the United States and abroad) is exactly one dollar or the equivalent per item—no matter how big the smile.

HOGWASH

Having spent at least half a lifetime perched shamelessly in the world's finest restaurants, I've learned to exercise remarkable self-control when faced today with such lapses and pretensions as three ridiculous pats of butter for a whole table, cute itsy-bitsy appetizers that look like insects on a plate, all manner of fruit oils and herb sorbets, open-shirted head waiters, customers with nose rings, and . . . well, you get the picture. While these are just annoyances I've come to accept, there are other real aggravations in restaurants that truly drive me up the wall and that I pray each night will blessedly and miraculously just disappear once and for all. To wit:

Cocktails in Wineglasses

There was a time when only the French would ever be guilty of this mannered gaffe, but today in the United States, even some of the most distinguished restaurants can be found serving martinis and gimlets and even vodka tonics in pathetic little wineglasses. The practice is certainly not chic, there are very logical reasons why certain glasses were designed for particular cocktails and highballs, and if it's a question of penny-pinching, my advice to restaurateurs is to check out the respectable and reasonably priced glassware at the nearest Pottery Barn or Pier 1. Don't ask me to explain exactly why, but I (and other serious boozers) literally can't drink cocktails in wine glasses.

No-Show Maraschinos

With righteous restaurateurs and the health police ever vigilant about red dye #2, I now go out to eat carrying my own supply of maraschino cherries in a small Advil bottle. What's a manhattan or whiskey sour without one? So secretly beloved are maraschino cherries by everybody, in fact, that I usually have to fight to keep others from casually plucking mine from my drinks (a manhattan or whiskey sour without a cherry looks naked and ugly). And how dangerous can those tasty sweet cherries be when, for heaven's sake, they haven't hurt Shirley Temple any all these years?

Water Rationing

It's irritating enough than many fine restaurants fail to place goblets of water at every setting on a table—especially when we're not in the middle of some drought. Of course, they're just praying that customers will eventually order rivers of grossly overpriced mineral water, today's fastest-growing beverage category and one that's twice as profitable as wine. But when one person in a party requests (or often demands) a glass of plain tap water and the waiter doesn't automatically bring the same for everyone, I go ballistic. Is a show of hands really necessary?

Massive Menus

I still haven't worked up the nerve, but I think that the next time I'm presented with one of those cumbersome, bedsheet-size menus that threaten to shatter every piece of glassware in sight, I'll ask the waiter either to hold it up for me to read or to set up an easel. (Also, when I see all the items on such menus, I can't help but wonder how fresh the food they trumpet can be.)

Women's Menus

Not listing prices for women is one of the most insulting and outmoded affectations I encounter in overly self-blown restaurants and one that nobody should tolerate. For restaurants that want to play that silly game, perhaps the question that might draw the right attention should be: "Oh, does that mean the ladies at the table dine for free?"

Absurdly Long-Winded Dishes

"Free-range Tacota Valley baby chicken grilled Kurd-style with Cajun spices and Salinas elephant garlic on a bed of hydroponic Raritan arugula, served with organic Peruvian creamed potatoes and Barnstable blueberry coulis." When confronted with this sort of menu jingoism, all I want to scream is, "Waiter, bring me a goddam atlas!"

Where's the Bread

Has anyone else noticed that bread—even in upscale restaurants—seems to be having more and more trouble making it to the table till the food orders are taken? No doubt this is a nefarious ruse to encourage famished customers to order more appetizers, but when confronted with this insult, I demand that we be given our daily bread—and promptly.

Low-Cal, Fat-Free, Saltless (and Lifeless) Anything

Studying a menu with these fatuous auguries scattered about, I wonder if I'm supposed to clear my dinner selections with my HMO. As the great Paul Bocuse once bellowed when asked why his cuisine was not more *healthy,* "I'm running a restaurant, not a hospital." Won't somebody please save us from those trying to save us?

Wine Before It's Time

The only thing that elevates my blood pressure more than being served red wine—*any* red wine—that's been fashionably chilled is watching a waiter open a bottle of wine before it's been properly presented and approved. Whenever I'm exposed to this inexcusable lapse of propriety—even in some of our finest restaurants—I can only view it as a matter of "bait and switch."

Undercooked Seafood and Poultry

Even our Neanderthal ancestors grasped the fact that food flavors are greatly enhanced by sufficient cooking. If science is not enough to dissuade you from ingesting roast chicken bleeding at the bone or ultrarare nuggets of fresh tuna (*pace* all sushi lovers), perhaps a tough bout with giardia (as I've experienced), salmonella, or the like will have you seeing red the next time such dishes are served.

"Lemongrass/Not So Pretty . . . "

Today in many fancy American restaurants (no matter the ethnic persuasion), lemongrass is infused in broths and stocks, sprinkled recklessly atop seafood and poultry, incorporated wantonly into sauces and risottos, used to flavor teas, soups, and salads, and even turned into witless sorbets. Chefs are still utterly *Thaied* to the pungent herb, making it harder to stamp out than crabgrass.

Keepers of the Lite

Legend has it that when Fernand Point, the late French master chef at the three-star La Pyramide in Vienne, ventured out to another restaurant, he would simply turn around and leave if he was greeted by a "skinny and dour" chef. My own reaction isn't quite so strong, but I must say, given the choice between a chef with a Jasper White waistline and one who looks fresh off a fashion runway, I feel much safer with the former. The spectacle of supertrim chefs parading about the dining room always leaves me very anxious, the reason being that I can't help but suspect that they much prefer being around a Stairmaster than a stove.

The Hoovers

You've seen them: those dolts who arrive at a deluxe restaurant thirty minutes after you do, indulge in little if any conversation, inhale three courses with the speed and efficiency of a new vacuum cleaner, and are up and out before you've even ordered dessert. Stopwatch dining seems to be a strictly American phenomenon, a disconcerting, sad mode of behavior practiced by those who are either miserable in a low-decible dining room, utterly bored with one another's company, or convinced that the chairs are to be rented by the hour.

"Phonies"

I'd be happy to furnish Letitia Baldridge's number to any clod who finds nothing improper about disrupting the decorum of an entire restaurant by making or taking cell-phone calls at his or her table. Such barbaric manners might be considered par for the course, if not socially de rigueur, in glitzy Hollywood venues; but if the business or long-distance babbling these lowlifes feel compelled to conduct in more civilized places can't wait, then they shouldn't be dining out in the first place. Get thee to the sidewalk!

THE QUESTION OF CIVILITY

MOST OF US AT LEAST SHOULD KNOW THE BASIC DIFFERENCE between good and bad manners, but from much that I observe on today's mutable restaurant scene, some people would be better off in a cage than in a reputable dining room. What we're now being exposed to is a whole new social order in even the finest restaurants, one in which strict rules have virtually disappeared and the line between what many perceive as right and wrong becomes fainter as each year of the new century evolves. Cackling customers decked out in synthetic field jackets, designer T-shirts, multiple ear rings, and even jogging gear; mineral water or Pepsi slugged directly from the bottle; overt amorous displays at the table; owners who plop down with favored patrons to rap instead of tending the shop; back-slapping waiters determined to conduct business on a first-name basis; chefs preening about dining rooms like peacocks—often I think I'm observing bipeds in a zoo instead of putatively civilized humans out for a respectable evening of good food and wine.

I hardly consider myself to be a stick-in-the-mud, hopelessly entrenched in outdated manners of the past, but there are limits to my tolerance of today's crude and irresponsible behavior in many first-rate restaurants. Feeling compelled to address the subject of etiquette for a changing era in dining out might appear ludicrous to some, but if somebody doesn't do it, the day is quickly approaching when going to a legitimate restaurant could be not unlike slumming at McDonald's.

No-Show Crime
Once, in polite society, reserving a table in a fine restaurant and failing to show up stamped you as a certified clod. (It also guaranteed sure financial

loss for the restaurant, as it still does.) Today, there are a shocking number of swells who think nothing of booking at two or three restaurants on a given night, then allowing their very impressed guests to state a preference—never bothering, of course, to cancel the two rejects. Understandably tired of being stung, most popular establishments now simply cover their potential losses by overbooking, the consequences being that, in the long run, everyone but the no-shows get hurt by their execrable behavior. If they had the courtesy (and good sense) to play fair, we'd all be better off. If not, it serves them right when their names are recorded and they're told not so politely to get lost the next time they call.

Bottom Breeding

Because most serious restaurants today are as much arenas for spectacle and entertainment as meccas of fine food and engaging discourse, the question of table seating has never been more important. Although I couldn't care less about restaurant theatrics and people watching, I do think it marks the height of rudeness to arrive at a table, purposefully grab one of the seats with the best viewing advantage, and leave others with their backs to all the action. (I know one couple in New York who actually make it a point to arrive well in advance of their party at a fashionable restaurant just to lay claim to the choice seats at the table.)

In equally poor taste are the hosts and hostesses who, in these liberated times, still insist on the silly practice of seating guests boy-girl-boy-girl, no matter what the mutual interests of these diners might be. The more modern idea of asking guests at dinner parties of, say, six people or more to move two, maybe three seats to the left after the main course may seem a bit tricky, but at least it serves as a safety net against possible incompatibility or boredom and helps spice things up.

Dress Decorum

Surely no rules on the current restaurant scene have been more relaxed (an understatement, to be sure) than those governing dress. Just twenty years ago, it was almost de rigueur for men to wear jackets and ties to any fine restaurant in cities throughout the United States (with the definite exception of Los Angeles). And even a famous couturier who once arrived at Le Perroquet in Chicago sporting a turtleneck beneath his blazer was shown the door—almost as fast as the bold-type socialite in satin tunic and pants who received the same treatment at "21" in New York. I still cannot imagine anyone with the slightest notion of propriety storming the premises of Taillevent in Paris or the Dorchester Grill in London decked out in designer jeans and sneakers, but, take my word, it happens—mainly with Americans.

There are sensible solutions to some sartorial shortcomings. I found nothing wrong, for example, when one of France's three-star chefs, no less, was recently stopped at the entrance of Manhattan's Le Cirque 2000 and informed with some embarrassment that he would have to slip into one of the jackets the restaurant keeps on reserve for those who don't respect the dress code. Generally, though, it has become perfectly acceptable for patrons to dress in tune with the more casual settings at small bistros, trendy New American shrines, most Italian restaurants, seafood houses, and even richly appointed hotel dining rooms. Not everyone, however, has developed an intuitive sense about what the limits are, showing up where they shouldn't in jogging shoes, T-shirts, or bomber jackets. As far as I'm concerned, these nerds should be offered no more than a table outside the restroom—or, better, given directions to the closest Burger King. It's one thing to dress smartly casual for a civilized restaurant; it's another to appear one step up from Neanderthals.

Just Shut Up and Eat

In the age of the instant expert, there now seem to be a disproportionate number of people who fancy themselves authorities on food and restaurants, and all I can say is pity the poor soul who has to sit next to one of them. Frankly, the last thing I myself (like James Beard and Craig Claiborne before me) enjoy discussing in any depth while trying to have a relaxed, congenial meal is complex gastronomic topics. And to be forced to listen to a foodie's running commentary on the dishes being eaten or on some hot new restaurant to which nobody else at the table can relate is almost as painful and vulgar as hearing the discourse of a self-appointed oenophile who lectures endlessly on the merits and faults of the wine list (and, of course, insists on ordering for everybody else). To me, it's almost as uncivil as yapping about current love affairs, babies, and exercises at the gym.

Table Talk

Long gone are the days when the reigning code of conduct forbade discussion of money, sex, or politics at a respectable dining table—not to mention the foul language you hear everywhere today. The range of acceptable topics now seems almost limitless, but because freedom always has the tendency to be abused, you might find yourself sitting beside some rube who tells vile jokes or discloses sexual matters best kept private. The sophisticated diner instinctively knows, say, that the bawdy story told in last night's bar is all wrong, wrong, wrong at this afternoon's lunch. Short of tossing a glass of wine in the face of such misfits, I've learned that the best reaction is no reaction at all—no comment, no smile or laugh, no awareness whatsoever of what's been uttered. Silence can be the deadliest and most effective of all weapons when confronted with such obtuse manners.

Ditch the Diet

When it comes to presumptuous behavior, the diet-obsessed are in a special class by themselves—possibly the most tedious creatures on earth. The savvy dinner guest or companion with legitimate dietary concerns courteously makes the issue known as far in advance as possible, then keeps his or her mouth shut. Those, on the other hand, who expect a restaurant to satisfy their every nutritional whim should really just stay home with a nice container of tofu or soy yogurt and pitchers of diluted decaf green tea.

Lazy Susan Dining

Like many Europeans, I find no display of American gastromania more plebian than the increasingly popular practice of passing whole plates of food around the table for everyone to sample. Naturally, the more pretentious professional foodies look upon this exercise as a show of sophistication; I consider it uncouth.

Don't get me wrong. Like anyone passionate about great food and drink, I'm often just as eager to taste what others have been served as they are to savor what's on my plate or in my glass. The proper solution? If I think those on either side of me might like a bite of my sea bass, I will very casually place a morsel of fish on a clean edge of their plates and ask them to do the same with whatever delicacies they might like to share with me. For the lady across the table yearning to try the bass, I simply gesture that she should extend her small bread plate for a sampling—and vice versa should I relish the sight of her venison.

As for tasting a tablemate's red Burgundy when I'm drinking a more appropriate white, I simply ask the waiter to bring another glass. The point is to make such exchanges as discreetly as possible, so much so that they go almost unnoticed.

Temper Control

Today I witness—and am usually forced to disregard—every form of bad behavior imaginable, but the one offense I cannot and will not tolerate from anyone at my table is the abuse of floor staff. Yes, it's true that most of the experienced, well-trained captains, waiters, and wine stewards of yore have been replaced seemingly everywhere by a new breed of less knowledgeable and adept servitors. But it's also true that I rarely encounter even the most awkward neophyte who, given a bit of encouragement, a friendly smile, and a word of thanks, won't bend over backward to help make my dinner a pleasant occasion. I also strongly suggest that the next time you're ready to let off steam at a waiter, you should pause to determine if the complaint should not really be directed at the kitchen or management.

Singles Sin

With seemingly more people eating alone in fine restaurants, the dinner companion of choice has become something to read. A paperback novel or small travel guide might be fine, but I find it nothing less than appalling when singles snap open a crinkly newspaper, spread out business documents, or commit other audible and visible gaffs that can subvert the restaurant's overall decorum. Have these loners ever thought of making the most of the occasion by actually studying the menu and wine list while not eating?

Après Vous

Finally, in these liberated, politically correct, often daring times, you might wonder if I still see fit to open the door of a restaurant for a lady, pull her chair out at the table, stand up when she goes to the powder room, and pay the tip to check her coat. You're damned right I do.

ACKNOWLEDGMENTS

Since some of these essays had another life in altered form in various magazines, I take this opportunity to thank those bold, open-minded, inquisitive editors-in-chief without whom I would never have been given the freedom to explore the broad range of eclectic, often controversial subjects that have interested me. Harold Hayes, Don Erickson, Patricia Brown, Curt Anderson, Barbara Fairchild, Gail Zweigenthal, Ruth Reichl, John Cantrell, Pamela Fiori, Marion Gorman, David Doty, and, especially, Frank Zachary—all were receptive to my ideas, all helped to shape my work and career, and all proved, still again, that an author can have no greater inspiration and, indeed, friend than a dedicated editor.

Suffice it that the driving force behind the creation, the format, and even the title of this book has been my gifted editor at John Wiley & Sons, Susan Wyler. Only she knows what I owe to her confidence, loyalty, literary intelligence, and cheerful stubbornness, a debt that might be paid only with a few dusty bottles of '61 La Tâche. Also, a peck on the cheek of Michele Sewell, the most efficient and steadfast publicist any author could ever hope for.

INDEX

Restaurants are identified by city.

McCardell, Ray L., 144
McThail, Tory, 40
Meat loaf, 122–126
  recipe for, 126
  stories of, 122–125
Meli Lupi de Soragna, Diofebo, 158, 161
Melville, Herman, 94–95
Menu items
  healthy foods, 292
  long-winded, 291
Menus, oversized, 291
Mexico
  potato salad, 148
  seviche, 197
Michelangelo (ship), 208
Michigan wild mushroom and parsnip
  chowder (recipe), 101
Microbrew beers, 3, 246–253
Moby Dick (Melville), 94–95
Model Bakery (St. Helena, Napa Valley,
  California), 80
Moonen, Rick, 228
Mora, Corrado, 161
Morocco, onion soup, 171
Mrs. Wilkes' Boarding House (Savannah,
  Georgia), 30
Mushrooms. *See* Wild mushrooms
Mussels
  eggplant, and walnut salad (recipe), 202
  potato salad, French curried with sugar
    snap peas and (recipe), 151
Mustard-dill sauce, Scandinavian gravlax
  with (recipe), 169

Napoleon Bonaparte (emperor of France),
  239
Nassauer Hof Hotel (Wiesbaden, Germany),
  143, 225
National Restaurant Association, 145
New England clam chowder, traditional
  (recipe), 97
New England Sampler (Early), 95
New England seafood chowder, 94–95, 96
New Orleans, Louisiana, absinthe, 209–210,
  213
New Orleans Sazerac (recipe), 217
New York: A Guide to the Empire State, 144
New York magazine, 138, 280
New York Times (newspaper), 122, 251
Nixon, Richard M., 231
Nobu (New York, New York), 280
Noodles with peanut butter-garlic sauce
  (recipe), 131

North Carolina-style Brunswick stew
  (recipe), 23
Norway, seviche, 197

Oak Bar (Plaza Hotel, New York, New
  York), 112–113
Ogden, Bradley, 82
O. Henry (William Sydney Porter), 210
Oink Express (mail-order business), 19
Okra, 27–35
  barley, and crabmeat soup, Maryland
    (recipe), 32
  batter-fried (recipe), 34
  Brunswick stew, 20
  gumbo, and Creole seafood (recipe), 33
  pickled (recipe), 35
  preparation of, 29
  stewed with tomatoes (recipe), 31
  stories of, 27–31
Olive Garden restaurants, 258
Olney, Richard, 208, 240, 244
Onion soup, 2, 170–175
  Danish creamed, and beer (recipe), 173
  English with Stilton cheese (recipe), 173
  Parisian gratinée (recipe), 172
  Portuguese (recipe), 174
  South American (recipe), 175
  stories of, 170–172
  Yugoslavian dilled (recipe), 174
Orange gravy, sweet potatoes with, baked
  fresh ham and (recipe), 15
L'Orangerie (Los Angeles, California), 260
Ordinaire, Pierre, 209
Ortolans, 206
Osteen, Louis, 30, 40
Oyster mushrooms, poached halibut with
  shrimp and (recipe), 110

Page, David, 113
Parker, Robert, 275, 278
Parker's Wine Buyer's Guide (Parker), 278
Parmigiano-Reggiano cheese, 2, 158–164
Parsnip and wild mushroom chowder,
  Michigan (recipe), 101
Pastrami, authentic, 271
Patisserie Française (San Francisco,
  California), 80
Peanut butter, 3, 122, 127–132, 261
  chocolate chip cookies with (recipe), 132
  garlic sauce with, for noodles (recipe), 131
  ice cream, crunchy (recipe), 132
  pound cake (recipe), 131
  stories of, 127–130